The Maddison Line

A JOURNALIST'S JOURNEY AROUND BRITAIN

Roy Maddison

HAYLOFT

First published 2003

Hayloft Publishing Ltd., Kirkby Stephen,
Cumbria, CA17 4EU.

tel: (017683) 42300
fax. (017683) 41568
e-mail: dawn@hayloft.org.uk
web: www.hayloft.org.uk

© 2003 Roy Maddison

ISBN 1 904524 06 0

A catalogue record for this book is available
from the British Library

Produced in Great Britain
Printed and bound in Hungary

To GBH, the Great British Hacks. May their battle to defeat those who wish to manipulate, spin and manage the news never weaken. And long may they continue to truly tell it the way it is. Their part in this country's democracy can never be over-stated.

ABOUT THE AUTHOR

ROY Maddison was born in West Hartlepool, County Durham and would quite like to have been an international cricketer for he can think of nothing better than playing the game he loves for a living - and doing so in year round sunshine.

Realism dawned in his early years and he became a journalist, happily settling for that - though where he now lives, on the fringe of the Lake District, is a considerable drive from Old Trafford and The Riverside.

It is a journey which he is happy to undertake for he is well used to life among the fells and lakes in England's north west and quite enjoys driving the A66 which takes him back to civilisation - which the M6 is sometimes called.

His journalistic career took him from Durham to Tyneside to Manchester and then to London's Fleet Street before the national newspapers moved to everywhere and anywhere, usually to Canary Wharf and always well away from the Street of Shame.

He has worked as a reporter, been on the news desk, was a sports editor and features editor all on regional evenings before becoming a weekly newspaper editor on Tyneside and in Northumberland and Cumbria. This occupied the last 18 years of his working life.

He has been a national President of The Guild of British Newspaper Editors and is now an honorary member of the Society of Editors.

He recently established his own business, lectured on media at the Cumbria Institute of the Arts and worked for the National Trust and the Prince's Trust.

He now considers his chance of a career in cricket is past!

A radio show called *Take it From Here* broadcast a sketch which Jimmy Edwards entitled *Night Train to British West Hartlepool*. It came through the ether sometime in the fifties - and so my home town gained a national notoriety which, allied to the tale of the hanging of the monkey, it could have lived without.

The monkey was hung by the crofters of old Hartlepool, a pleasant little place from which West Hartlepool had sprung several centuries later, the pair of them existing side by side and both clinging to the north east coast of England. Old Hartlepool has more than a thousand years of history and part of the town's folk lore is the story of the monkey.

It goes like this:

In the early 19th century word filtered through to the little fishing port of wars with the French. France was at the other end of the world so no one was unduly alarmed. But, within a few short weeks of this disclosure a ship, the *Chasse Marie*, was wrecked off the coast, in the Tees bay and, washed ashore on the drifting wreckage was a monkey, dressed in a sailor suit. A French sailor suit.

The crofters had not seen a monkey before and neither had they seen a Frenchman. And so the poor little hairy chap, whose language made no sense at all, was collared and hung from a gibbet on the foreshore as a warning to any other foreigner who might be considering aggressive action and preparing for invasion of the town.

The tale was, and remains, a burden to people born in the town and on many occasions fisticuffs have ensued when an incomer has asked 'Who hung the money?'

The reply is usually along the lines of: 'Why, is your father missing?' and soon the air is filled with flying insults, and occasionally furniture. This was not unknown at The Friarage, when Hartlepool Rovers rugby team had taken enough jugs of strong ale and abuse from visiting clubs.

Hartlepool has quite a history, which was added to as recently as 2002 when the town's football club mascot, who wandered the streets dressed in a monkey suit and called himself H'Angus, was elected mayor.

Whether this elevation to the wearing of long red robes and the fur collar was the embodiment of dissatisfaction with politics or a joke is left to the reader to decide. It surely did not do a great service for the Heughers, as the folk of old Hartlepool are called but, as for the people of the 'new town' of West Hartlepool, well, what do they know of history?

But H'Angus got himself a proper and decent suit, vowed to further the cause of the good burghers and, as we live in a democracy, there he was in a very decent office though it is not known if he offers peanuts when serving visitors aperitifs.

~ ~ ~ ~ ~ ~ ~ ~ ~ ~

St Hilda built one of England's earliest monasteries in Hartlepool; it was the birthplace of Reg Smythe who immortalised the shiftless trying ever-so-hard-never-to-work Andy Capp and his oppressed wife Florrie and it was the first place in the UK to be bombed when, on 16 December 1914, a series of shells fired from a German ship standing off shore blasted several streets in the old town.

There were fatalities and many casualties and so Hartlepool, with yet another unenviable piece of history heaped upon its good folk donated more cash to the war effort than any other town in the country. And after all this, Mr Edwards came along with his radio show.

It has to be said that the town where I was born was, at that time, much as any other in the industrial north and wasn't showing a lot of initiative. A boy growing up in an end of terrace house near the North Cemetery was not expected to have much future; rather he was patterned to behave like his contemporaries, do as well as he could at school, get a 'decent' job, marry - and then quietly pop off without a blemish on his character leaving those remaining to enjoy a weep and a ham tea at the Co-op.

Assuming, of course, any one could be bothered with the token sniffle which probably arrived later while Camerons' beers continued to be served thereby allowing emotion to take a grip and gallop all over reality.

And at night the Wagger Moon at Seaton Carew (where the night sky was illuminated with a fierce red glow, diffusing into orange and yellow as the slag was tipped at the steel works) would shine upon the lot of us.

It was said a tramp, trying to keep warm on a bitter winter night, had curled up at the bottom of the tip, insulated internally with several pints of Strongarm ale and seeking a little heat and comfort on the outside.

In the early hours of the morning a train trundled out of the works and chuffed its way across the lines at the top of the tip. There it let go its load of red-hot ashes - on top of the poor lad below whose problems were all ended in a rush of glorious technicolor. It wasn't, particularly, anyone's fault; but it made for a good fireside tale to be exaggerated and sighed over on dark nights in the terraced streets.

~ ~ ~ ~ ~ ~ ~ ~ ~ ~

Our house was in a small street. 'Stoned' front steps indicated a pride by the woman of the house in its interior which, it could be assumed, was equally bright and scrubbed. We were independent enough in our two up and two down houses with the wireless to keep us in touch with the world.

It was war-time and my mother told me many years later of how she listened to Lord Haw Haw, the German propagandist on the radio, this making an entertaining change from the British propaganda as the sneering one started his broadcast with: 'Germany calling...Germany calling...'

It was chilling, but what was frightening everyone was when the bombs dropped as enemy aeroplanes sought the magnesium works on the coast at West View or the docks and if they escaped the searchlights then the windows were rattled with their efforts. And the next day stories of who had been hit and where the bombs had dropped occupied shoppers hunting meagre rations and seeking gossiping information.

My memories are of being scooped up by neighbours and carried from my bed along the street to the cellars of the Nursery public house on the Hart Lane corner. The smell of the beer in the casks imbued in me a taste for decent ale which, thankfully, has sustained me through many years of convivial public life.

Across the road from our house an old woman had people popping in and out of her front door day and night as, in her darkened front room with the curtains tight closed to prying eyes from the pavement, she told their fortunes.

The street gossip was all about other local ladies who, while their husbands had gone off to fight for King and country, had taken themselves off to local pubs and dance halls and been seen returning home in the moonlight with servicemen who most assuredly were not the ever loving whom they had so recently kissed goodbye on West Hartlepool railway station.

It was a life-shaping time, early days when, lying in my bed in our corner house above the Richardson Street pavement and hearing, before 7am, the shipyard workers' boots clatter on down the pavement, heading for Middleton Road and then to the docks every morning made me good and sure that this was not going to be the way my life would be heading.

There was one set of hobnails which tramped the street, winter and summer, with a tread measured as a Buckingham Palace guardsman. Whether there was snow on the ice cold ground or the sun was already up and warming the air, the man's steps didn't falter. Not once. Though he did, invariably, cough. A rasping, Woodbine-effort, a deep-down in his boots catching of breath which usually concluded with a half crown hawked up then deposited at the end of what would have been a nicotine-brown stream from his lungs and into the gutter.

But he never broke stride and while the years of breathing in the ship yard's rubbish, allied to his smoking, would probably see him off well before his time it seemed, if he was to be judged by his unremitting progress, as though he couldn't wait to get through the gates and set about his noisome, dirty business.

I never saw him, though I imagined him well enough. It wasn't hard for he was one of so many. When the siren blew in the early morning and at evening time the hordes poured through the shipyards' gates and along the road which lead into the town. They all wore caps which were old and pulled this way and that to suit them and a battered jacket on top of their bib and brace overalls or boiler suits. Work dress designated the tradesmen, one from another and any one in a collar and tie more than likely worked in the drawing office. And so there was a pecking order, unmonitored but definitive, which sorted out the staff from other workers.

A concession to the biting wind, which always seemed to howl off the North Sea and frequently whipped rain and winter sleet into their faces, would be an old gabardine mac which they pulled over and around everything else and buckled or tied around them. Heads down, they would walk on seg-studded boots to the buses or, if they lived close enough to home, to tramp the distance on foot.

There was no way I was going to work in the shipyards - or in Richardson's Westgarth or the Central Marine Engine Works where young men, after leaving school, went to learn engineering and then go to sea to get their 'tickets' which, eventually would allow them to become draughtsman 'in the office'. Give me a drawing to follow and a bench full of raw materials and I'd probably build something which would sink. Quickly. Not for me the usual technical route to the usual West Hartlepool career. There had to be another way.

~ ~ ~ ~ ~ ~ ~ ~ ~ ~

I was laid low so often in those early years with asthma attacks dreadful enough for me still to remember - the fighting to be able to breathe, rolling around the bed gasping and the disease being made worse by the prospect of a visit by a one-legged doctor who made me dreadfully afraid.

Kerr Muir would arrive at our house and, when just inside the front door, mutter for a few minutes with my mother. He would then clump up the stairs to see me, sound my chest, poke with icy forefinger around my protruding ribs and, without speaking to me, go outside, close the bedroom door and murmur once more to my mother.

She, after he had stumped off to his car, would go to the chemist with his prescription and return with some sort of jollop, a patent asthma cure which she would burn in the bedroom and which would give off a smell pungent enough to knot my stomach with cramps. It didn't do any good at all and after I suffered one particularly violent attack the Old Queen decided she would take the matter into her own hands.

I had spent an entire night sat up in bed, afraid to lie down because the moment I did so breathing became nigh on impossible. And all the time the cough rasped and tore at me, making my eyes water and nose run. When daylight broke I was exhausted with the effort of forcing air into my lungs - then fighting to expel it.

That night she rubbed my chest with Vick, placed Thermogene, a sort of red powdered cotton wool, over the well-rubbed area - then gave me a hot drink. Within minutes my temperature took off. I was generating enough heat to power the QEII across the Atlantic.

Just as I was about to expire mother climbed the stairs to check on progress and, seeing my beetroot red face and gaping mouth realised even a doctor who couldn't alleviate the problem with his duff prescriptions was probably doing marginally better than she was with her Draconian home made remedies.

I survived, and yet another entire, wretched night was swept into almost minor significance during a long illness which meant I lost weeks and months of school as I lay in bed wheezing and coughing and then catching colds whenever I stuck my head outside the door. Well, it surely seemed that way.

~ ~ ~ ~ ~ ~ ~ ~ ~ ~

At this time of my life school and I were comparative strangers, though I did, on occasion, drag my gasping self through the school yard gates. A comparative stranger to my classmates, I was quickly to become used to bullying - courtesy of the Harker gang who would trap the unwary then dig and punch and thump those who took their fancy or whose turn it was to be bashed.

Perhaps that's the way it was, and remains, at most schools and though Harker himself was a sorry, weedy specimen, he showed considerable managerial talent by surrounding himself with bigger, older boys who would do his beating up for him. It would now be called, by a human resources officer, delegation.

When it was my turn I took it like those others who were less organised than Harker's mob, but there remains with me an incident which was part of growing up and understanding all men are most certainly not born equal.

There arrived one morning, in the playground at break time, Jimmy. Plump, socks collapsed around his ankles, woollen jersey with collar buttoned up to his neck - and always smiling. He didn't say much and, because there was always a teacher near him, he was, for a day of two, ignored. He stood and looked at us until, one morning, he appeared on his own; no teachers in sight, but still smiling, still not saying anything.

We, because he was no longer chaperoned and us being full of curiosity, approached and stood in a circle around him. Just looking at him. He looked right back and the smile on his round, beaming face didn't flicker for a moment.

There was a silence until, slowly, he began to make circular movements with his right hand. He still watched us and we stared right back. The hand began to move faster and as it did so Jimmy began to sing. It wasn't anything we could recognise, no title sprang to mind. And then

Jimmy began to dance around and around, still smiling.

And then we knew what he was doing. He was winding up a gramophone and treating us to what a gramophone did - it made music and people danced to that music. Little kids ran from all over the school yard and stood to watch Jimmy, all of us now smiling with him as he skipped around and around and sang.

Then through the crowd came Harker, for the moment not being the centre of attention, unable to understand that and seeking the cause of this gross insubordination. And so he pushed through the crowd - and punched Jimmy in the face. Jimmy collapsed onto his ample backside, clamped both hands to his nose - and howled.

Harker, realising he had gone too far, melted into the crowd of us while teachers dashed from everywhere to scoop up Jimmy and whisk him away and into the corridors of Lynfield School.

We were never to see Jimmy again. He couldn't have been badly hurt - small boys don't punch hard enough to do lasting damage, but he was, presumably, taken to a special school to be treated as gently as his condition demanded.

I went back to attending when I could, but spending most of the time in a sick bed and, even at that young age, to wonder what made people like Harker tick.

~ ~ ~ ~ ~ ~ ~ ~ ~ ~

And so I hated my first senior school for, having been at Lynfield School barely long enough to take the exam, I passed the first part and failed the second part of the 11-plus.

Instead of getting the promised bicycle if I passed (Lord alone knows how the Old Queen would have afforded such an amazing present) I got gasps of horror from aunts and uncles who predicted for me a life of labouring on the roads (where the fresh air 'would do me good') or being pushed about the place on wheels as the asthma got worse before totally incapacitating me.

Prospects which had never been brilliant were now, after due adult consideration, deemed to be the south side of average following my failure to win a place at a local grammar school.

Socially, my mother and I were quite isolated, she having been widowed during the war and left with a baby who was a sickly pain in the neck (or the chest with the asthma sometimes making me sound like a juvenile Paul Robeson). The pair of us were thus labelled 'widow with ailing lad'. It made for a solitary existence... about as cheerful as the BBC's light programme on Sunday afternoons which could have made depressives out of us all.

But education of some sort had to go on and so, at eleven, I started at secondary school and began a most uncomfortable and unhappy phase of my life.

The corridors of the huge Dyke House School had been brilliantly decorated by an art teacher who, along every inch of the wall had created a frieze of brightly coloured figures which depicted a history of England. It was superb work and as a mark of appreciation the pupils wet their fingers and drew from the nether regions of the men lines which looked like willies - which disfigured entire corridors.

We lunched in the assembly hall with a senior pupil heading a table of six. My 'dinner' companions were blessed with a more senior, sallow youth who charmed us all by leaning forward and, thrusting his head over our plates, where he would belch. This, depending on our hunger and whether the food was edible, would allow him to finish his own plate before scooping up what remained on one of ours for he was also inclined to dribble on our lunch when he broke wind. Charm and style were not his forté, but this was lower division British West Hartlepool.

While I could handle the dinner hall digestive peculiarities and antics and try to understand the graffiti down all the corridors I was truly scared of two teachers. One shook uncontrollably and school yard whispers said he was shell shocked because of the war and to add to our every day apprehensions he had as his first lieutenant the tallest hunchback I have ever seen. They were Messrs Fearon and Paul, a Hammer horror duo who, between them, would savagely beat boys for misdemeanours which were too often minor.

The cane was part of scholastic life, but Paul was particularly dreadful. He would carry a stick up the sleeve of his jacket, holding it there, almost out of sight, the end in his cupped hand - always ready for action. His stiff-armed march around the quadrangle and school yard made him intimidating, fearsome and someone to be avoided - always. Inevitably, at this joyous time of my existence, he was going to beat seven bells out of me.

Student teachers came and went - hopefully to rejoin an outside world where they never, under any circumstances, put into practice what they had witnessed at my school. We had one, bless his untutored ambitions, who had been with us a week or so.

He was working under Paul and had left the class for a few minutes and so we chattered instead of working. When he returned the noise had risen and so, to emphasise his new found authority, he picked one boy to stand outside the door and await the arrival of Paul who had also been away, but was in overall charge of the class.

He chose me and so I stood in a sweat of apprehension for I surely knew what was coming - and I was not to be proved wrong. Paul came marching down the corridor and, seeing me standing there, paused mid-stride, opening his hand to allow the cane to slip out of the sleeve of his jacket, clutching it at the last moment by the taped binding at the end just as it looked as though the hard bamboo would fall to the ground.

He then went into his routine, making made me hold out my hand, palm up, which he lashed time after time, sometimes hitting my wrist, sometimes the very tips of the fingers. He then made me hold out the other hand and repeated the performance.

I always tried to look up at him, straight into his eyes and not let my gaze flinch as he went on, and on flogging me. But this time he was beside himself and, breathless with the effort, he lashed away until my eyes dropped and my head went down.

Eventually even he decided I'd had enough and so, trying hard not to be labelled a wimp, I slunk back into the classroom, sitting at a desk at the back with arms crossed and hands cradled under my armpits as I tried to ease the appalling, throbbing pain.

The repeated thwacking noise of the extremely severe beating in the corridor had been heard indoors and shocked the class into silence. The student, realising just what kind of lunatic behaviour he had made me suffer, put aside protocol.

Ignoring Paul now at the front of the class, red faced and open mouthed with his effort of disciplining the unruly (he hadn't asked why I was outside the classroom door before he beat me up) the student came to the back of the class and sitting next to me, murmured again and again: 'Sorry, I'm so sorry.'

It was a toss up which of us was about to start blubbing first, but I think we called it a draw and hung on. Just. But I couldn't hold a pencil for the rest of that day and all of the following morning as my hands swelled and the bruising came out. It looked as though I was wearing multi-coloured mittens.

I suffered the happy pair of Fearon and Paul and their ghastly institution of alleged learning for two fearful, uncomprehending years, all the while trying to avoid further punishment and determined to get away somehow.

I borrowed text books from the public library and, through them, studied at home as the coughing and wheezing confined me to the house for week after miserable week. And when I did go through the school gates it was as though I was being dragged into somewhere which figured in a Dickens' novel - which, in all sanity, no school should ever be.

In later years I wondered what Mr Paul did for kicks when there were no more little boys to beat up. Sure, discipline is necessary for growing lads; unmitigated thuggery has no place in school.

I even thought of going back, when I was fully grown, and asking him whether he would now to like to give me a hiding, but he had probably retired and no useful purpose would have been served. But I will never forget him.

~ ~ ~ ~ ~ ~ ~ ~ ~ ~

I also wondered, as most of us small boys did at Dyke House, about a middle aged woman teacher who had a huge bosom, wore strangulation tight sweaters and taught, as well as the bottom of the heap kids in her form, Scottish country dancing.

As she leaped up and down demonstrating reels with heel clicking springs into the air of considerable vigour and much snapping of fingers and shrill shouts of 'och aye', she was a heaving sight to behold.

When she descended her huge breasts were still in the ascendancy - and then the process was reversed. Wide-eyed amazement was rampant with little boys wondering what was happening to them before their very eyes - for it made them feel increasingly uncomfortable in other regions.

Why she was allowed to behave in this provocative way could never be established. It probably did something for her lonely spinster fantasies as she heaved up and down in front of an audience of little lads who sat and marvelled, accepting only under the most severe, uncompromising instructions, her invitation to the dance.

To confront her in a musical twinning was to be embarrassed as only little boys can be with sexual happenings beyond their understanding.

And so it was, with the greatest possible sense of release, I passed examinations at the age of thirteen which took me to the West Hartlepool Technical School. Oh, blessed relief; there was, indeed, a God.

My asthma disappeared within months and I embraced my new school with an affection which remains with me.

~ ~ ~ ~ ~ ~ ~ ~ ~ ~ ~

As we couldn't afford the complete school uniform I was bought only the cap which, as I grew (and I was shooting up), became no more than a diminishing dot fixed on the back of my head.

This was disparagingly remarked upon by a youth in the form ahead of me and, as honour needed to be satisfied I took a swing at him. He hit back and there we were, slugging it out in the school yard. It was winter, he had woollen gloves and though I managed to get out of the way of most of his punches those which slid by, brushing my face, lifted off a few square centimetres of skin.

I was later to learn the fight had been watched by two teachers who let us get on with it until it seemed I was about to be flattened and that was when they stepped in.

No recriminations, no punishment. My opponent and I shook hands and vowed not to do it again. I learned not to fight big lads wearing woollen gloves, was given Dettol and water to wash my face by one of the staff - while my sparring partner ignored me for the remainder of our school days. But he never again made remarks about my lack of school uniform.

I was awash with a considerable amount of hero-worshipping during these days of my early teens. And I was never disappointed by teachers who did not, when collecting dinner money, make a point of calling out the names of those who were being fed free which in earlier days had always been a cue for pupils, whose parents were paying for the school's very average meat and two veg, to make comment - which had got them a little something from me for afters.

Learning to fight was part of growing up in British West Hartlepool. To fight with discretion and common sense was to be learned much later

There were other reasons for life starting to swing upwards. A physics master, who was also my form teacher, made me form captain. He encouraged me to play more cricket, for I was now nearing 6ft, though still only fourteen - and I could be a bit swift when bowling flat out.

Another who qualified for my adulation was a chemistry master called Flint whose broken nose and flattened brow indicated a sporting youth and, perhaps spotting I had a modicum of ability, he gave me my first pair of cricket boots.

By now I was playing for the school first XI - and Flint sent me to Park Drive, the home of West Hartlepool CC, and a beautiful home it is, for coaching. England's green and pleasant land is epitomised by some of its truly lovely cricket grounds. Park Drive is up with the best, its manicured grass surrounded by mature trees and situated at the very top of the town surrounded by big, detached houses with beautiful, cared for gardens.

My 'new' boots pinched a bit, but they had studded soles and stopped an aspiring Fred Trueman spread-eagling himself on his backside when following through off a long run - this impersonation of a starfish not being unknown and usually performed to the delight of form mates. But the boots helped to make me progress enough to play, at the age of fourteen, for West Hartlepool Under-16's in the North Yorkshire and South Durham League.

When playing away from Park Drive we would meet at St George's Church, in York Road, and be taken by taxi to still more beautiful cricket grounds. By taxi! It was transportation for toffs and here I was being driven around like Lord Nuffield. That and my ability to play to a reasonable schoolboy level left me with a deep affection for the great English game which blossomed as the years passed and so I continue to travel long distances to watch cricket.

School was now good and enjoyable. There was no more snivelling into a shirt cuff after floggings for now I was being lifted to a comparative academic paradise where I was spoken to and not shouted at; where good teachers took their classes way beyond the school gates and the time table and the curriculum and the regulation call of duty.

Mr Agar, of blessed memory, took us out into the Durham countryside on Sunday afternoon rambles. After knowing only the town's streets I was not only being transported by taxi to play cricket all over North Yorkshire and Durham I was becoming aware of vast fields where there was more than cricket stumps and pavilions. I gazed on forests and hills and I could stand and listen and look into huge green space with the North Sea coast far below us, blue and merging with a horizon which was far enough away to be forever.

It was wonderful and so different; my horizons which had been confined to dreaming after watching the films at the West End on Saturday nights (a few coppers to get into the dog end and hopefully leave alone and not carrying a little livestock) began to have a shape and form.

I had joined the Boys' Brigade, at St Luke's, where the clergy was always more understanding than St Paul's, which was my parish church, but which divided the diocese as though with an ecclesiastical knife.

Those in the east end were not in the world inhabited by the more fortunate who lived up Nob Hill towards the park and so I appeared to be excluded from many activities - though I was encouraged to join the choir and for a short time I did so.

To get to practice I had to walk along Murray Street and negotiate passage past the hated Harker gang, still apprentice Harlem hoods harbouring memories of junior school days - and still living around Murray Street's environs.

They considered anything from which they were excluded to be part of a world inhabited by cissies. And so they beat up the inhabitants of this 'other world' which was beyond their understanding.

I would run along side streets to get out of their way and arrive breathless (the asthma was in its last throes, but still apparent) at Mr Ransome's practice where Alan Strike sang as all boy sopranos are supposed to sing - with a pureness and clarity nothing short of beautiful.

The choir was fine with the choir master leaning from his lofty seat at the back, close to the organ, to clip with a Bible the ears of those who sang rather less well than Strike. I was never sure that the Good Book was designed for such a purpose but the Lord no doubt approved of the end result for we sang his praises much the better with head singing as well as voice.

Mr Ransome was particularly exercised when we sang, as we frequently did, Lord now let us thy servants depart in peace. All too often it came out as: Lord now lettuce they servants depart tin peas.

He, who propelled himself around town on a huge three-wheeled bike to compensate for his lameness, would lean forward over the choir stalls and all the might of the saints and the Old and New Testaments would cut a young lad off in mid verse.

But St Luke's was different to St Paul's and the Boys' Brigade presented an opportunity to get away from the books with which I continued to surround myself. And part of the BB was camp, which was always in the school holidays and was on the banks of the Tees, at Eggleston, near Barnard Castle where huge tents were pitched and some of the officers' wives would spend a week cooking for the Brigade.

I never asked to go to camp because the Old Queen, always being short of readies, would surely have been unhappy about her lad being left at home.

Not telling her about such things skirted the problem until one day there came a-visiting the vicar of St Luke's, Mr. Goldie who, in deep conference with my mother not only told her there was such an event as summer camp, but left her to tell me I was going to be there. Whether he paid for my week in the schoolboy paradise of the Brigade or the church came up with the cash I never knew.

I did know this good man took me to the bus station in Clarence Road where we caught two United buses (changing at Darlington) and I found myself at camp.

Mr Goldie stayed for a few days and one afternoon presented himself in bathing costume which looked like a prop from a Mack Sennett comedy, it having arms and legs and high, round-neck collar.

There was much behind-the-hand chuckling from the boys as the vicar strode down towards the river - until he dived straight in and began to swim like an Olympic champion.

Lads love heroes and the man who was already one of my most favourite guys achieved awesome recognition from the rest of the Brigade with a powerful Australian crawl across the big pool in the River Tees.

The school, the teachers, Mr Goldie... I had always suspected there just had to be something beyond Hopps Street; had to be more to life than just existing in this small conurbation in the industrial north where men worked at all hours of the day and night, making the town ring with their rivet hammers and behaving like Pavlov's dogs as they obeyed the unceasing, interminable hooter which told them when they had to start... and when they could finish.

It was said at my new school that I was moving in the right direction and that I would make good academic progress; my always fertile imagination was encouraged, my passionate love of English was being nurtured and I was very eager to learn. But life's practicalities were already getting in the way.

~ ~ ~ ~ ~ ~ ~ ~ ~ ~

The Old Queen and I existed on her widow's pension for almost all of my early life - and it was inadequate. While still at school I had to make money.

Cricket, the Boys' Brigade, homework - all had to be fitted in and around a source of income. Any source of income. And so I got the best errand boy's job in town. Not for me the early morning and late evening newspaper lad's hours, oh no, posh I was and the money was very good (12s 6d per week).

I went along after school with my bike which had been given to me by Sister Rosemary Bray, a friend of my mother's and another lady possessed of a bosom big enough to eat your tea off, such appendages still being a source of much red-necked wonderment to a young lad developing acne, a red neck and suffering many an uncomfortable bed time.

The bike surely wasn't a Claude Butler, but had probably been ridden by Wilson who, as any schoolboy who could get his hands on any of the comics of the day knew, dressed in long black underwear, lived in a cave, probably in Scotland, ate sparingly of roots, drank only water and was a world champion all round athlete - at everything.

It was a sit-up-and-beg machine of great age and possessed of much rust which I would propel around the pound note areas of West Hartlepool, delivering posh frocks to wives of the gentry, a job which not only paid top dollar, but yielded the odd tanner tip to supplement a sound income. The additional benefits, sometimes in terms of an occasional shilling, were very good news indeed.

The routine at the Misses Carr Modes, whose shop was at the corner of Grange and York Roads did not vary. I would arrive after school and pick up the monster bicycle from the back yard. Barbara, the shop assistant, had packed the posh frocks in tissue paper, then neatly placed them in brown cardboard boxes, tying one to another with string and then placed them into some kind of geographical common sense to allow me to map a route around town, dropping off boxes at glossy front doors at the end of long gravel drives.

And when the day was done home for tea then head down for two or three hours of homework. But Saturdays were different.

~ ~ ~ ~ ~ ~ ~ ~ ~ ~

Ladies wanted new dresses for the high times at the Grand Hotel, or the Staincliffe that night for this was the weekend and many times I cycled up the same road twice in a morning as dresses were sold by Barbara and the Misses Carr to the early Saturday shoppers, all of whom were absolutely insistent that the dress had to be delivered that very day.

And so the Saturday morning shift, which started at 9am, could sometimes stretch until mid afternoon. This required a strategy to be formulated by a boy riding a Monster. A plan had to be engineered.

If tips had been good I could, on alternate Saturdays, afford to see Middlesbrough and The Greatest Footballer in The World play. He was up there and beyond The Cannonball Kid, Roy of The Rovers and would have displaced anyone in Baldy Hogan's first team. To see Wilf

Mannion play football was worth just about anything.

Ayresome Park was always full for The Golden Boy. It took men wearing flat caps and mufflers and smelling of tobacco smoke up and away from their hard working, down-the-river, shipyard or chemical factory lives, lifting them with great gusts of loyalty and roaring enthusiasm to the ultimate sporting experience of watching Borough beat... whoever.

And Wilf was our star for he played as we all wished we could play. He, in a soccer dream world of Raich Carter, Tom Finney and Stan Matthews, was our man fulfiling our sporting ambitions for we could never hope to play the game, which was then still beautiful, as he did.

But to see Wilf needed a field marshal's planning. I had to leave the powdered and scented world of Misses Carr Modes and my friend Barbara behind me at midday. Then there was a sprint down Grange Road to the bus station, opposite the *Northern Daily Mail* offices which was, much later, to start me on my career.

The Port Clarence bus left around 12.30 and wound its clattering way through the town's suburbs, through Seaton Carew and thus to the Transporter Bridge which crossed the Tees.

Men and boys crowded onto the Meccano structure to travel the couple of hundred yards or so to the Yorkshire side then wait for the metal gates to clang open and release us - those who could afford it to get the bus up to Ayresome Park, the rest of us to walk the miles, through the town and out towards the General Hospital where the patients on their beds of pain tried to judge which way the game was swinging and how Wilf was playing by the cheers and groans spilling over the dividing wall.

When it was all over, when you were hoarse but jubilant, then it was the long trek back to the Transporter, the charge off the bridge at the Durham side to get to the waiting bus and not have to wait for the next one. Then home - frequently damp, invariably cold, but still totally exhilarated if Boro had won.

Came the January day of the Arsenal visit and the Christmas coin still jingled in my pocket as I delivered Saturday morning dresses to the wives of the town's grandees.

I had arrived for work as the shop opened and was quickly off carrying as many parcels as I could, barely able to see over the top of them as I hooked my thumbs through the string binding them together and gripped the handle bars, soles of the shoes always ready to be jammed down on the road to compensate for a highly dangerous lack of brake power.

I had made three runs by 11am and already, through the drizzling rain, I could see Wilf dancing and dazzling his way through the Arsenal defence; in my mind I was already there, cheering and shouting and jumping and dodging around trying to see past the men blocking my view.

I made my fourth run of the morning and arrived back at the shop to park Monster in the yard. Barbara, always a conspirator in my efforts to get away on match days, was looking agitated. She stopped me and said one the shop's best customers, who lived up West Hartlepool's mahogany end, was hitting the local high spots that very evening, had made a big money purchase which I had to deliver, right now, to the top of the mile-long Park Road.

Wilf's wizardry vanished before my eyes and I stood defeated at the prospect of missing the big match. Barbara and I looked at each other, saddened. I breathed deeply. And then I made the decision.

'I won't do it,' I said, 'I've done enough today. I'll work late on Monday.'

She looked aghast: 'But the dress has been promised. You've got to deliver it - no choice.'

I looked at the ceiling and Wilf looked down, smiling at me eyebrows raised in query. My courage or my cowardice was about to be examined. All schoolboy emotions twixt and between must have chased across my features; I was in turmoil. We looked at each other for several long seconds.

'I won't,' I told Barbara, turning and heading for the door. 'I'm going to see Wilf Mannion.'

And so the first errand boys' strike in the UK got under way.

It wasn't a very big strike - just one of us on the walk out - and throughout the journey to Ayresome my mind was occupied with the very real prospect of losing my job, for had not one of the Misses Carr come from out of the curtained booths in the back of the shop and asked why

I was hanging around in my allocated position - behind the front door and out of sight of the customers? She told me not to just stand there, but to get along and deliver.

She then disappeared into the changing rooms and I, as instructed, disappeared out of the front door - quickly.

As the bus rattled along and the steam from the travellers' breath clouded the windows I was convinced my defiance would certainly see cards and coppers in my hand on Monday and most assuredly would put me down the road - and all because I wanted to see Wilf play.

And Wilf did play. And he was brilliant, but even as I applauded and shouted to tell him how wonderful he was the prospect of losing my job swirled over me in clouds during the match.

All through the weekend the proverbial high jump, which was surely awaiting, occupied me and so came the Monday night when all my bravado had vapourised as me and the Monster reported to the shop and I stood, as usual, behind the door, hands behind my back, head lowered, waiting for the hard word.

Barbara, very business like, all black dress and bustling, came from the back of the shop, arms full, and presented me with a pile of cardboard boxes. She told me to get about the business of delivering - and double quick.

Then, looking hard into what must have been a very miserable face, she winked. Perhaps she had delivered the Dreaded Last Saturday Parcel. Perhaps one of the Misses Carr had driven up Park Road with it. I never found out.

But I had kept my job and I had seen Wilf Mannion play football - which once again seemed to be worth anything in the whole wide world. But I bet he, my very own super soccer genius, never knew he had been the cause of the first errand boy's strike in the UK.

~ ~ ~ ~ ~ ~ ~ ~ ~ ~

Middlesbrough Football Club were a source of great enjoyment for so many Teesside men for they had in their side players of enormous character - like 'Gorgeous George' Hardwick, who played left back for the club and for England, both of which teams he captained.

Good looking enough to have been a film star, more handsome than

Clark Gable (both had a moustache and George didn't have to have ele-phant-like ears taped back before he walked the streets) he would lead the team onto the pitch and while they were shooting-in before kick off he would trot around the perimeter of the penalty area. Back and forth and never touching the ball until the game had started, it was an idiosyn-crasy which the crowd loved and, indeed, I have never seen such a per-formance since.

Behind George was the Italian goalkeeper Rolando Ugolini who was something of a gambler and when, after half time the crowd shouted to him and asked for the results of the horse races which had taken place earlier in the day, Ugo could give them first, second and third at meetings all over the country, this information having been gleaned at half time when he should probably have been listening to what the manager was shouting instead of cocking an ear to the radio.

Lindy Delapenha was the West Indian winger who could run like a gazelle and there was always a huge roar when he had the ball for he would set off down the touch line like a full throttle express train.

In the crowd was Asta, a huge black club comedian who took the same spot on the terraces at every home game. To roars which would rattle windows in surrounding streets Delapenha would start a run to huge encouragement from Asta who would yell: 'Go on, our kid.'

They might never have met, but no one cared; it was all part of the Saturday afternoon cabaret and when Asta produced a box of matches from his pocket, struck one and held the flame close to his face the crowd waited for the line they had heard a hundred times. Asta never failed them: 'Light,' he would bawl, 'on a dark subject.'

The laughter could be heard in the town centre.

Good, harmless days when violence in football was unheard of, when crowds were never segregated and men could go to the match on the bus without a thought of assault or abuse from someone who supported the other side. And they had only dreams of the next game to occupy their minds.

I had been able to soak up all these occasional good days by being able to pay for them out of my delivery boy's wages - and still have a few bob left to contribute to the household budget.

But money in the Maddison household remained desperately short. I was adding weight to my considerable height and was now wearing an uncle's suits, which had seen better days (and he had also given me a pair of white flannels which he had worn for tennis and I wore for cricket).

They were half mast jobs, the legs finishing well above my ankles, but a blind man on a horse galloping around the boundary might have said I passed muster. I was the only 45-year-old teenager in town. But now was the time to move on. My education was ended; I had to leave my much loved school and get to work. I was fifteen.

Arthur Bray, husband of Sister Rosemary Bray, was a top union man for the Typographical Association and arranged for me to sit an entrance examination in English and maths which I passed and so became an apprentice compositor at the *Northern Daily Mail*, the town's evening newspaper.

I think I repaid, to some degree, his kindness and twice won his union's national essay competitions which meant I attended their AGMs - one of which was a week in the Isle of Wight. For a young man who hadn't travelled beyond Bishop Auckland it was a trip abroad.

But I have long wondered how life would have turned out if I had been able to stay at school and gone on to higher education. That dream, along with my aspirations to be coached to a top standard at cricket, was so much nonsense for it was beyond the realms of reality. Practicality is all and starting life darn near the bottom of the social and economic ladder doesn't leave a lot of room for dreaming.

I began night classes for an English qualification, for a City and Guilds in typography and design and layout and examinations in this, that and two more which galloped away with my nights when I could have been exploring life in a rather more exciting way instead of staggering around under an army surplus khaki rucksack stuffed with books and coping with an imagination fertile enough to make me ache to find out if girls did more than giggle.

I suppose, in part, this knee-knocking trepidation came from a mother who sent me off to night school with the promise that if I went out with girls I might 'catch something I wouldn't get rid of in a hurry'. Sad or what? Better believe it for girls frightened me to stammering embarrassment - to the extent that I probably made a total ass of myself by boasting and strutting and swaggering when the reality was I was all chat and absolutely no follow through.

Indeed, I was in my very late teens when, as it was so elegantly put in West Hartlepool, I broke my duck. I did so with a pneumatic woman, several years my senior. The daughter of one of the town's head honchos, she drove a Hillman California, cream and red with white wall tyres - an ice cream sundae of a vehicle and she, not being one of nature's retiring creatures, wore wispy, float away light coloured dresses and white, high heeled shoes.

She lived with her top brass dad in a wonderful Victorian terraced house on the sea front and we intimately found each other in the snowy softness of her bedroom on the third floor with the moon illuminating the bay, the beams creeping through the window and a dreamy Radio Luxembourg playing quietly, romantically. in the background.

And so I entered, in every way, the higher echelons of the town's society.

~ ~ ~ ~ ~ ~ ~ ~ ~ ~

But before all this, in the painful teenage years of erections and flushes, through the days of being broke, I worked any and all hours offered for the overtime money. And the *Mail* trained me as a compositor.

A journeyman, called Bill punched me on the chin for pushing past him, and Tommy Hanby looked after me when I did silly things like starting to smoke and when I went through a period of posturing and pretending I was a man because I had a fag in my hand and I'd bedded (been bedded?) by a lady who drove a new car with a bright red fold down hood.

Syd Alderson, Jackie Stonehouse, Arthur Richards, good men all, remembered still with affection, for these were the old sweats, the men who had fought in the second world war and had wondrous tales to tell of soldiers and airman which, for a lad raised without a father's presence, were pure magic. They played to a most appreciative audience.

Jackie had flown for the RAF in Africa and the Middle East. Arthur had been in Japanese prison camps for most of the war and, try as I might, he would never tell of his experiences, but would tell stories about the Army and the brief time he had before being captured. It was all very character forming and opened a world which had been beyond my imagination.

The years went by with a turkey at Christmas from the company and money from a bonus scheme which paid even grubby apprentices quarterly and then annually with sums geared to the profitability of the company. Portsmouth and Sunderland Newspapers were a good outfit.

Certainly, my mother couldn't believe her luck when the pay packet was tipped up, for she could now have coffee at Binns where residents of the town's equivalent of a Knightsbridge bistro spent their mornings shouting at each other in cut glass tones.

She even managed to do some shopping at Knights, the grocers, in Church Square, where a large and loud chap in white overall demanded to know what the women arraigned before him wanted. He would then repeat the request, loudly, and this constituted a quite excellent sales technique which is worth noting.

The customer would never ask for a couple of ounces of boiled ham and a few broken biscuit and have the order bawled out for the world to hear. Oh, no, there had to be an order of some significance which he would shout out and this probably inspired those waiting for the honour of being served to up the ante and ask for a couple of tins of something exotic hoping, when they got home, the old man would find the contents edible.

The Old Queen had always been proud of the fact that we didn't really live in a totally terraced house, but in the two up and two down at the end of the terrace - but as the kids played football against our wall she lived in fear of the ball shattering the kitchen window, bringing that extra sharpness to our dinner. It all served to remind her and keep her very aware of who we were and where we were coming from.

But now here she was with a lad working at the *Mail* and able to afford things which had, for so long, been beyond her. And why not?

Working at a linotype machine, duplicating the words composed by others, was soul destroying. It was the creativity of the journalist which mattered; it was his by-line at the top of the story and the guy who set the type was merely a cog in a production machine. But it didn't take rocket science to realise the future for such workers was insecure.

There could not be a start-of-work-to-retirement prospect for someone who was merely duplicating the work of others, but such was the power of the craft unions it would have been a brave management to tell them this.

IT, computers, transmission of pages and pictures over dedicated 'phone lines, they were only dreamed off, and then to a very limited degree. Such hallucinatory innovation did, however, get their use to a dreamy, pencil and the back of a fag packet experimental stage. But these experiments would mean linotype operators and compositors would lose their job if direct input by journalists came about. And that was going to be fought. Viciously.

For many years still to come, the Typographical Association, now the National Graphical Association, was to rule - even more so in Fleet Street where I was once told by a Father of the Chapel (shop steward) to 'get the hell off the floor' because 'there are too many so-and-so journalists in here'. I did. Quickly.

No one argued, for to raise a syllable of protest was to tread a highly dangerous path. If the NGA said that's the way it would be then that was the way is was - otherwise they might stop production of the newspaper and management got quite huffed at this for many thousands of pounds would be lost and circulation would be conceded to rival publications who, far from showing sympathy and managerial solidarity, increased their print run to take up any slack going from the unfortunate title which had not managed to hit the streets that day.

There was no togetherness among the owners and their top managers; if one paper was in trouble the others took as much advantage as they possibly could.

The production unions, of course, knew this; were aware they could ask for the moon - and probably get it for no newspaper wanted to lose ground to others and so their demands escalated.

Indeed, during a dispute in Manchester a member of SOGAT, a long term malingerer was, after much soul searching and many a conference, eventually fired. The remainder of his stereotyping 'team' refused to work until they were 'fully manned'. Application had to be made to SOGAT headquarters in the city - who sent along to the office a guy to make up the numbers.

He just happened to be the same one who had just been fired. He got 'call out money' and an increased salary for he was now regarded as a freelance.

Quite, quite ludicrous, but whosoever challenged the 'craft unions' had a professional death wish for the company would certainly bounce the journalist, or anyone else in the office, who had been inconsiderate enough to upset 'the lads'.

But those stories are for later. At the time of which I write I was one of the guys tapping out hot metal slugs to be collated and locked into a forme which made up the page, which was then cast in a foundry and the resultant plate locked onto the press. When all the pages were done, we would roll and 'hit the streets'.

There was a kind of romance and there was pride in the times off stone (when all the day's pages had been sent for casting to the stereotypers) and on to the streets. On Saturdays the Green 'Un went out with reports and results of all the football matches and though play didn't finish until 4.40pm it was not unusual for the presses to roll at 5.05 which demonstrated the slick dedication of the journeymen compositors.

Down in the despatch delivery boys crowded as the presses roared, the newspapers were automatically counted into two dozens and carried by a conveyor belt into the howling, shouting throng to be labelled and distributed.

They were over seen by Mrs Hart, a small lady of indeterminate age and considerable girth, wrapped around in a grey coat which reached her ankles, atop her ginger hair a Queen Mother-type hat. She was possessed of a vocabulary which would have brought a blush to the stubbled cheeks of a three-badge stoker. When she started her tirade the small boys would shout back at her and quite often qualified, if she could catch them, for a clip around the ear which had been known to lift them off their feet.

But she got them and their stuffed-full bags out onto the winter streets and into the pubs and clubs, their raucous yells inviting anyone and everyone to buy and, in days when only those who had wads of cash had a minuscule black and white TV, the Saturday night sports edition sold.

Through all this, the days of composing and learning, the nights of overtime or night school, I was continuing my sometimes painful growing into manhood... all the while wanting so much to be rid of the composing room and what was clearly going to happen to it and, whisper it, try to become a journalist.

But the present had to be dealt with. The need for money remained undiminished. I took my City and Guild examinations for layout and design and passed with credits which took me above those printers from the jobbing shops in town - and earned me a few extra shillings.

~ ~ ~ ~ ~ ~ ~ ~ ~ ~

And there were add ons! Because I was tall I was asked (for a princely fee of £1 10s) to be the Press Ball doorman at the Borough Hall in old Hartlepool, where St Hilda and the Vencrable Bede had brought Christianity and now I was to bring order to a load of locals hell bent on a good night's thrash.

I was seventeen and so thin I bordered on physical embarrassment. But it was extra cash and so I stood, taking the tickets, quite resplendent in another suit of my uncle's.

The Press Ball, along with the Mayor's Ball and one or two tennis club knees-ups, were the places to be if one figured in the chattering classes in West Hartlepool. And here I was. On the door, smiling and wishing one and all a very good evening.

However, any semblance of competence and pseudo-Hollywood toughness evaporated like snow off a dyke when a local farmer, rat-legged with alcohol came with three others and made to walk past me. I stood in his way and asked for his ticket. He turned and as he spun grabbed me with his left hand, pushing and pinning me against the wall.

He was pulling back a right hand big as a ham shank when a staggering (drunk) woman, presumably the ever loving, carolled: 'Leave the silly little bastard alone, Harry.'

The little bastard was much relieved at this, but Harry, nevertheless, thrust his scarlet and port face into mine, the veins pulsating and his spittle covering my newly ironed shirt. He described my ancestors, then my present condition and made a forecast which cast considerable doubt on my sexual future.

A small enough incident, but at that Press Ball was one of my heroes (and how little did I know that, one day we would drink side by side) Charlie Summerbell. Charlie lived on Embassy tipped cigarettes and Gordons gin. He also wrote like a dream for the sports pages of the *Daily Mirror* but remained a Hartlepudlian for all of his days despite various bosses trying to get him away from the north east and to the headquarters of national newspapers in the north, Manchester.

He stepped between us and suggested to Farmer Giles that he had the charisma of the inhabitants of one of his sties and led me gently away as the eloquent one was taken, staggering, weaving and waving - and still swearing, into the dance hall by his friends.

It was a happening which I was to recall many years later when, alongside Charlie, I was to spend many hours leaning on Nancy's bar, at the County Hotel, in Newcastle with other sports writers before and after United's games at St James's Park. Charlie, built like a question mark, heart like a lion, would smile at the memory, when I reminded him, say nothing at all about it - and offer me another drink.

Not that he was ever lost for a crisp word or two. Time was when German visitors arrived in Nancy's which was akin to another invasion for this was the journalists' watering hole. Charlie had fought in the war and when some overture, fuelled by booze, was made by the visitors along the lines of we are all friends now and everything is forgotten, Charlie looked at them sideways and said: 'Buchenwald, Belsen and Auschwitz pal.'

He then turned away and drank long from his glass of Gordons, the saddest of memories no doubt crowding in on him. He then looked back into the glass and drew deep on his cigarette. It was a short, but absolute put down and maybe we should not have expected anything else from a man of great eloquence and long memory.

My efforts to become a journalist started when I covered football matches. When I could get a Saturday off work I would go, unbidden, to a wind-swept field (and the wind always blows in West Hartlepool) stand on the touch line and afterwards get the names of the scorers to go with the result.

I would then, on Sunday, painstakingly write up the notes and push them through the editor's door before the sun was up on Monday mornings.

It was sycophantic rubbish - fawning because I wanted to go back to cover the same team and once the players had been favourably mentioned why, then they made me welcome.

But lessons were learned. I had my first piece in print and, although there was no by-line, it was still my own work. I wasn't copying anyone else's efforts as I did as a linotype operator. It was mine alone.

And the second point, well made and understood, was names mattered. If I wanted to see my work under a by-line then readers also enjoyed seeing their names in print.

In fact when the local amateur theatre group (The WHODS, West Hartlepool Operatic and Dramatic Society) performed it was obligatory. Miss out one name and there would be a letter of bitter complaint to the editor, so even the guy who brewed the interval tea got a mention along with the principals. The performance was, of course, always a 'resounding success'.

When local dignitaries suffered the same fate as the rest of us and popped off a reporter was dispatched to sit sat at the back of the church before the mourners filed in, each of them determined to give his name to be noted by the hack regardless of whether they had known the deceased well, or even at all. To be associated in any way possible with a town notable added a certain credence to their future posturing and posing.

When they wished to be seen around the duffel coat brigade, leaning on the bonnet of an MG roadster, their social ambitions were enhanced by the fact they had been there, at the funeral, when dear old Bloggins had shot through and they had known him so 'very well...don't ya know?'

And if a 'mourner' did not get his name in the paper then his sadness, his soul searching agonies at the 'friend's' passing somehow transcribed into vitriol and a demand was made to the editor that the errant reporter similarly be boxed and sent on a one way trip down the aisle.

~ ~ ~ ~ ~ ~ ~ ~ ~ ~ ~

For weeks nothing happened when I pushed my copy through the editor's door, but Frank Dines, of most blessed memory, would smile at me as we passed in the corridor and one day I took it upon myself to ask his secretary if I could see him.

She, as secretary's frequently do, had an over zealous protective instinct for the boss, but said she would allow me a slot - to be announced when she deemed it appropriate.

The days rolled by. Nothing. Not a blip in the oiled machine that was the editorial department - and so I waited. What else could be done?

Eventually, I tried again, cautiously asking the Sentry at the Gate whether she had forgotten me. She glared, I made a scuttled exit and went back to the composing room in a sweat of apprehension. And two days later I was sent for by Mr Dines.

The corridor I walked seemed to be a mile long and me fresh from the loo with hair plastered down with water and printers' ink scrubbed from under my fingernails until the skin had lifted and damn near bled. I had taken off my long, brown ink-stained overall, put on a jacket and so I stood for several seconds before knocking at the door.

My Dines smiled, told me to sit down and asked what I wanted of him. He sat with his back to a window which overlooked a municipal car park and then on to Binns store. I wondered if the Old Queen was having her daily intake of caffeine with the town's shouters and realised I was tongue-tied.

Mr Dines raised his eyebrows and smiled: 'What is it Roy?'

Crumbs, he called me by my first name!

And suddenly it was like turning on a tap. I told him how much I wanted to be a journalist, that it was me who had pushed the match reports under his door and could he please take me on because a guy I know had been moved from the telegraph (wire) room to the editorial room at our sister paper in Sunderland and could I follow in his footsteps? Please.

He was gentle. He said he understood. He said he'd think about it but was I aware there would be much studying to be done, much work to be completed and attitude and fitness counted for so much.

I assured him I was fit. And I was. I would have run to Middlesbrough and back to prove it. I said I totally understood the work involved, the examinations to be taken and promised I wouldn't shirk. My enthusiasm made him smile and he said he'd get back to me.

Three days later he did. He said he would take me on as a cub reporter. He told me it hadn't happened before at the *Mail* and that overseer Tom Hanby had agreed to release me from the composing room and he would make sure the editorial staff would accept me.

Even now I recall the elation, the most fantastic, overwhelming joy, the sheer can't-believe-it emotion which swept over me.

The kid from Hopps Street was to be a journalist; on the edge, the very edge, but with a finger tip hold on the same profession as James Cameron and William Connor and Hugh Cudlipp and yes, sure, this was West Hartlepool and I'd only been to London once and never to Fleet Street and God love and save us all, the work that had to be done.

But for now it was home and I walked in a drizzle of North Sea rain, along Hart Road and through the back streets to our house, floating above the puddles.

'From Monday,' I told the Old Queen, as I sat down to tea, 'I will be a journalist.'

'Good Lord,' said she. And wasn't that just about the right response?

~ ~ ~ ~ ~ ~ ~ ~ ~ ~

Journalists were always the newspapers' elite. And rightly so. Advertising reps and their managers (these days called advertising executives and advertising directors) will say it is they who create the revenue, who generate the finance which allows the product to continue - and there is not a lot wrong with that argument.

But it is journalists who truly create; the reporter presenting facts in a balanced and professional manner and the writers who, from their experience and their research and sometimes writing from within their very souls, who present the deeper, more considered piece.

And I was on the brink, about to be one of them; it was a joyous prospect which consumed me - even if one or two in the *Mail's* news-room considered me to be most definitely to be from the wrong side of the tracks. This I could handle; I knew this was exactly where I wanted to be.

There remain, as there always have been, people who will buy a news-paper for just one writer, that writer who has the capacity to touch chords and illustrate almost personal feelings which are shared and understood with the reader. He or she who, sincerely and with integrity, presents and reflects the common sense opinion and who will not be persuaded other-wise by extravagant lunches and facility trips to somewhere exotic - there is never a free lunch.

For newspaper journalism can require a bravery and determination to publish as Harry Evans did with the scandal of thalidomide when he suf-fered all manner of pressures to kill the stories before the presses rolled, but he went ahead and got some form of justice for those who today still carry the legacy of their mothers taking a drug which left the children with malformed limbs and subsequently severely diminished lives.

I was never to meet Harry Evans yet he was geographically so close to me in those early days, he being editor of the *Northern Echo*, at Darlington, just 25 miles from West Hartlepool.

He was to go on edit the *Sunday Times* in the most stylish and charismatic way and I would have given a great deal merely to have been alongside him - at his conferences, when he was talking to the troops, laying out his pages, designing them for maximum impact and briefing writers who could make the language caress the mind and sing a recog-nisable tune to readers as they followed him through one of the most wondrous periods of my life in journalism. But here I was, making a start and about to taste the magic - and raising eyebrows in the newsroom of the *Northern Daily Mail* as typewriter ribbons rather than printers' ink stained my fingers

Among my first jobs I was sent to court to watch Mrs Wainwright, JP, chairing the Bench, she with her nervous tic pulling back her lips. Many a lad appearing before her considered this a most favourable sign, for was she not smiling at him? He was frequently disappointed when she then banged him up for a month or two... lips twitching the while.

Then there came the brilliant defence by Rose Heilbron of a local solicitor, Louis Bloom, who had taken Mrs Wainwright's daughter, Pat Hessler, home with him one night.

Pat was the daughter of two local solicitors and a frequent occupier of a high stool in the cocktail bar of the Grand Hotel where she smoked through a holder, drank with little finger raised and made conversation with the high flying men about town who, on their way home from work, had just popped into the Grand for a scotch, a little intellectual stimulation... or whatever else might be on offer.

But the night she went out with Louis was to have a violent conclusion - and leave vacant a hallowed corner of the cocktail bar which had become almost her own. It was to be the last meeting between Louis and Pat for, after a long relationship, he had wearied of her as a lover and, as he was to later to tell the court, he wanted out.

In fact the last night's tryst between the 39-year-old woman and the 35-year-old lawyer was arranged in a civilised manner. They would, they agreed, go to a show, have a drink and then, separately, go home. Early.

In the beginning the evening went as Bloom, son of a former mayor of the town, had planned. Until she suggested they prolong the farewell for just a while and so they went to his offices in Upper Church Street - where they both began to drink gin from a bottle.

She was still in the office many hours later and the more drunk she became the more loud were her protestations as Louis tried to ease his way out of the relationship. She shouted about her lack of luck with men and how she wanted to stay with him always - and he became increasingly agitated and worried.

The night passed in a cacophony of bitter recrimination. And now the sun was rising and it was becoming time when Bloom's staff would arrive for work and the shop on street level, below the offices, would also open for the day's business. But by now Hessler was screaming at him and his statement to the police later said he had taken her by the throat to quieten her. He began to squeeze - and still she screamed. He exerted even more pressure... and suddenly she was quiet. And dead.

The plea entered on his behalf embraced anatomical medical evidence with which was allied a declaration of lack of intent to kill. It worked. Louis Bloom got a light jail sentence when he could have been contemplating the remainder of his days walking around without his shoe laces in Durham.

The case set Hartlepool agog. We were not used to such *News of the*

World happenings in down-town Church Street; it kept us in gossip for weeks and I well remember watching, from the *Mail* office windows in the days before the police used body bags, Pat Hessler's corpse being carried from the Upper Church Street offices in a rough wooden coffin and into a black van. It was a huge story for a town even as tough as Hartlepool undoubtedly was. But we locals were to gain even more notoriety.

It was the era of the Teddy Boy, tough guy buffoons who dressed in long, velvet-collared jackets, black drain pipe trousers and crepe soled shoes. A white shirt, sometimes frilled, and bootlace tie completed the ensemble - and you laughed at them only if you had a penchant for hospital food.

Our own precious lad was one Captain Cutlass who, along with his first lieutenant, Eddie the Gent, was a frequent visitor to the pubs in town. And there were lots of them. The Royal Back bar, the Devon, the Shades, all were moved in on by Captain Cutlass and his lads, always looking for money, booze and trouble.

They figured in local folklore alongside Jimmy the Murderer, who sang at anyone's request and recited 'The Charge of the Light Brigade' to the accompaniment of rattling beer trays and banging glasses as he shouted: 'Cannon to the left of us... Cannon to the right of us.' Both were to be avoided.

Yet another Poor Jimmy. He got his ridiculous name through a lurid and ridiculous story for it was alleged he had terminated all of a cat's nine lives with the aid of his mother's mangle.

His name was to live for ever more in West Hartlepool tales along with that of Ducky Merryweather, the town's first cross-dresser who, with posh frock and painted fingernails would mince through the streets and probably qualified for a bravery award as he posed in the pubs for the dockers and gangers who were drinking in the town centre.

But Jimmy was deranged and Ducky was sad while Cutlass was dangerous and after many of his violent skirmishes were reported in the *Mail*, one or two stories got into the national press and so a reporter headed north from London.

His name was Procter and he used we local hacks only for reference, keeping himself to himself and residing, thanks to a considerable expense account, in the Staincliffe hotel at Seaton Carew, from where he only journeyed to town to get close to Cutlass. He managed to concoct a story the outcome of which was the inadequate Cutlass challenged the heavy Teddy mobs of London to a fight to the death - which was rather like pitting Thomas the Tank Engine against the Orient Express. But it is presumed some folk believed this tabloid tosh.

Meanwhile Procter, having done with this nonsensical set-up was also getting quite close to several policemen in town, including one Superintendent who, one bright and sunny morning, laid devastating hands upon me when I went around to cover magistrates' court - and he pitched me out onto the pavement.

It came as a considerable shock to me - and also colleagues at the *Mail* who had been safe and warm in the newsroom while I was becoming closely acquainted with the stone steps of the police station.

The court was housed in the same building as the police station and the cells. The morning routine for the duty reporter was straightforward and established over many years. The duty sergeant was called on and asked whether anything new in the incident book was worth reporting and then it was off to the coroner's officer who would list those who had died overnight.

Having picked up what was on offer the reporter would then head on upstairs to the court and complete carving his initials into the press bench while waiting for the first case to be called.

Also upstairs, alongside the court rooms, were the police administration offices. Came the morning I headed on up - and the superintendent came in the opposite direction at a considerable rate of knots. He grabbed me, spun me around and ran me down the wide and curved Fred Astaire staircase and there I was, blessed by him and on the pavement debating whether it was Christmas or Easter and why was my head spinning?

It transpired our friend from the nationals had been caught in the superintendent's office, looking at papers on his desk and so all journalists were banned - forever and from everything.

It was a singularly stupid response to what was a moderately sinful happening which had availed Procter no gain at all. Courts have to be covered and to be so extreme was a mistake. Our national newspaper friend had gone back to London, leaving Cutlass' fighting ambitions thwarted - and us to pick up the pieces and we duly did so. But it took several weeks for routines to be restored and bruised feelings massaged into what then passed for normality.

This incident apart, these were the days when policemen and journalists worked well together - as, indeed, they did when the heavy lads from Durham headquarters came into town, sealed off Lynn Street, then the principal shopping and boozing street, and one dark night set about a pub crawl, nicking everyone who wore a velvet jacket.

It was said Teds who were not transgressing in any possible way had a beer bottle stuck in their pocket and were thumped hard against a wall. The bottle smashed, the guy was then arrested for being in possession of an offensive weapon and invited to prove his innocence at a later date. Job done.

Cutlass, whose actions had sometimes ranged on a higher criminal plane than that of his contemporaries, was an unpleasant character and went down for several years along with a few of his team - all for crimes of violence. The police were thanked most sincerely for their actions which, these days, would be unheard of, and the town breathed easily once more.

The pub trade picked up and Jimmy the Murderer could sing along without fear; the girls could totter along Clarence Road on their white, high heeled stilettos swinging their hooped skirts and their handbags as they headed for the Queens Rink dance hall.

And Ducky Merryweather could wink at the lads - much to the horror of the late night boozers in beautiful down town West Hartlepool.

~ ~ ~ ~ ~ ~ ~ ~ ~ ~

Some two years into my life as a cub reporter there came an event which was to have the most far reaching effects. I had just come back from a story which brought a brilliant picture from one of the photographers.

The local brewery was, in the interests of efficiency and expediency, selling off its dray horses and was to use lorries, capable of transporting many more barrels of beer. Huge, magnificent and well loved beasts, the horses were show animals, pulling the flat carts, piled high with the wooden ale containers around the town. But their day was now done and the last groom was there to see the last horse off to its retirement fields on the edge of town.

He had been promised access whenever he wanted to see the beasts, but this little jockey of a guy, wiry, bow-legged and tanned, with his best shirt and strides on and sporting a clean neckerchief for the occasion, was inconsolable. Tears poured as he buried his face into the horse's neck and it, sensing the man's distress, shuffled uneasily on its huge feet, the metal shoes clomping and ringing on the cobbled yard as it tried to get even closer to a friend who had cared for it for many years

The photographer got the picture and it was just right with the horse, bending its huge neck and resting its magnificent head on the groom's shoulder, almost posed.

I asked, as one had to, how he felt about not coming into work every day to look after and groom his horse, to muck out and dress it in livery which glittered and gleamed and made folk stop in the street to admire his work... and his giant, beautiful horse.

He looked up and the tears brimmed and spilt again.

'I would,' he said, 'rather lose the missus.'

It could have been a comment which cost him dear.

Back in the office I tried to save him from his emotions and write the story light-heartedly and encompassed it in an extended caption for, so good was the picture, it didn't need much more written illustration.

I hope I succeeded and his wife understood. There were women in town well-used to waiting outside factory gates on Friday night's to claim their man's wages before the money went over the bar; ladies well used to hard times and dusty roads and who, if they thought they had been in any way demeaned, would make husbands pay for it by withholding everything from him - except his breath.

And for some, if they considered the old man had really let the family down, they might have tried to take that away on a permanent basis. Would the groom escape with his dinner, his sex life and his future intact?

I handed the copy in and went back to the newsroom where the chief reporter, who I suspected had never really approved of an inky crossing the great divide from composing room to editorial, said the editor wanted to see me and smiled a smile which intimated he knew something I most certainly did not know and that what I was about to hear suited him very well.

He looked down at the riding boots he would bring into the office from time to time. They would stand, disembodied and sentry-like, with their trees keeping them immaculately straight these signatories to the sporting life he probably dreamed of living, where he could sip a stirrup cup then gallop away and away over sun kissed fields far from the office. Perhaps, in darker moments, it crossed his mind that, if such a roistering country life was not to be then we, especially those who had crossed the Great Divide should, as an alternative, receive a boot and spur heartily applied to the posterior.

~ ~ ~ ~ ~ ~ ~ ~ ~ ~

It took years for me to understand that, whenever someone in authority sent for me it was not inevitably going to be bad news. I was still at the apprehensive stage on this fine Monday morning, but had not things been going well? Had I not made progress and all jobs on the diary been completed without complaint?

Mr Dines was waiting for me, ran a finger up the side of his face and, looking very thoughtful, asked what I knew about sport. I told him I'd played as much as I could as a schoolboy, maintained an interest since and watched whenever work commitments allowed.

He then smiled, said my appointment as a journalist had paid off (oh, blessed relief) that he was satisfied with me and it was time to move onward and upward.

'Would I,' he asked lifting his eyes to look at me, 'like to move out of the newsroom and be the *Mail's* sports editor?'

Perhaps because relief overwhelmed me I didn't pause to even think about it. 'Sure,' I gushed, 'and thank you for your confidence.'

It was knee jerk stuff, a reaction which came too quickly and, on reflection, I needed more time on hard news. But what the hell? The boss was pleased with me, the wearisome night school years had paid off, I was moving to the sub editors' room - and into management.

Well, some sort of management for there was only me to be in charge of... me, though I had several stringers and not a clue about sorting the competent among them from those who were useless and in it only for the few bob which was paid to them.

And so they stayed on, anonymous and professionally inconspicuous for by-lines were ridiculously naive and copy appeared under names like Linesman and Touch Judge so no one owned, or had heightened responsibility for whatever they wrote. Their names did not appear above their copy and the extra edge to the writing which would have been endemic, was missing. Mistakes were made anonymously; the writer was unrecognised and too often slipshod because of it.

But these were early days for me and what I would never have tolerated later in my career was accepted and part of the journalistic scene in the very early sixties and, after all, was I not to be Sentinel and covering Hartlepool's United?

I was also to place my boney rear end into the seat with hollows worn therein by Charlie Summerbell for, many years earlier, he had been Sentinel. I was also to be in the same office as the news sub editors who were over seen by chief sub Tony Tyreman, a huge man with slicked-back grey hair who came to work in shiny black shoes, pin striped trousers and dark jacket - which he removed before donning a holed old cardigan.

He would then settle in a wooden bosun's chair, with aged cushion to protect his ample backside. A pipe smoker, he would allow the bowl to almost rest on his collar, which rested on his chest, which reclined on his belly and he was, for all the world, an authoritative Buddha.

One of his stunts and tricks was to have new reporters stand respectfully to the left and slightly behind his chair as they reached forward to place their treasured copy within reach of his left hand. Then they would wait.

After several minutes he would pick their copy up, scan the first couple of paragraphs and drop it into the waste basket. It was most unnerving sending, as it did, the would-be hack slinking back into the news room to whimper and whine to a senior and ask for guidance. The introduction to the story would be changed, the chastened one sent to tip-toe back to the subs' room and place, once again, the copy at Mr Tyreman's left hand.

Again the wait; again the soulful, deep, what-kind-of-garbage is this sigh as he reached for it, read the introduction, then dropped it on to the pile of copy in the centre of the subs' table for one of them to pick up and start work on it. It had been accepted and the reporter scurried back to his colleagues across the corridor, smiling.

Many years later I met Mr Tyreman. He had retired from the *Mail* and was producing a house magazine for one of the shipyards. He was absolutely charming, delighted with my progress - but I was still too in awe of him to ask why he was so silently brutal to youngsters.

~ ~ ~ ~ ~ ~ ~ ~ ~ ~

Hartlepool's United and I were to endure a relationship which grudgingly functioned, but was not particularly easy as the team struggled in the lower reaches of the Football League. They were without money for decent players, picking up instead lads who had failed to make the grade at Sunderland and Newcastle and were heading for soccer oblivion - and some locals, too. They tolerated the local press (me) because the big boys from the national newspapers only made occasional contact and then only by telephone as they directed their efforts towards bigger conurbation's with teams playing leagues above United. Much more reader friendly.

It was common sense to do so whereas I, a brand new Sentinel, damp behind the ears and eager, made the daily trip from our offices to the Victoria Ground, there to talk with the manager, Billy Robinson, who had played in an FA Cup Final for Charlton, coached at West Ham then found his way back to the north east to manage United. Lord knows why he moved so far down the football hierarchy and neither He nor Billy was telling.

I gathered Billy's job did not pay too well, though he had enough money to chain smoke, a necessary evil as Pools frequently produced performances which could have driven men not only to many packets of the weed, but to strong drink in exasperation.

I was now able to afford my own suit from Jackson the Tailor in Lynn Street and had even bought an Austin A40 Somerset which most assuredly had not been pre-owned by one nervous nun. Indeed, when I took the Old Queen for a ride to Durham City I drove through a pool of water and she got her feet wet.

But Billy asked to borrow the battery from my aged and ailing vehicle while I was away for a summer weekend because his own was flat and I wouldn't be needing it for a couple of days would I? The financial misery of soccer teams in the lower reaches of the professional game was, clearly, well spread around the club. Billy's solitary brown suit was shining like a sea front lighthouse.

His second in command was Ned Westgarth, son of a famous former manager Fred, who reputedly, once told the Blackpool management to remove themselves from his presence when they, a First Division (equivalent now of Premiership) side, kindly, almost charitably, offered to sell Pools a player who had been good, but was reaching the end of his first class career. Fred considered the fee was too much and, in his subtle north east manner, made his view forcibly known.

Ned, huge of girth and fleet of foot was the club's trainer in the days when buckets and sponges constituted primary on-the-pitch medical care, and was possessed of a turn of speed which was lightning quick as he sprinted to the stricken who had received a leather boot in a painful place. Ned's gallops were cheered every twinkling step of the way by the crowd as he sprinted cross the playing field. His imminent arrival at the 'catastrophe' had been know to make those with broken limbs spring to their feet as Ned hastened towards them, bucket in fist.

During the ensuing week, Ned would lay the suffering one on a dressing room table and suggest their sexuality would be in doubt if they allowed what was probably a massive contusion or an agonising muscle pull, to impair what ability they had and put their place in next week's team in jeopardy.

Ned didn't do pain, had no truck with real or imagined suffering and was probably under definitive instructions to get the first team onto the park in any condition for the reserves were not a particularly sparkling bunch of likely lads.

Indeed, Ned suggested turning around the seats at the Victoria Ground to put them back to front to enable spectators to sit facing the back of the stand thereby allowing them to escape the sight of Hartlepool's United labouring on an off day.

Heaven knows how he would fare today when players earning nigh on £100,000 a week fall over their handbags and lie writhing and gesticulating in an agony that exists only between their ears and are allowed to do so by administrators who see no wrong in their cheating habits.

44

But the days of which I write were cash strapped for soccer players in the lower divisions and the maximum wage, even for the top men, was very much in evidence. And so United went everywhere, regardless of how many hundreds of miles, by Bee Line coach. Any meal stop we had would see the manager issuing instructions not to order steak or scampi, which would cost a few shillings more, and ordering everyone to stick to the cheapest food on the menu.

Today's players have pasta or toast or nothing at all before a game, but nutritionists and calorie and protein intake control was not part of a pro footballer's life in United's footballing days in the sixties, though most players had enough sense not to eat too much before kick-off.

Early Saturday mornings would see us climb aboard the bus with Ned occupying his usual front seat into which he sank, never to speak unless spoken to - and then reluctantly and monosyllabically - and off we would go up Park Road to the mansions behind Ward Jackson Park, one of which housed the club chairman.

The coach would back up an unmade road with the springs creaking and the vehicle pitching in the potholes as we painstakingly made for the bottom of the drive to wait what seemed a lifetime until 'the Boss' deigned to walk down from the house and board the bus to a sycophantic chorus (possessed of a considerable depth of insincerity) of: 'Morning Mr. Chairman.'

He loved it and I have little doubt it suited him to be such a damnable inconvenience, to make us motor to his home and then keep us waiting forever. When he'd completed his ego trip we were eventually off, back towards town and heading off to... wherever.

~ ~ ~ ~ ~ ~ ~ ~ ~ ~

We travelled, more often than not, on the day of a match for overnight stops in hotels cost money the club could ill-afford. Rail journeys were rare - a full coach made much more fiscal sense than the cost of train tickets for players, manager, directors and Ned. Any meals we had on return trips were frequently restricted to visiting a fish and chip shop and many was the night, after a defeat at Accrington or Crewe or Chester, we would drive the many miles home stopping only for a pee at the side of the bus with beaten and outraged management, in fear of future employment, ignoring pleas from further down the coach for sustenance.

It was the way it had to be. Big clubs, Middlesbrough, Sunderland and even Newcastle were well within reach for the true soccer fan and Hartlepool's United then, as might still be the case, found life financially difficult.

It was a Catch 22. They had to play well enough to attract the crowds and generate revenue. But if they did not perform on the pitch the fans stayed away and the financial position became so critical they could never afford to buy players. Like hamsters on a wheel they were unable to get off a treadmill which was leading nowhere.

But there was a pride in the town and always, but always, the hope that this season would be the one when they would be promoted and no longer have to play at Lincoln or Darlington or Carlisle and make the trips to nowhere land to play the local cloggers.

They were the days when it was never thought necessary to be aware of good publicity; to understand the local newspaper was a mightily vital tool as they tried to engineer, season after season, survival. And all these years later there are still soccer clubs who are uncomprehending when it comes to the can't-be-bought value of favourable publicity.

But here I was, fresh faced and full of vim, a sports editor and well established in journalism.

~ ~ ~ ~ ~ ~ ~ ~ ~ ~

The first match of the season was away at Southport, who were managing to hang on to League status, but not, as it turned out, for much longer. They competed for local support with teams like Liverpool and Everton, which was no contest at all and one which they gave up shortly after our visit which saw us unloading from the coach stiff and weary after yet another long, cross-country journey from North Sea to Irish Sea, crossing the Pennines en route.

It was no way to treat athletes (well, Billy Robinson said they were) who were to be on the park inside a couple of hours and playing for their honour, the town's glory and the couple of quid win bonus.

As we filed off the bus one of the players, pointing over his shoulder at me, said: 'He's not with us.'

It was to become a whiskered gag and one which, as the months went by, I inwardly groaned about, but had to tolerate.

Such problems of identification came with the job and at every home match I would carry a portable typewriter from the office to the ground, there to type my copy in the press box at the back of the main stand. Completed, it would be given to a runner (a youngster earning a few Saturday shillings) who ran back down Clarence Road, into the office, up the stairs and delivered the goods to the sub editor.

Every time, as I headed with my typewriter for the gate marked 'officials and press' before the game and passed the queue mufflered and lounging against the fence which surrounded the dog track, someone would shout, to the joy of his mates: 'Are you Sentinel?'

Red-faced I'd plead guilty and the yelled reply always was: 'You weren't at the same match I saw last week.'

Ho hum, ho hum. The lads laughed loudly, I smiled weakly.

It was all light and frothy stuff except the time, at Southport, when the guy on the gate, aged and uncertain, stopped me going in.

'If you're not with the team where's your ticket?'

'They were joking,' I said.

He breathed deeply, had a scratch at his blue nose, looked to the heavens for guidance and once more demanded the magic ticket.

So I searched all my pockets for I had, indeed, applied earlier in the week for a press pass and Southport had sent me one... which I couldn't find no matter how many pockets I emptied.

'Can't find it,' I said.

'Can't come in, then,' said Methuselah, now mind made up, legs astride, feet firmly planted, face set and determined.

I paused for consideration. Time was ticking on, I had to make my first call to the office in an hour.

We examined each other and he stood, four-square, the light of authority gleaming in his rheumy eyes, for was he not the arbiter of who was who and what was what and wasn't this an official entrance? I looked past him onto the yawning, empty terraces where tufts of grass were cracking the concrete steps and suggested to him that he was not really thinking too deeply.

'Do you consider,' I said, 'I would travel from the north east coast and cover all those miles to watch your ghastly team unless I had to?'

My tone was crisp and perhaps I paraphrase for I was somewhat miffed - not to mention apprehensive as the clock ticked down to let's ring the office time. Not being entirely without sensitivity and under-standing anger verging on rage he stood to one side, I went in and took my place at the back of the stand.

I picked up the receiver of the telephone we had hired from the local freelance reporter - and the line was dead. Not a buzz not a peep. Nothing. Panic rose within me. My first away match and the Green 'Un would go without its principal report. This really couldn't be happening to me and I desperately scrambled to the other 'phone in the box, picked it up and, most blessed of moments, it was 'live'.

I rang for help and the panic in my voice must have helped for an engineer arrived just before kick off and made useful again the telephone I had rented. I made contact to a relieved office and staff, some of whom had undoubtedly been saying: 'Told you so, knew he couldn't cut it,' and started my report.

That night the Green 'Un hit the streets. On time. Hartlepool fans were satisfied; I was knee-shakingly relieved and the boss was quite happy, too. It had not been the smoothest start to my career as a sports reporter - but it was under way.

~ ~ ~ ~ ~ ~ ~ ~ ~ ~

Covering Hartlepool United was as good a way as any to cut sporting teeth. The chairman threatened to ban me after one report when the team were beaten umpteen-nil for he thought I had been unduly harsh by detailing this unpalatable truth; the centre-forward threatened to drop me in the bath, but realised my future reports might be somewhat coloured if he ruined my prized Jackson the Tailor suit - and on one auspicious night they left me totally in the dark.

The team were playing under floodlights which were just about pass-able by the Football League's standards of those days, but the press box, at the top left hand corner of the main stand, was a bench with a seat behind it. Charles Dickens had written by candlelight in more comfort-able surroundings for illumination came courtesy of a single, naked bulb dangling and swinging from a flex which was plugged into a point some-where down below in the office.

This single glow was, like the occupants of the box, left to the mercy of the winter weather on the north east coast. And on this night it gave up, departing this life with a small tinkle of exasperation, thereby leaving me, literally, in the dark.

I hastened downstairs to the office and explained my predicament. There was no replacement bulb to be found, but a candle was tipped out of a box of bits and pieces in Ned's dark and deeply out of sight treatment room, a box of matches borrowed and back I scattered, up the stairs to the back of the stand where the wind whistled off the docks leaving me to cup my left hand around the candle (which contrived still to frequently blow out) and make notes with my right hand. Welcome to the reality of reporting of football in the lower divisions, where sometimes the games were so awful the match report should have been in the obituary columns.

But I had by now got enough money together to buy a riding mac which, heavy and made of rubber, kept out the wind and rain and, when all the buttons and buckles were fastened, it was like living in a tent. It would sustain me during many years of covering sport.

~ ~ ~ ~ ~ ~ ~ ~ ~ ~

After home matches at the Victoria Ground had ended, when I had finished my interviews and had enough copy to write up the next day, Sunday, then get it into the first edition of Monday's paper, I would go home.

After a bath (to warm me up) a meal (to create a sponge which would help me soak up the evening's alcohol which was to come) I would head back into town to the West Hartlepool Rugby club's headquarters, which was opposite the Wesley Church.

Upstairs, and fortified by a pint or three, I would join the singing which was of a remarkably high standard, sometimes good enough to bring lads from the downstairs bar to stand and listen to about 20 of us as we went at it, sounding like a decent quality glee club - and we surely were a happy little band of choristers.

Then, as the street lights came on it was off to the dance at the Town Hall, which reckoned to attract those a cut above the clientele at the Queens Rink, down Clarence Road, where the tough guys bopped and boogied, and let the evening develop. It wasn't the Ritz and it surely wasn't Park Lane, but as I knew nothing of such things it just didn't matter.

Life was going along smoothly enough and I wasn't complaining.
Enter Alan Sleeman.

~ ~ ~ ~ ~ ~ ~ ~ ~ ~

We had been friends from our early days at the *Mail*, he a journalist,
me an apprentice printer, but truly good pals for all that. By the
time I graduated to the news room he had headed for Newcastle and the
Chronicle and *Journal* which, situated in the city's Groat Market, was the
Valhalla for reporters in the north east. There were, as there still are,
three publications from the office, the *Journal*, the morning paper, the
Evening Chronicle, serving the city and surrounding area and the *Sunday
Sun*.

It was a time which registered the height of newspapers' successes,
with the *Journal* selling 120,000 every morning and the *Chronicle* a massive 260,000 every night. It seemed the presses never stopped rolling for
on Saturday night and through to the early hours of the following morning the *Sunday Sun* was published under its entrepreneurial editor,
Norman Batey, a local man who had, since he started at Thomson House,
developed a charisma which grew as all good stories should, for he did
the unlikely and accomplished the unheard of.

And as his reputation hit the high spots so his circulation increased,
almost week by week as Geordie enjoyed his read before the pub and
Sunday lunch.

Batey was something of a Saturday night bully as his sub editors' desk
was full of freelance shift workers from the *Chronicle* and *Journal* editorial, all looking for a few extra bucks to help them through the remains
of the weekend.

But if he picked up copy which had been subbed and was ready for the
composing room he had the unattractive habit of shouting to the journalist who had just handled it: 'Mr Smith, don't you know how to
spell...whatever?'

Smith would grumble, under his breath: 'Here we go,' but aloud would
say: 'OK Mr Batey,' and walk to the back bench, where the editorial
bosses worked, to retrieve the copy.

But Batey hadn't just spotted one mistake, there might have been three
and the process would be repeated, again - and again until he was satisfied

the copy was correct... and the sub had been made to look a complete chump. No one wanted to be on the receiving end of another Batey shout of 'Mr ... don't you know the difference between...'

And so clean, well presented copy was usual when it wound its way to the composing room.

But the editor's thinking was deeper than that and went way beyond rocketing sub editors. He started giving more and more space to sport.

The north east lives for its soccer - and Batey, being a local man, knew all about it. He went further than anyone had dreamed of and gave the result of every match in every area which was embraced by the *Sunday Sun*. Wherever a ball was kicked there was someone who, for a few shillings, would 'phone in to the Thomson House copy takers the result of the match and the team and scorers. Everyone had their name in the *Sunday Sun*.

He frequently was able to publish short match reports, too, and the mention (for it was little more) of lads playing for some obscure team on a slag heap of a pitch meant another dozen or more copies sold. It also meant there was a huge amount of territory to be covered and this, in turn, opened up a happy little earner. Well paid shifts for the *Journal* and *Chronicle* journalists on Saturday nights producing many editions of the *Sunday Sun* were very good financial news, indeed.

It made economic sense, too, for Batey did not have a numerically strong full time staff to pay, relying, instead, on his Saturday night hacks to get the product off and onto the streets.

He and Alan Sleeman were meant for each other with Alan's huge, booming, infectious laugh, carrying all with him, for was it not he who, when reporting a Sunderland match at Roker Park, left three inches of space in the middle of the report... absolutely blank.

He wrote underneath: 'This space was reserved for something nice to say about Sunderland.'

Wearside was not best pleased - but they all bought the paper to curse the writer and they could hardly wait to see what Sleeman would write next week about the love of their lives, Sunderland AFC.

Alan was banned from the Roker Park press box, another of soccer's incredibly silly decisions for he and Batey made great play of this by inviting readers to read the report of the Man They Cannot Gag.

And as Alan sat in the stand at Roker the photographer on the pitch got a picture of him looking suitably studious as he penned a powerful piece while sitting with the spectators - and everyone in town just loved the sheer tomfoolery of it all. And the circulation increased as Alan went on to be more outrageous week by week.

One day he pitched up at West Hartlepool and invited me to join him at the Devon in Church Street for a small refreshment. After large, Runyanesque hellos, we got to careers and what was happening where with us. He told me he had been watching my stories, thought they were good and I basked in these tributes, all the while understanding there was a massive amount of progress I had to make.

But flattery's oil is a beguiling fluid and I happily listened to him as he intently made his pitch. He said there was a job going on the *Journal* sports desk and would I be interested?

I surely would be and, within 24-hours he had made an appointment for me with Norman Batey for the *Journal's* editor, Eric Dobson, was on holiday.

~ ~ ~ ~ ~ ~ ~ ~ ~ ~

Thomson House was large and inspiring with a huge front office, rather like a city bank's and a back entrance called The Lodge. Davey the lodge keeper knew everyone, was possessed of a duff arm and a sense of humour which was delicious in its irony.

He had a knowledge of everyone who worked there - and there were several hundreds going about the business of newspaper production in this massive centre. He bade me welcome, said he knew I was arriving that night and smiled conspiratorially as he signed me in - which left me totally confused.

But the job interview was quick and easy. How did he know? The position was mine and would I start very quickly. It was another lesson to be learned. If you really want to know what is happening in your world don't go to the top - ask the van drivers or the guy on the gate. They ferry around the high and the mighty or they see them coming and going. They put two and two together and, now and again, come up with a correct answer.

Back to the *Mail* office to resign and, a party of us went to the old town of Hartlepool and the Harbour of Refuge pub for the farewell thrash and a late-night under the full moon skinny dip in the ice cold sea.

You might consider bathing in the North Sea at any time of year is not to be recommended, but if Irvine and Mallory could climb Everest in boots and tweeds then brash young north east lads could manage such numbing cold at sea level.

I was later told Mr Dines was not best pleased that I was leaving, no doubt feeling he was instrumental in my arrival into journalism from nowhere and I was now getting ideas above my station - and all too quickly, for I was just 24. I have since thought about that and, indeed, to move so comparatively quickly might have inferred ingratitude.

But I had fulfiled everything he had wanted from me and probably exceeded his expectations. I had been promoted in no time at all at the *Mail* and done the job others, much more senior, had not done as well. My salary was in the region of £13 weekly and here I was, about to get £15 and move to a comparatively massive title and all the opportunities it presented. If Thomson House was ready for me then I was surely ready for it.

~~~~~~~~~~

My first job was to sort out accommodation and, having sold the shot-through-with-rust A40, paid off the bank and therefore being without wheels I had to hire a car. With a sense of style as befitted the occasion I rented a Vauxhall with wings, or fins or whatever at the rear end which made it look like something from Las Vegas.

It was brilliant red and as long and wide as a bus and I fairly zoomed into town, parked up and made my first trip, as an employee, into the office with a very confident hello to Davey who greeted me - by name. What a man!

There was a notice board in the news room which announced forthcoming parties, usually with nurses from the RVI and General hospitals, carried advertisements for restaurants and pubs - and told of other journos who had accommodation for rent.

One of these was Jack Saltman who was writing between the programme jingles for Tyne Tees Television, the type of thing which was read by talking heads like David Hamilton who was with TTT at the time. Jack would write, and David would announce: 'And tomorrow night on Tyne Tees don't forget to look in at 8.30 and watch...'

It was no job for a hack but, as Jack told me: 'I write for TV!'

His flat was in Fernwood Road, in Jesmond, and was delightful, being on the first floor with an outlook over the Mansion House gardens. There was a lounge with a partioned-off kitchen where we would boil up a stew (to which we would add vegetables as money dried up and the pub could not be afforded) and a bedroom.

This had two single beds and a deal was made whereby if either of us was entertaining while the other was out, on the return of the pub-bing/working one decency demanded a knock on the bedroom door before entering in case the stop at home was entertaining a lady.

This worked most of the time but frequent attendance at the Jesmond boozers did make us somewhat forgetful from time to time and so a card had to be pinned to the bedroom door when it was in use.

~ ~ ~ ~ ~ ~ ~ ~ ~ ~

Jack taught me a great deal about city life. A Mancunian, he had been with the *Chronicle* before moving to television and embarking on a career which was to carry him light years beyond writing jingles. In later years he was to produce flag ship programmes for the Beeb, including *Panorama*.

But that was for then and this was for now and Tyneside was an oyster for two young, single guys. And a particularly succulent dish she was with good restaurants, most warm and friendly pubs and an awakening night life which was to become quite amazing.

The club scene was in neon lights. Hollywood came to La Dolce Vita and Jayne Mansfield and Perry Como and so many of their contemporaries came with it, though the management could never quite nail down Sinatra. London's star cabaret artists were keen to travel north and we flocked to see the singers and top of the bill 'turns' - as Geordie would phrase it.

Jack and I explored it all before he took off for BBC Manchester and, eventually, for London there, no doubt, to continue to charm London with his Errol Flynn looks and a line of chat which could have put a smile on the face of a bag of spanners.

I vowed that, when he died, I would have him cremated and the ashes placed on the mantelpiece for everyone should have a pinch of Jack early in the morning to set them up for the day. He would just grin, tell me he'd outlive me and because that was a copper bottomed fact he'd hold on to that ten bob he owed me because if I was to go first there was no point in my relatives benefiting.

~ ~ ~ ~ ~ ~ ~ ~ ~ ~

In the flat below us, in Fernwood Road, lived Jack Haig, an actor who, dressed like Charlie Chaplin, would entertain children in a lunch time production by Tyne Tees called the *One O'clock Show*. Jack was later to be in lots of television, perhaps most memorably as Monsieur Le Clerc in *'Allo 'Allo*.

He was hard of hearing and when the telephone, which was in the hall, but close to his ground floor room, rang, one of us would shoot down stairs to let him know it could be the London Palladium calling. Don't suppose it ever was, but an actor's life can be very hard as bookings are sought and contacts maintained and the telephone was important to him.

Scottish comedian Jimmy Logan appeared in pantomime at the Theatre Royal while I was in Fernwood Road and he, in theatrical terms, was at the top of the Christmas tree. He lodged further up the road from us, his Rolls Royce with the personalised number plates parked outside the flat. He threw parties which brought the most beautiful girls from his show to Jesmond - and one evening we were invited to meet them. And we certainly did.

Above us was the top floor flat rented by a gloriously good looking prostitute called Helen, a lady who dispensed, at what we were assured was a very considerable price, happy times for the city gents. When I was working nights on the *Journal* and arriving back on the all night around the city bus, I was still in my bed the following morning, catching up on sleep long after Jack had headed for TTT on City Road. It was then Helen would knock at the door and shout: 'Hi, Roy, anything you want today?'

She meant did I need any shopping for she was heading for the village stores. But it was a super offer!

The downside to this cosy arrangement was Helen's boyfriend, a former PT instructor who was insanely jealous of her - which was not good news for a lady who sold her favours at the town's Haymarket pub and brought the punters back to the flat they shared.

The boyfriend was under instructions to clear off at certain times when Helen was expecting to be doing business and, one assumed, spent many hours during his enforced exiles, in the pub. This, one damp and dark evening, became too much for him and he arrived home staggering - and much too early.

Helen was most unhappy at the intrusion and, though barely five feet tall she had a temper which was legendary. As the punter legged it down four flights of stairs in a state of semi-undress and out onto the winter streets fearing for his life, the boyfriend raged at his ever-loving.

Helen was having none of it and grabbed a milk bottle. She hit Mr Wonderful so hard the glass shattered whereupon she hit him again and the jagged edge sliced through the palm as he held up his hand to protect himself.

His screaming hit a different note and he staggered on down to us with a blood stained towel wrapped around a dreadful wound. Jack bundled him into his car and drove like crazy to the Royal Victoria Infirmary where he deposited him at A&E.

The boyfriend wasn't seen in Fernwood Road again. The lovely, diminutive, fearsome Helen continued to pursue her occupation and to knock on my door and, as I slowly opened my eyes, ask if there was anything I wanted. Peace was smilingly, blissfully restored.

~ ~ ~ ~ ~ ~ ~ ~ ~ ~

Thomson House was a revelation. The journalists therein were so good the *Sunday Times* (also part of the Thomson group) not infrequently pinched the top men who headed for London and the big time. Some writers were quite outstanding and I was under the wing of a good one, Walter Peacock, a Bradfordian who took a shine to me as I showed sound judgement by looking to him for guidance.

They were heady days, with characters proliferating on the editorial floor and I was fascinated by a breed of men, now lost to journalism, who were old, probably crippled and answered to 'boy'.

When cheeky young sprogs like me finished subbing a piece of copy we would hold it up, shout 'boy' and over would hobble a geriatric on turned-in feet, or wearing surgical shoes, to take the copy from us.

He would then stagger across the open plan floor, put it into a container which would, in turn, be placed in a pneumatic metal tube which would suck it up into the ceiling and a mass of connecting pipes before disgorging it into the overseer's basket in the composing room.

Tommy was our, man, a Brummie of considerable vintage with a laugh which was half a cackle, lighting up the dreariest evening. To start this maniacal chuckle a hack had only to mention Randolph Sutton who had, it seems, been an actor when Tommy had been a call boy in one of the Birmingham theatres.

Randolph had taken a shine to the lad and with pursed and rouged lips frequently pursued him. Tommy, whose feet were presumably a lot better in his early days, legged it swiftly backstage where he dodged among all manner of props and apparatus while attempting to contain that laugh as Randolph cooed along in his wake, trying to coerce the lad into his dressing room.

Another of the messengers, Jack, declared he and his neatly cultivated moustache, were absolute lady killers and, as our shifts ended around midnight, frequently regaled all on the editorial floor with tales of his latest conquest.

But came the night Jack didn't turn in for work and there was much ribald speculation. This was to increase as the weeks went by without Jack showing up until one night he turned in to work with plastered leg and arm following, he said, a sojourn in Gosforth with a lady who was married, but whose husband, she assured Jack, was many miles away on business.

But he wasn't and he came home in the dead of night as Jack was lavishing attention on the wanderer's wife. Seizing his strides in one hand and his boots in the other Jack courageously leapt from the bedroom window, aiming for the front lawn. But he missed.

Landing on the concrete path below he broke an ankle and an arm and so lay there moaning and beseeching help. Hubby, who had by now sought his beloved's boudoir, heard the commotion, looked out of the open bedroom window and observed below our hero in dire discomfort and dressed only in underpants and nattily patterned socks.

Being a man of some intelligence it took him no time at all to assess the situation and with a snarl to his wife which indicated she should not be relying on a happy time in the immediate future, he headed downstairs - and into the shed in the back garden. There he donned his ex-army boots, which he wore for gardening and which had long since lost their National Service shine on the toe-caps.

He then walked slowly back around the house to where Jack lay begging forgiveness and a doctor, but not necessarily in that order. Hubby was not possessed of the milk of kindness and caused Jack further injuries, courtesy of equipment formerly used by Grenadier Guardsmen. These were so severe they gave rise to speculation by doctors at the Royal Victoria Infirmary about whether Jack, when he eventually arrived, had been run over by a corporation trolley bus. Jack thought that assessment was reasonable and went along with the story.

~ ~ ~ ~ ~ ~ ~ ~ ~ ~

To have a sense of the outrageous and be possessed of a flaring imagination should be part of a journalist's intellectual portfolio. The ability to understand and then draw a defining line between fact and fantasy separates the top people from those who always dwell in fantasy land. Robert was difficult to assess.

A reporter on the *Journal* he also lived, as most of us did, in Jesmond and outside his flat was parked a Mini Cooper - which he drove very quickly indeed. He said, which sometimes was believable for he was a big, dark, brooding sort of a fellow with lantern jaw and the capacity to look very sinister, that he had been chased out of London.

The next very obvious question was 'why' and Robert said he had driven get away cars for the underworld gangs in the east end of the city. To prove his point he would almost put his size ten boot through the floorboards as he hunched into his small car and gunned the vehicle around Newcastle, making tyres scream. He would return to the office with tales of the local constabulary being unable to catch him as he broke all the motoring laws.

He once took out for the evening a girlfriend who was staying in the flat while her bloke worked a night shift on the *Journal*. She went despite warnings about Robert's character and his dreadful driving.

On her return after midnight she offered a brave face and retired, with a milky drink and a digestive, to bed on the couch, forsaking the large

Scottish medicine she had been known to take to induce sleep.

Just two weeks later Robert creamed himself on the Coast Road. It was said the ambulance people had been unable to separate him from the metal of the motor and so a considerable part of Robert was lifted, with the Mini Cooper, onto the back of the breakdown truck. But there was enough left for the undertaker's purposes.

He had been heading, at a zillion miles an hour, for the flesh pots of Whitley Bay, progress being interrupted by a lorry travelling in the opposite direction whereupon Robert found himself doing 70 mph - backwards.

~ ~ ~ ~ ~ ~ ~ ~ ~ ~

We on the *Journal* sports desk continued to take supper at Nancy's bar in the County Hotel. Supper was intended to be taken in the canteen and only those with experience of nosebags taken between shifts on newspapers really know how awful the grub can be and so we headed, every working night, for Nancy's place.

A lady of considerable proportions she ruled with some determination and those not considered to be among the city's gentlemen were given 'the look', this being calculated to sour milk and remove the unwanted presence after the first pint.

She did, however, allow a geriatric with a rheumy eye, extremely large brown boots and a never ending supply of roll ups to sit at the back. We would greet him as we went in and he, adopting a Tyneside accent so exaggerated he was nigh on impossible to understand, would return our good evenings and mumble a while.

He was the local bum and usually got a pint or two every night for it was as though we, who were working and had money, owed him, who seemed to have so little. If we got fed up a nod to Nancy would see her giving the guy the hard word and we would be left to chat about which sporting person had said what and when.

Nancy would, on high days and holidays, produce home baked pies which were a treat and life for a young guy finding his way could not have been better.

One of our number, Ken McKenzie, was covering Newcastle United, a gem of a little man who, though amazingly forgetful, managed a minimum of a story a morning for readers of the *Journal* - who were spread throughout the city and the north of England.

It was said Ken (who had spent most of the war in Japanese prison camps having walked off a troop ship and straight into Changi) had a memory which now played many tricks. Indeed, it was rumoured he had once pushed his son, in his pram, from his house on the outskirts of the city, into town, a distance of several miles.

Weary he caught the bus back up the West Road and walked home where Mrs McKenzie confronted him with the very reasonable question: 'Where's the boy?'

'Crumbs,' said Ken, and caught the bus straight back to town to reclaim the pram, with baby still inside, from outside Binns store.

~ ~ ~ ~ ~ ~ ~ ~ ~ ~

After an away trip the football team had arrived late at the Central Station due to a train delay. One of the club directors, Roddy MacKenzie, from Seahouses, a village on the Northumberland coast, had offered Ken a lift in his taxi. Arriving at his house Ken left the cab forgetting he had asked Roddy in for a drop of something sharp to help him survive the journey north - and slammed the door on the disembarking Roddy's fingers which caused the director's eyes to water and Ken to miss out on several months of good stories.

Alf Greenley covered Sunderland and League cricket, John Pargeter rugby and golf and a young Arthur Lamb and I were left to round up anything and everything we were bidden to tackle. It was a sound team and I was learning all the time from professionals who looked after me.

The world took a more specific turn when Walter said he was looking for a horse racing tipster (the *Journal's* man rejoiced in the title of Underhand) and would I be interested?

Certainly, I said, and there I was, tipping horses for a trusting, unsuspecting public. I knew absolutely nothing about racing.

The *Sporting Life* had a naps table which allowed punters to compare the performances of tipsters in the bigger newspapers. The *Journal*, under my uncomprehending stewardship, headed very rapidly, helter skelter, for the foot of that table.

This could not go on and one day words were very obviously said at editorial conference for the editor had probably been getting considerable earache from readers who were many quids lighter through following my racing tips.

I was throwing other people's good money after bad for, though I was able to understand why jockeys travelled long distances for one ride at a meeting and I could read form and knew which trainers were doing well, I was tipping long shots to try to make up lost financial ground from my early racing days. And these nags were almost being followed around by corned beef wagons.

Walter, usually a most gentle man, took me to one side as I reported for work one afternoon.

'Look, son,' he said with unusual emphasis. 'For God's sake just tip favourites.'

I did as I was told, one or two horses won and in one memorable afternoon at Newcastle (when fields were poor because there was frost in the ground and trainers wouldn't risk good horses on treacherous going) I went through the card, which meant I tipped the winners of every race.

The reason for this was fields were small and there was an obvious winner in each race. Even if punters had rolled up every bet from race to race the accumulation of their winnings wouldn't have bought a decent night out at Curly's bar behind Eldon Square.

Much was, however, made of this achievement in the front page 'puff' the following day, which detailed successes and trailed to the latest wondrous offerings inside. Nothing was said about the failures which had preceded it.

~ ~ ~ ~ ~ ~ ~ ~ ~ ~

The *Journal* continued to be almost a home for me. I would start early just for the pleasure of being among my contemporaries and we would head for coffee at Pumphreys in the Bigg Market and occasionally for lunch at Carricks, where Newcastle's equivalent of the Lyons House Nippies called you Pet and Hinney and walked slowly to the kitchens on their varicose veined legs to get you ham and peas pudding stotties, probably with a bowl of chips to enhance our healthy eating.

The poet Basil Bunting who had a great deal of facial hair and was much given to looking into reference books and sucking the blunt ends of pencils as he tortuously made his way through the copy he had to work on, was one of our sub editors.

One of our reporters would walk backwards into the newsroom when he was late, which was more often than not, pretending he had been in the office at the time he was due to start and no one would notice if he reversed his approach to his desk.

He had two overcoats, one of which he always left on his chair thereby giving the impression he was in the canteen or out on a job close by the office when, in fact, he was out on whatever personal business which was occupying him that day. It was a deceit to be adopted many years later when, we are informed, our representatives in Brussels and Strasbourg took time away from their European Parliamentary duties leaving behind them, over the back of their chair, a jacket.

Perhaps the politicians not only learned from people like Joe but considered no one else had done so and the rest of us could never possibly guess what they are up to. Their arrogance, their condescension is, so often, overwhelming.

I am amused when, to dodge a question one of their favourite lines is: 'What is really important, and I know this because I hear it when I go around the country, is....'

The geographical 'around the country' line probably doesn't extend too far from Westminster, Pimlico, Chelsea and Kensington where some of them have in-town flats to make their hectic lives just that fraction easier.

I am constantly lead to the conclusion that being a politician is a super job for those who might otherwise be sweeping factory floors or trying to teach kids who, these days, know their rights before they can multiply ten by six. Not an easy job.

The politicians' travelling expenses, the salary, the 'fact finding' trips around the world make most of them fight like fury to retain their jobs and status and if they have to be economical with the truth - well, who will remember such a small lapse one week later?

The top interviewers of these ducking and diving smoothies are John Humphrys, Jeremy Paxman and Andrew Marr. Long may they continue to try to pin these people down to hard fact and an acceptance of liability.

L ife, among the dedicated and the idiosyncratic at the *Journal*, moved smoothly along. Freelance Dudley Hallwood, white haired, beautifully spoken and quite ancient, but possessed of a super wit and humour and a man well used to the healing qualities of Nancy's bar, drew caricatures of sportsmen and their teams, these appearing every Monday in a panel on the *Journal's* back page. More use should be made of cartoonists who, if they are any good, are compulsive reading and lighten the pages of any title.

Then Walter, despite my many miserable (and, for the punter costly) failings as a tipster, asked me to start writing a series of features which would culminate, after several months and many interviews, with an awards ceremony It was an idea which was to flourish for many years. The North Sportsman of the Year started in September, 1961 with the winner to be announced in January.

It was not a competition for the great and the good, rather it was to laud and applaud the guy who marked the pitch on Saturday morning, the person who kept the accounts and the club running while the lads were on the park. It was for those who didn't hit the headlines and Vaux Breweries, from Sunderland, were to be sponsors with the awards culminating in a lash up dinner and presentation at one of their hotels, the Seaburn.

I started work on the pilot and the entries poured in from all over Durham and Northumberland. Soon I was chasing around every which way to interview the most deserving sporting people, light years removed from St James' Park and Roker Park and well away from the big cricket clubs.

The first prize eventually went to one of Britain's paraplegic athletes who lived in Ponteland and this was to be the start of many years of the North Sportsman of the Year which the *Journal* readers enjoyed almost as much as those who came from comparative obscurity to the well deserved big time - even if it was only for one glorious night of acclamation.

My brief was widening and not only was I writing for this competition and working on the desk, I was sent in a van across the Pennines every week to Carlisle. It was not a comfortable journey and was not intended to be so, for the van was shared with a reporter, feature writer and photographer and we huddled together before being tipped out in the Great Border City's elegant centre and dispersed to pick up as many stories as we could during our single day. These were then written up on our return to Newcastle and 'slipped' in special editions for the west coast.

This meant we would, back in Newcastle, on a daily basis, strip pages within the newspaper which had contained news appropriate to our north east readers and insert special stories for those in the north west. I would liaise with our sports correspondent in the north west, the former England international footballer, who had played for Newcastle, Ivor Broadis.

Ivor was a great humourist, a most chucklesome Londoner who had a unique ability among his peers. He could write decent, readable and, occasionally, very clever copy.

I was later to work alongside Jackie Milburn, the Geordie dream of a soccer player, so popular they erected a statue of him, and Len Shackleton, the Sunderland inside-forward, both of whom had been internationals and first class at their chosen work... but were the south side of average when it came to writing and reporting.

Journalists at head office would have to pick up their work, make sense of it, try to convey their feelings according to what they were attempting to express - and then it would appear in the newspaper, usually a national title, under the famous footballer's name.

There was a time when the National Union of Journalists took a stand and insisted on the rewrite man being credited, but his name went in five point while the footballer's would appear in very large type and probably alongside a picture. Journalists' names do not sell newspapers; star players' opinions, which don't usually amount to a hill of boot studs, do.

Broadis was the exception to this and when a *Journal* editor tried to persuade him to give up his life in the sticks and come to Newcastle he refused. There was a dispute and Ivor stayed in Cumbria, picking up a job with the *News and Star,* the evening newspaper for the county. It was, without doubt, the *Journal's* loss.

But for me the work was piling in and on top of it all I was asked to produce yet another feature series, to last for one week (six stories, one a day) on gambling. It was manna from heaven for Underhand who, by now, was tipping favourites and one or two of them had won. I knew a thing or two about gambling!

I wrote of horse racing, went to Brough Park dog track, spent time in a bookie's shop; I interviewed compulsive gamblers and stood with the tic-tac men on the rails at Gosforth Park. The words were hammered out of the typewriter; it came so easily and as Geordie, a great gambler, was a suitable subject, so I was ready for publication.

There was, at the *Journal*, a quite excellent features man, a New Zealander called Brian Gridley and my copy went to him. And it was Brian who devised a title and skillfully used pictures and graphics for illustration all the while talking with me, getting into my mind, picking up my thought processes. He was the epitome of a good sub editor, doing just what a lay out and design man should do.

And there it was, my first by-lined feature series for a quality morning newspaper. It was well received and I waited for the next job from Walter. It came after just one week, but it surely was not expected.

~ ~ ~ ~ ~ ~ ~ ~ ~ ~

I jumped off the trolley bus from Jesmond and headed for the office for the usual graveyard shift, which started around 4pm and went on until the job was finished - which could have been well into the early hours of the following day.

Past Davey at the Lodge and up the stairs to the editorial floor where Walter was seated at the head of the group of desks which formed our small department. He looked up as I took off my jacket and hung it up, smiled and nodded across the room. 'The editor want to see you,' he said.

'OK,' I said, confident as though this happened on a weekly basis, but as I walked the 30 yards slowly, I was going back over recent times and thought if there was a problem Walter would surely have dealt with it; there really couldn't be too much to worry about...

Nevertheless, it took some courage to knock at the door for behind it was the big boss in the room where all the decisions which mattered in the newspaper were made. 'Come in,' shouted the editor.

'Sit down,' he said and as I waited, tense, he went into a few minutes of asking how I was enjoying life and was I coping well and he then added he had enjoyed the gambling series.

'Thank you,' said I - and, feeling rather less apprehensive, waited some more.

'Stan Bell is retiring before the start of the football season,' said Eric Dobson, and took a deep breath, peering over the top of his glasses. 'I want to offer you his job.'

Stan Bell had covered Newcastle United for the *Evening Chronicle* for ever. He had seen them through FA Cup Final victories and was one of the best known men in town. Every football fan in the north east recognised Stan if only by his pork pie hat which he wore, jauntily, above a craggy, well lined, almost emaciated face. He, too, was not known for his huge appetite and, more often than not, shared Nancy's bar at lunch time with other sport writing hacks, getting nourishment in a liquid, time honoured journalist's way.

I paused - but only for a moment. Again I said: 'Thank you.' This time with feeling

'It's a massive job,' said Mr Dobson. 'Everyone in the area has an opinion about United; it's a way of life for hundreds of thousands of people, they need their football probably more than anyone else in England. Are you aware of that?'

'I think so, yes.'

'You'll start on Monday with your first back page lead. And I do mean lead; no side panel stories and certainly no down-the-page fillers. Tyneside expects more than that.'

I sat trying to absorb all this. It had been the quickest of interviews and I later thought minds were made up long before I was called in. I was dumbfounded - but not so overawed that I didn't ask one big question.

'Will I get a pay rise, Mr Dobson?'

Mr Dobson sighed, harumphed into his ever-present pipe, and looked hard at me.

'£18 a week is the going rate which will lift you by £1; is that acceptable?'

'Certainly is sir,' I said and thanked him again before walking out of his room, weak-kneed but floating.

Walter looked across, saw me coming and winked. 'Feeling good?' 'Oh, yes,' I replied.

And why wouldn't I be? I was 25 and about to be the lead sports writer of one of Britain's best selling evening newspapers. Was it just three years since I was pulling proofs of journalists' work and handing it, with inky fingers, to them, wishing all the while it could be me on the receiving end?

It was, indeed, a wonderful life. Time to practice the vernacular by shouting: 'Howway the laads,' and proclaiming, 'I could have fanned that in with me cap,' when an open goal was missed.

~ ~ ~ ~ ~ ~ ~ ~ ~ ~

The job was massive. The minimum of a back page lead every night in the *Chronicle* was routine. More stories were expected every day, these to be devoured by a public who would, if given the opportunity, read about a United player's hair spray.

In addition I had two tabloid pages inside the Saturday sports edition given to club gossip. The Pink 'Un also had a 'runner' which was the match report on the day of the game and which covered the front page and two further pages inside as well as a match verdict, which was about 150 words - and the selection of a man of the match. All to be tele-phoned and completed by the time the final whistle was blown.

There was also a programme edition for the home games which sold outside St James's Park before the match, the vendors mixing with guys carrying huge banners telling us the end of the world was nigh or, as a happy and positive alternative, the wages of sin would be death.

This midday edition detailed the home team and gave potted biogra-phies of the visiting players, their manager, back room staff, former play-ers... you name them and they were there.

When United played away the *Sunday Sun,* who did not always send a reporter away with the team, this not being financially expedient, needed 800 words for their title and this had to be delivered within an hour of the match finishing. This would hold for the first edition and then quotes from man-ager and the players had to be incorporated in a rewrite (usually done on the rain heading north) and telephoned from the nearest station en route.

And all for £18 a week - though I did, eventually, manage to squeeze first class travel out of the *Chronicle* for the directors would only travel that way and my plea was I needed to get close to them after every game for their comments. Too easy? Too right! Let me at it.

~ ~ ~ ~ ~ ~ ~ ~ ~ ~

The routine of these days and weeks stretched ahead and were patterned as though stamped in steel down in a riverside factory. But the style of communication between a huge and expectant public and the club was dictated on day one. Let me rewrite that. The club attempted to dictate.

Joe Harvey, who had seen United through to FA Cup successes as a player in the fifties and had subsequently served a managerial apprenticeship at Workington, who were still in the lower reaches of the Football League, had crossed the Pennines and was back in his beloved Newcastle. We started our respective jobs within days of each other as the 1962-63 season got under way.

Much was expected of the former army sergeant major, but he was, in terms of a club saviour, unknown. Newcastle were in the Second Division, which was absolutely disgraceful for a city so big and possessed of a public so desperate for soccer success.

Joe, who had been with them in the glory days was employed on a mission of hope. What was expected of me by the club was equally clearly defined. And ignored.

~ ~ ~ ~ ~ ~ ~ ~ ~ ~

My first day in journalism's big time arrived and I set off for St James's Park. I made my way from the office, up Newgate Street and headed along to the open air Green Market. Then it was up the Gallowgate incline to a flight of steps long enough to have been a Busby Berkeley Hollywood set. These led to the glass doors behind which dwelt those responsible for a city's sporting dreams and ambitions.

Among those on the board were Alderman William McKeag, a lawyer of some standing in the city and Stan Seymour, who had a sports outfitters in town. It was Seymour who was at the top of the steps and waiting for me. Not for Stan the proffered hand, the warmth of welcome in the voice and the wish that we all might work well together and prosper. 'Is thoo,' he demanded, 'the new reporter?'

I pleaded guilty as charged.

'Well, if you behave and do as you're told you'll manage.'

The comment was so amazingly crass it was laughable - and while I didn't laugh aloud I did raise a smile which he perhaps took to be acquiescence for he turned his back, let the glass door swing back on me, leaving me to climb the remaining steps, push at the door and ask of a cleaner working in the foyer where the manager's office was.

A small man, Seymour had played for the club as a winger and risen through to the board - where he and McKeag worked really hard and put in many hours dedicated to deeply disliking each other.

McKeag the educated, almost languid, small, tubby guy with pince-nez glasses and ribbon spread over his ample black waistcoat to prevent the glasses being lost and Seymour, a bruiser who would, vocally ferocious, make his point, his Geordie accent and jabbing forefinger punctuating his points as his voice rose. Their dislike for each other was the cause of great amusement among the sports writers.

There has to be some speculation about how a United board (united as in unison and totally co-operating) might have fared for these were dreadful times which had come about at St James's. And yet the crowds still rolled in, 40 or 50,000 regularly turning up. But Geordie never ever said, while watching classics like United v Swindon Town, he would rather be at Roker Park watching Sunderland.

As one feeling, caring director of those days remarked: 'If we opened the gates in summer we'd get 10,000 to watch the grass grow.' He was right. Geordie's loyalty to his club was blind, transcended the rational and probably responsible for the club faring so badly. The fans would pack in regardless of the awful performances on the pitch. So... no worries, United.

And so Newcastle and the local press frequently sparred, each only grudgingly aware of the importance of the other. We needed to carry all the news we could about Newcastle United and they had publicity they could never have afforded if they had to pay for so much space.

Always there was the threat of banning the press because of a bad match report ('bad' not being inaccurate, but a report they didn't like) or because a player had complained about this or that or two more, or because the breeze off the Tyne was coming from the wrong direction.

Nevertheless, I managed, during my four year tenure of the job, to travel in the team coach to away matches and share train compartments and was always able to visit the ground daily. It all worked well enough, probably rather better than it does now for sports reporters, and, most of the time, we got along.

There were many Tynesiders who would have given anything (and I do mean anything) to cover Newcastle United for the *Evening Chronicle* and, for a young man doing the job it did have a degree or two of charm and brought with it an aura and maybe more than a touch of charisma. I was invited to speak to clubs and societies all over the north east. Dinner was occasionally on offer and I comfortably grew into the job as more social functions tumbled my way.

Then I, with Kent Walton, the TV wrestling commentator whose opening line in every broadcast was: 'Greetings, grapple fans,' made a television advertisement for Vaux Breweries' splendid ales. I was asked to do so because the advertising company handling the work thought I was a 'sporting celebrity'. I was happy to go along with that and the exercise put my face not only on TV but on huge posters as a 'still' and these were displayed on massive billboards all over the north east.

Whether my million-miles-wide smile started the day irretrievably badly for the thousands of motorists travelling over the Tyne Bridge into the city is not recorded, but it did much for a young man's ego. Maybe too much.

The *Chronicle* was also producing posters with my face on them and the legend 'Follow Newcastle - follow Maddison.' These were all over town and, on one bright and sunny Tuesday morning (Tuesday was always my day off), I took a bus to town and wandered, all sort of laid back and wide eyed, to stand beside one of these contents bills on Newcastle Central Station - pretending I was waiting for someone.

I wanted people to look at the poster, then look at me - and recognise me! Tyneside scattered by and got on with their business. Unsurprisingly, no one recognised me. What a downer.

But I was not in the least fazed by this; I was enjoying many good times with lots of entertainment. Among many guest appearances I judged beauty competitions at the Mayfair Ballroom. It was a great platform and the *Chronicle* did not object. I was their lead sports writer and had to be seen to be part of Tyneside life. It also fed my mushrooming arrogance - and as Arthur, one of the subs back at the office was to remark: 'We all know what makes mushrooms grow.'

When the crowded dance floor was cleared for the competition and the judges introduced to the throng of dancers I strolled (sauntered?), smiling, across the dance floor to the official long table while the Mayfair Big Band played 'It must be Madison'. I would have preferred, for accuracy's sake, to have the title spelt like my name, with two d's, but the pronunciation was the same, so I could breathe gently on my fingernails - and live with it.

The air was filled with Old Spice after shave and Evening in Paris perfume and the girls lined up in bathing costumes, most of them parading on a circuit which took them from one beauty competition to another, all around the north east, each of them hoping for the big break into national competitions, but picking up en route around the local dance halls a useful wad of cash.

Came an autumn night and another of these meat markets and I was to survive an attempted attack by an irate minder when, along with the other judges, I retired to an ante room for beer and wads, which was a most acceptable grub for a guy living at the end of the week on stew and sliced white bread.

Cold meats and sausages, pies and pickles came embellished with crisps and fancy bits and pieces on toast all of which were gratefully consumed.

We had hardly been able to wait to declare another young woman Miss Sleepeasy - or whatever - after she had shaken her considerable curves, then told us she wanted to be a model, do charity work and travel. We said 'oh, really', and headed smartly for the goodies.

But the boyfriend of another girl entrant, who had not won, decided we didn't know cellulite from celebrity and came a-pounding on our door inviting all behind it outside for an assignation with his considerable knuckles.

Norman Kemp, the gentle manager of the Mayfair, showed his diplomacy was not a veneer and manoeuvred Godzilla away from the door and outside - aided, it should be added, by a couple of big lads employed for just such an occasion.

Just one incident as nights rolled by in a haze of clubs and pubs and when funds were limited, which they frequently were, I would cross the Tyne to Gateshead where a guy who looked like a very young Groucho Marx was a genius of a pianist at the Coffee Pot, in the High Street, and we swelled it along, posing and pretending this was London for the era of the coffee bar was making its impact here, too.

I was up there with the best of them, behaving as though the pockets were lined with large bucks when I probably was wondering whether there was enough petrol in the car to get me across one of the Tyne's bridges and back to Jesmond.

Don Robinson, truly an entrepreneur who came up from Scarborough to the Newcastle City Hall brought with him a team of wrestling midgets. These guys knocked each other over and tumbled around the ring like tennis balls, inflicting minimal damage - a course of non-action which communicated itself to two huge guys one of whom rejoiced in the title Giant Haystacks. And they rolled around with lots of aggressive gestures and grunting and masses of malicious intent. Wrestling was, as it is, 90 per cent show biz and 10 per cent perspiration.

Don filled Newcastle's City Hall for a week and, because I had covered the event, invited me to London and the Savoy for the Variety Club of Great Britain's Christmas lunch.

I swapped my day off, got out of bed before the sun was up, hastened to the Central Station and took an early morning first class train ride to Kings Cross, eating a huge breakfast en route. The cab then took me across London to the Strand and in I went to the Savoy's massive, brilliantly seasonally bedecked ballroom.

Don and I stood at our tables as Kenneth More made his entrance and I was surprised that such a little guy could have been the hero of so many macho films, regularly winning the war and saving the world. But he smiled a lot and when he spoke we were spellbound by his diction.

But it was Ingrid Bergman who was the principal guest and I was overwhelmed by her beauty as, small and porcelain-like, she walked, almost floated, into the room, already laid for a sumptuous lunch and where all manner of stage personalities, TV and film stars were gathered to feed beneath the crystal chandeliers. She was as gorgeous off screen as ever she had been in Casablanca. Every man in the room looked at her and sighed... and wished... we were a black pianist called Dooley Wilson and she wanted a favour from us.

But Time Went By all too swiftly and the Miss Christmases, in white fur trimmed red capes and mini skirts fussed and teetered around on their high heels dispensing champagne and warm, welcoming words. None was another Ingrid Bergman, but who was I too complain? And so I smiled at the memory of a very different day out. as the train rattled on north.

~~~~~~~~~~

I became a member of the Football Writers' Association, a collection of sporting hacks who held their annual dinner at London's Cafe Royal when all soccer's biggest names gathered for an award ceremony (best player, best young player) and to get drunk.

Each member could take a guest and so, diplomatically, I had with me Joe Harvey who, in turn introduced me to many top players I had watched on the park but never met. It was good for business and my contacts book grew.

It was a perk of the job. After a long, hard season of freezing in press boxes, being out in all weathers and still being around after unremitting get-the-paper-out pressure the Thomson organisation took all its lead sports writers to London for the FA Cup Final.

They entertained us to lunch in the mahogany end of headquarters, in Grays Inn Road, then ferried us by coach to Wembley where we sat in the biggest press box I have ever seen and covered the final, regardless of which teams were involved, for our individual newspapers.

Peter Tinniswood, one of the brightest young men I had met, was to write classic comedy for TV, epics like *Tales from a Long Room* and *I Didn't Know You Cared*. He was also a desperately keen Liverpool fan and when I was able to produce a Cup Final ticket for him when his team was playing his joy was almost embarrassing. He was to go on to be one of the best comedy writers this country has produced, his work for radio and television, vehicles for his delicious humour, delighting millions. His early death in 2003 was, indeed, sad.

But there I was, right up there, meeting them all, influenced by a life style which had, just a very few years earlier, not even been dreamed of. I began to believe I was part of this amazing world by right and wondered how the city of Newcastle had managed to live without me in the previous 1,000 years.

The stories were rolling in, the boss had told me he was pleased and I strode the floors of Thomson House expecting applause around every corner on every corridor. Along one of them I met Walter.

I had occasionally seen him when the *Chronicle* and *Journal* shifts overlapped, the evening paper staff making way for the morning hacks coming on duty. But this time it was just Walter and I in the corridor and I wished him a hearty good day.

'Hello,' said Walter, 'everything OK?'

'Great,' I said, 'just fabulous.'

'Don't think so,' said Walter, standing silent for a while and looking at his boots and then at the ceiling. His gaze eventually settled and he looked straight at me.

'You are,' he said, 'not the lad you were. In fact you've become something of a pain.'

He walked past me to his desk leaving a very red in the face, indignant sports writer with a severely dented ego.

I had always owed him respect and so realisation about the size and the responsibility of the job and my ambitions to sit at the right hand of everybody famous began to dawn. And with it all came a heightened enjoyment.

~ ~ ~ ~ ~ ~ ~ ~ ~ ~

Newcastle United meant so much to Newcastle people... and still does. More needed to be done and so, in addition to the daily news reports, I recalled roots and tried to be more sensible and understanding by starting a weekly column in which I wrote about sport nationally.

It presented still more work for me, but it was necessary for it was needed by a sporting population along the Tyne which was massive. And I needed to be aware of the well quoted fact that any journalist is only as good as the last story he wrote.

I started going to the Strawberry pub, at the Gallowgate end of the ground, on match days rather than taking my refreshment at Nancy's bar. The bread and butter lads were there, the fans who paid the wages and had watched through all the miserable years as United tried, unsuccessfully, to recapture some of the style of the fifties.

I took a load of lip and masses of ribbing, but I smiled a lot, agreed (and genuinely so) with most of what they said and so, after several weeks, they accepted me face to face rather than through the *Chronicle's* columns.

Being, even briefly, an apprentice poseur was put on the back burner in favour of a bit of honest graft.

~ ~ ~ ~ ~ ~ ~ ~ ~ ~

It was at this time of professional light dawning, that the January snows came as they frequently did in an area on the north east coast where the wind seemed to come straight from the Siberian wastes.

But it was 1963 and this time the snow didn't stop after a day or so, but lay on the ground for weeks. Rivers froze, we had front page pictures of people trying to ski to work... and the temperature dropped to many degrees below zero as Britain hugged itself and shivered for weeks on end.

It was a time when under-the-pitch heating was unheard of and days followed weeks of there being no play on break-your-legs football pitches, rock hard and frozen solid. But still the back page had to be filled.

I grabbed at anything which would make a line and sports news was replaced by sports features when I wrote about trivia as varied as the laundering of the kit to the number of cigarettes Joe Harvey was smoking in these stressful days. Anything, any story at all.

One thing I never did, then or ever, was resort to sports writers' speculation, rampant even today, when a manager is sacked and they then print the names of half-a-dozen probable successors. If one of these eventually becomes manager then the writer screams...

'...as I exclusively revealed last Wednesday, Bloggins is to be the new manager of Didsbury Cloggers...' This 'exclusive' line is put on copy which amounts to an ego trip for the writer sacrificing accuracy and never being of consequence to the reader, though the theory is that if Farnsbarns tells the tale often enough, declaring his story is 'exclusive' fans will believe he has something to offer which is not to be found elsewhere.

Footballers, in this rubbish style of journalism, their managers and officials, never speak. They 'rage', 'snarl', 'snap' - and do so 'defiantly', 'courageously', 'triumphantly'.

I never did, and still do not know, if the public is fooled by this type of nonsense writing; I like to believe there is enough between their ears for them not to be so. Surely there is more sophistication among supporters than that, although a 50-year-old guy with a beer gut wearing a Manchester United shirt with the name Beckham on the back has to be marvelled at. Is he so devoid of character and personality he has to pretend to be someone else?

The replica football shirt is a massive con trick advertising, as it does, whatever product or company is sponsoring that team. And so our supporter buys a shirt thereby paying for the privilege of trotting around the streets looking ridiculous and advertising something he knows nothing about. And that, in anyone's language, has to be a promotional stunt as smooth as silk

It's rather like driving a car with the name of the garage from which you bought the vehicle displayed in the rear window. You are a mobile advertisement for an establishment which sends you motoring around the country to promote their name. For this 'privilege' they charge you very large bucks when you buy the car. What a stroke, but then most PR people try to put lipstick on a gorilla.

Football teams are run by managers, most of whom have failed at other clubs. Yet they are hired to do something which they have proved to be totally incapable of doing elsewhere and that is to bring success.

The chair is occupied usually by an ex-player who signs a contract with a clause written in to cover his sacking - which usually follows as surely as night follows day. And when the inevitable arrives he accepts a huge pay off, picks up the golf clubs and heads for Spain for a month or three.

When he returns to the UK another club steps in to hire him after the newspapers have creamed themselves into a froth of speculation over whether a singularly incapable ex-footballer can be the next manager of their local team and lift them from obscurity.

Players are still as one-footed as ever they were, yet get paid massively more for their ineptitude and many would be struck dumb if the 'F' word was removed from the language. They don't know the words of the National Anthem (or choose not to sing it before England games) and surround and push at referees, each of them incapable of accepting a decision against them made by the official.

Too many, too often, behave like the slobs they surely are - on and off the park. As role models to those young people who aspire to be professional players they are desperately inadequate.

Their ability to articulate answers to straight questions comes close to incoherence - and when listening to some of the game's commentators who tell you: 'The boy done brilliant' and 'We're looking for a result' anyone who cares about the language could seek a large handkerchief to hide the pain and wipe away the tears.

~ ~ ~ ~ ~ ~ ~ ~ ~ ~ ~

But that is now and in the short, cold winter days of the early sixties, when Jack Kennedy was issuing dire warnings to Nikita Kruschev and the Tyne Tunnel was receiving planning permission - all of which were detailed on the front page of the *Chronicle* - I had to start my week by filling the back page, or go a considerable way down the line, every day of the week, towards so doing. And it stayed so cold the Tyne had ice floes on it.

Postponed matches, players unable to train, snow, snow and more snow with me metaphorically trying to keep my nose above the drifts and desperate to report on something... which just wasn't happening.

The Northern Ireland full-backs, Dick Keith and Alf McMichael were at Newcastle and Dick, with an easy charm and fund of stories some of which were vaguely printable was a good source of bacon-saving information.

Alf, too, told stories one of which was how he would take care of Stanley Matthews when we played Stoke and he related how Matthews, when they had been in opposition at club and country level would dance towards him dribbling the ball, bobbing and weaving and talking all the while repeatedly saying: 'Don't kick me,' and 'Mind me legs, mind me legs'.

Such heart-rending requests left Alf unmoved and, occasionally, he managed to stop him by one means or another (the other being to kick Matthews). Both had played under Charlie Mitten, the former Manchester United and England winger who, while managing at Newcastle, had showed a great fondness for gambling, betting by telephone from his office at the ground and also by visiting courses.

Reporters had taken exception to Charlie locking himself away and not answering the door when they arrived with copy deadlines hovering. The manager was unmoved and continued his 'other business' of betting and talking with dog and horse racing contacts.

Came the day Dick had been injured and he duly reported for treatment one Sunday morning, the day after the match, only to find he was not able to gain access to the treatment room. He knocked loudly. Then he knocked again.

Eventually physiotherapist Alec Mutch unlocked the door and, peering around it, asked where the fire was. Dick replied in equally crisp and caustic fashion and demanded treatment.

'Can't be done,' said Alec.

'Why not?'

'Busy,' said Alec - at which point Dick pushed past him into the area which housed the physio's couch. Lying on the off white linen covering was a greyhound with the infra-red lamp shining on a back paw.

Alec looked down at his boots, shrugged and said: 'Manager's orders, mate.'

Dick, quite reasonably enquired why a dog took precedence over the club captain on the treatment table and afterwards, in quieter moments, wondered whether the hound was a Brough Park winner - and why he didn't have a bet on it if it did win.

Welcome to the Great Groin Strain Syndrome, rampant and unfettered.

~ ~ ~ ~ ~ ~ ~ ~ ~ ~

Things began to change under Harvey. They just had to. Even Geordie, good natured as you like and welcoming to everyone, was reaching the stage where he'd had enough of the second class and so Harvey even hinting at better times was looked upon as a Messiah.

And good signings were made - along with the occasional duff player, but who said football, like life, would be perfect? Indeed, one forward suffered such permanently damaged ankles, his feet stuck out at an angle. Trainer Jimmy Greenhalgh had to tape and swathe them in bandages before every game enabling the guy to raise a hobble fast enough to score goals.

Jimmy, a little, bandy-legged Lancastrian hard man, could fairly be labelled something of a visionary for he decided in those early days players' diets were important.

But the boys enjoyed their steak and chips on the night before a match and while they were sensible enough to obey club rules about drinking before games (well, most of the time) they were not as disciplined as players would surely become in these more enlightened times.

But there was an upside for they played in the days when players were allowed to be individuals and could talk to the newspapers.

Jimmy, despite his failed attempts to bring sensible eating to soccer players, managed to retain his sense of humour. As the team lined up in the tunnel before running out on to the park he would shout to them: 'Good luck lads - and for crying out loud don't play your normal game.'

Barrie Thomas, a centre forward who could run so quickly he could have caught pigeons, solemnly told me one day, after a long spell of injury, that the doc had told him he had muscles too big for his body. But Barrie's escapades were as nothing compared with Cas the Gas.

I met Ron McGarry at the Central Station on a bitterly cold day when he arrived to sign for United. He wore a blazer with a Bolton Wanderers badge on it (the team from which Newcastle had just signed him) and an open necked shirt. Blue and through chattering teeth, I bade him welcome.

He was a tough guy, apparently impervious to the biting cold of a north east winter and thankfully possessed of a huge sense of humour as sharp as the east wind. This prompted him, while he was out of first team favour at United, which he frequently was, to have printed business cards with the legend Have Goals Will Travel - this being a straight pinch from a television series entitled *Have Gun Will Travel*.

He was called Cas the Gas because he couldn't stop talking (and Cassius Clay, later to become Mohammed Ali, was starting along a glittering road and he, too, found it hard to keep quiet).

Ron was, in his later days at St James's Park, to kick Bobby Charlton so hard he left Ashington's local hero in a heap in the centre circle. The crowd booed Cas for the remainder of the game - and he was playing in front of his own fans.

John McGrath, the Newcastle United centre half, had a choice when he was a youngster in Manchester. He had the build of a cruiser weight boxer and could have earned a living in the ring, but his father stopped him entering the world of split lips and cauliflower ears and so John became a footballer, first with Bury and then, after playing for the England Under-21 side, with Newcastle.

He was a man who could, and let me put this kindly, look after himself. But after a brutal match at Elland Road I asked why Newcastle didn't take on Leeds United at the heavy stuff. His reply was simple. If Bremner doesn't get you then Hunter will. If Giles doesn't sort you out then Jackie Charlton will. They just line up... there are too many of them.

John had, nevertheless, a happy way of dealing with the suffering and dying on the park. When a player went down in a heap, moaning and protesting at a foul tackle, John would walk by the prostrate one - and stand, very heavily, on his hand.

The reaction defined whether the injury was genuine. If it were not then the 'injured' player would be galvanised into immediate retaliation, leaping to his feet to threaten John, thereby invalidating his claim of grievous and lasting hurt. John, craggy and hard as the Cheviot Hills, would smile a lot.

~ ~ ~ ~ ~ ~ ~ ~ ~ ~

Leeds United plastered their press reception room at Elland Road with newspaper cuttings which detailed unflattering reports the club had received over the years about some of their tough guys. And there we were, at half time and after the final whistle, drinking their whisky and eating their sandwiches surrounded by our headlines which declared our hosts to be anything but a decent lot.

Huge characters and intriguing football stories came so easily in such atmospheres and there was a precious moment before a game which will live forever.

The press box at St James's Park was on the top of the main stand, tiered theatre style, and I, as the representative of the local evening newspaper, had a corner seat on the front row with the pitch laid out below like a chess board, a brilliant vantage point.

Behind, others had seats reserved by their newspapers in this sloping layout. But there were, inevitably, those who wanted to be there for the view of the match and had tenuous connection to the media if, indeed, any connection at all. They certainly did not appear to be working. We tried to get rid of these confounded nuisances who were not properly occupied - and sometimes succeeded.

Not among them was a national newspaper reporter who was never averse to earning a few extra bob and, because he didn't have to file his copy until the game was ended, he would also broadcast updates to a local radio station as the match went on. So, there he sat, with huge 'cans' on looking like something from outer space, a Mekon from the Eagle comic.

For one game he arrived particularly early to check his line to the radio station. While he was doing so a telephone at a nearby desk began to ring. And it rang and it rang until our man picked it up.

'Hello,' said he.

'Ah,' said a voice, 'is that Bloggins?'

'Nope,' said our man.

'Oh, dear,' said the voice, 'it's the *Daily Telegraph* here... is there any sign of Bloggins, we're getting quite concerned because he should have rung in by now?'

'Nope!'

'Oh,' said the *Telegraph*, 'if he doesn't turn up at kick-off perhaps you could oblige us with a report, old chap, we'll pay, of course, just give us 1,000 words at full time.'

'Hinny,' said our man, 'I divvent knaa 1,000 words.'

~ ~ ~ ~ ~ ~ ~ ~ ~ ~ ~

There was the photographer, known for his lack of tolerance and regarded as something of a character by the tens of thousands who took their positions every game, at the Gallowgate end of the ground.

United were playing Grimsby Town and Charlie Wright, the Grimsby goalkeeper, was called upon to take a goal kick shortly after kick off. John the photographer sat with his colleagues behind the goal and Wright found his run-up to take the kick blocked by the squatting John and his cameras.

'Move,' said Wright, somewhat unceremoniously and in a tone which was understandable, for it was business, a Football League game was being played - but it was not appreciated by John who, ever one for etiquette and manners, enquired who the goalkeeper thought he was talking to - or words to that effect.

There ensued a mutual exchange of ignorance culminating in the comparatively diminutive John, glasses askew, huge coat about to be stripped off, standing up, looking up - and offering to part the huge goalkeeper from his breath.

The crowd loved it and a patrolling policemen got between the pair and moved John a couple of feet to the left. He sat down to massive applause and a smiling Charlie Wright took his goal kick

~ ~ ~ ~ ~ ~ ~ ~ ~ ~

Photographers are usually an odd lot. Most of them are frustrated reporters and never listen to anything the reporters say - for which they should be fired for it is up to the snapper to illustrate and illuminate the story not shoot off at tangents. Trainees frequently suffer at their cynical, been there and done it, hands.

They handle young reporters as though they are there to be trodden on - but if this can be sorted through and a good photographer happens along then he is to be nursed and cherished and paid top dollar for he will surely make a page sing.

A photographer with whom I went on a job did not come into that great and glorious category. We were to interview Henry Cooper, truly a sporting hero, who was in town on a charity mission to raise money for disadvantaged children. The fund organiser was delighted to have brought the fighter up from London and we were very ready to take a picture.

On the way the photographer said he had a brilliant idea and I made 'oh really', noises for the man and brilliance were separated by light years. But he rattled on about this 'idea' all the way to the middle of the city.

We duly arrived, met Henry and the organiser and the photographer said: 'Henry, would you mind just pretending to punch Harry on the chin?'

It is to Cooper's credit that he didn't groan: 'Oh, Lord, no, not again.' Instead he raised a fist to the chin of the organiser, smiled through teeth clenched as tight as his left hand, the camera flashed... and we had a truly whiskered, rubbish picture.

~ ~ ~ ~ ~ ~ ~ ~ ~ ~

The telling of stories is a photographer's forté and it is worth repeating one about a job on a railway station from which a contingent of poor souls were heading for Lourdes. The photographer's diary had been heavy and our man arrived at the station to see the train bearing the pilgrims pulling away from the platform. Three nuns were turning away after putting their charges on the train and the photographer approached them.

'Sisters,' said he, 'I'm going to be in big trouble because I've missed the picture the news desk wanted. Can we do a salvage job?'

'In what way?' asked one nun

'Could you,' asked the photographer, 'look down the platform and wave as though you are seeing the children off on their journey?'

The nuns went into a huddle and one of them eventually broke away and said: 'We're not very happy about that.'

'Why not?' asked the exasperated one.

'Because it would be a lie.'

'But nobody would know, sister.'

'God would know.'

'But he doesn't get the ruddy *Gazette*,' shouted the snapper and wheeled away.

~ ~ ~ ~ ~ ~ ~ ~ ~ ~

Fighters played a big part in the north east sporting scene and one bright morning a Clydesdale horse was brought to the Newcastle Central Station, there to meet Sonny Liston, the American heavyweight champion of the world.

The huge, black man, wearing almost incongruously a too-small pork pie hat, was helped up and on to the magnificent white animal which was then led through the city's streets toward St James' Hall boxing arena, which was next door to the football stadium. Colossal Incorporated!

Crowds cheered and Sonny looked blue and bemused as the horse plodded up and past the covered market, past Eldon Square and towards the stadium. But even a lad who communicated in grunts had the wit to raise his tiny hat occasionally and smile now and again.

That night he fought an exhibition match and I was overwhelmed by the size of the man. When I was introduced and we shook hands it was like putting my fingers into a pillowcase. Then he went to the dressing rooms, stripped - and got down to a little light preparation.

He skipped to the tune *Night Train* and the floor of the ring began to bounce as he jumped up and down from one foot to the other and the music beat a rhythm which suited his ponderous style.

He then sparred with 16oz gloves and, when bending his arms to push his hand into them his biceps came out so far they nearly touched his wrists and I thought such a huge man could never be unshipped by any boxer. He'd be the heavyweight champion of the world forever.

Within months young, slim, lightening fast and lippy Cassius Clay had beaten him - twice.

Liston was to end his short life in a New York gutter, the victim of gangs and drugs. The unbeatable heavyweight at the top of the world's rankings when he was paraded through Newcastle so soon afterwards died the death of a resident of Palookaville - a no hoper.

~ ~ ~ ~ ~ ~ ~ ~ ~

I enjoyed covering boxing and did so whenever my Newcastle United duties allowed. I travelled not only to St James' Hall for the fights, but to the Engineers' Club in West Hartlepool and the Farrer Street Stadium in Middlesbrough where, during one fight, a boxer took a punch, shook his head - and covered me and my notebook with blood, sweat and water from the trainer's bucket - which taught me to sit a little farther back in future.

Boxers are a journalist's dream. They train for months for fights which either lead to the top - or see them on the so dreadfully familiar road to nowhere.

But they always interview after the event. Covered in sweat and cut and bruised they will talk. Sometimes through loose teeth. If they have won they're bursting to lay claim to a title and want to name the next opponent. If they've lost there is ground to be regained - and they need publicity.

The north east produced good fighters, title winning men frequently from National Coal Board clubs, men desperate to get away from working in the pits and trying to win enough money to ease their way through the rest of their days in God's good light and not miles out under the North Sea.

Maurice Cullen, George Bowes, so many of them worked out in little more than seaside sheds with punch and heavy bags strung up from rafters around a makeshift ring and, year round, when the sun shone or when the early dark of winter days made the roads slippery and dangerous, they pounded along seeking fitness and readiness for the next fight.

~ ~ ~ ~ ~ ~ ~ ~ ~ ~

Jack London, a British heavyweight champion, had been born in West Hartlepool and his son Brian, who fought out of Blackpool, came one night to St James' Hall to battle with a fresh-faced all-American boy. Oh, dear.

The preliminaries completed, the six rounders and no hopers out of the way, among whom was a lad from Gateshead who cut very easily, had his fights stopped early and must have been in despair as the crowd invariably greeted his entry to the ring with cries of: 'Here comes the blood donor.'

But the top of the bill pair arrived and were early in the fight, to tangle in the middle of the ring.

The very last thing a boxing referee says as he speaks to the fighters is: 'Defend yourselves at all times.'

They then go to their corners and come out fighting. So it was and when these two heavies clinched the referee shouted, as he should have done: 'Break and stand back.'

The American did so at once and, bless his starred and striped soul, dropped his hands - whereupon London, who had neither stood back nor dropped his hands, hit him very hard on the chin with an up and over right hand - and a cultured, thoroughly decent Yankee boy went down like the proverbial sack of potatoes.

The American's corner men and manager charged the centre of the ring, waving their arms and loud in their protests. Incensed and shouting about the Marquess of Queensberry, they demanded a re-match, retribution and a few quid from the till, which would translate to a cut of the purse. Their man, now lifted onto his stool, was still debating which side of the Atlantic he was on and not taking much part in all of this when his still furious corner-men asked where the referee, Jim Folland, was from.

Jim was from Greatham, near West Hartlepool... and the boys from across the pond already knew London senior was from... West Hartlepool. What had passed before was as a zephyr. They exploded in a welter of waving arms and screaming accusations.

The inquest continued late into the night, by which time Brian London was on his way back to Blackpool's bright lights and, eventually, to a fight with Ali (he who had been Cassius Clay) - which saw our local man metaphorically on his bicycle as he tried to escape in the square ring only to be caught and severely unshipped by the greatest athlete the world has seen. What goes around...

London, when last heard of, was fine, but too many fighters end their days mumbling about the bout when they were 'robbed' of the verdict and some then dive into the bottom of a bottle. The fight game is only for the level headed who get out with a few bob while they can still talk using words of more than two syllables and think in, more or less, a straight line.

~ ~ ~ ~ ~ ~ ~ ~ ~ ~ ~

But football mattered most to Newcastle and smoke shrouded Joe Harvey, while keeping the cigarette companies solvent, was building a team which looked capable of putting United back in the First Division.

His best signing in these years when the ground filled with nearly 50,000 to see such footballing stars as those playing for Rotherham and Bury, was Stan Anderson, an England international who had played for Sunderland since schoolboy days.

Born in Durham, Anderson was possessed of great football ability and it was he who steered the team to a position, on Good Friday, 16 April 1965, where they would win that promotion to Division One if they beat

Bolton Wanderers at St James'.

Wanderers were a team of some quality. Francis Lee, who was to play for England and later to become a businessman of some note around Manchester, was good and they also had a Welsh centre-forward called Wyn Davies who was big and rangy with a flat forehead. When he headed the ball it went with a bullet's velocity. The City was expectant - but apprehensive.

And so it came to pass John McGrath kicked Davies in the first few minutes and off the striker was carried. McGrath told me later that, when the referee booked him for the dreadful foul he had added, with some sadness: 'John, I knew you when you were a good player.'

McGrath, who saw the First Division and the extra money looming tried, without great success, to look contrite.

United won and the players pushed through delirious, pitch-invading fans, to the dressing room and then made their way upstairs to stand in the directors' box where they waved to an ecstatic crowd who covered every inch of turf on the pitch at St James's Park.

Anderson took off his shirt, swung it around his head and threw it to the crowd. Immediately the other players were stripping off their shirts and throwing them down to the cheering, roaring crowd; people who were, next season, to see the best teams in British football.

No city deserved it more; no spectators had shown such unswerving loyalty in such massive numbers towards a team which, so often, had not deserved it. Now the disappointments, the nearly-but-not-quite seasons were all past. I flew to London for the season's final Saturday match with Crystal Palace with the Second Division champions of the Football League.

We drank so much champagne at the ground and on the way to the airport we got aboard the flight already floating way above the earth as we eased our way through the greeters and weepers crowding the lounges and foyer.

Settling in our seats, I raised yet another glass and looked blearily out of the window.

'Stan,' I said to director Seymour, 'we'll never get off the ground at this speed.'

'You're right,' said he. 'We're still taxi-ing.'

The 1965-66 season got off to the expected start. Newcastle raised their admission prices and the cost of a place on the terraces went up by 25 per cent, from four shillings to five shillings.

The TV licence was increased to £5 - and all Geordie's entertainment was shooting up because the price of ale was rising, too. But he couldn't have cared less about any of this added cost. United were in the First Division and international players were coming to St James' with Arsenal, Manchester United and Liverpool and the rest.

My commitments were, as they had been, and the sports pages of the *Evening Chronicle* had to be filled - but the names I wrote about were rather better known.

Sometimes this did not present a problem, but there were those who did not wish to speak to local newspapers. Don Revie, the manager of Leeds United was, in years to come, to keep me waiting at the Inn on the Park, in London, for four hours while he had dinner - then after leaving the restaurant, he walked past me saying it was too late for interviews and he was going to bed.

Being quite sharp there was not a lot got past me and I knew, at 11pm, it was getting late and I could have done with turning in myself after sitting around on the foyer for all that time. It was not necessary to behave like that and I did not forget his cavalier treatment.

But there were others who made the job more worthwhile. Newcastle United, when staying in London, used the Great Northern Hotel, at Kings Cross, which was crazy. All night long trains clattered in and out and, after one particularly noisy night, Ron McGarry came downstairs for breakfast complaining he couldn't sleep because a guy with a green flag had been running in and out of his room all night long.

Other teams weren't much better and instead of taking their players away from the city to ensure a good night's rest many of then stayed at the Royal Station Hotel in Newcastle which is situated - right on a station platform.

On Saturday's I would turn into the office early, for there was the programme edition to fill, and another page lead to be written for the first edition which was on the streets shortly after midday.

Much of this work could be accomplished in advance, but I was always hopeful, ever ready to try for something different. And so I would telephone the hotels where the visiting team was staying. The responses were almost routine.

'Who's calling?'

'Maddison, *Evening Chronicle*.'

'Mr So and So has given orders not to be disturbed.'

'OK,' and I would hang up.

Occasionally I would go across to the hotel and wait around hoping for an interview - and was usually disappointed. Neither players nor manager would emerge much before 11 and then the manager wanted a team talk, or it was close to lunch - and, in any case, the first editions had gone to bed.

But the day dawned when United entertained Liverpool. The routine was not to be varied: I rang the Royal Station and asked for Bill Shankly, then waited to be fobbed off with the statutory answers.

To my amazement a gruff voice made more distinguished by a heavy Scottish accent, came loud and clear and Bill Shankly asked: 'What's your name, son?'

'Maddison.'

'No, son, your first name.'

'Roy.'

'Right, Roy, have you got a car?'

'Yes, Mr Shankly' (already I was in awe of the man).

'Will you take Bob Paisley (his No. 2) and me to Gateshead; Durham and Northumberland schoolboys are playing this morning and I want a look at a couple of the lads.'

'I'll be at the front entrance in 15 minutes,' said I, unable to believe my luck. I was to have an entire morning with Bill Shankly, a legend of a manager - and I would be the only reporter there. I rang Gateshead.

'Hi, Roy,' said the secretary, 'what are you doing ringing us on a Saturday morning? Have United cancelled their match?'

'I'm bringing Bill Shankly to see the schoolboys' game.'

The sigh was very audible: 'Roy, I'm busy, don't mess me around.'

'I'm telling you, Bill Shankly and Bob Paisley. We're leaving in ten minutes.'

And so we left with Bob tipping up the passenger seat and cramming himself into the back and Bill Shankly in the front seat of my small car.

They could have ordered a limousine, a Roller, a Beamer, a Merc; they could have made a spectacular entrance and swept into Redheugh Park; they could have demanded ankle deep red carpets and fine wine.

But they chose to go with the local newspaper reporter in his aged, rattling vehicle and talk to him about their football club. And when they arrived they asked for... a cup of tea.

Big men - big enough to know where they had come from for Shankly was born in a coal mining village in Scotland and Paisley had started life amid the pit heaps of East Durham.

It was an episode I was never to forget and when I was, many years later, to be confronted with politicians who had certainly forgotten their roots and were deep into believing their own publicity, I could very easily remember Bill Shankly and Bob Paisley and taking them to watch schoolboys playing football in Gateshead.

It would not have surprised anyone at that time to know that Shankly was aware that one of the players on view had already been signed by city rivals, Everton, but Jimmy Husband was not his target - he just went to watch and assess.

Professional? You'd better believe it!

~ ~ ~ ~ ~ ~ ~ ~ ~ ~

Newcastle went through that season winning some and hanging on to their new, elevated status. The fans were well enough pleased as the weeks went by and I continued to enjoy a life which was becoming if not easy, comfortable enough.

Aside from the hard work - and there was lots of that - there was a lighter side and on a late July day we played a pre-season friendly at Burnley, a team which was stuffed with Geordies, thanks to a brilliant scout.

Jack Hixon could spot young players who would make the professional grade probably better than anyone before or since. His talent was remarkable and several of his discoveries went on to play for England, including centre forward Alan Shearer.

Jack would stand on the touch line at colliery welfare pitches all over the north east in pouring rain and biting wind watching, waiting and always hoping that a young player would show enough skill and aptitude to go through the ranks and become a top footballer.

He should have been working for Newcastle United, but wasn't, and so he sent lads across the Pennines to Turf Moor which almost became his second home as he made trips to see the boys he had sent to north east Lancashire make progress.

Newcastle cruised in their luxury coach to Burnley on a sparkling Saturday for a game designed to ease players into the new season which awaited them.

It was customary for all sports reporters, when the team they covered was playing away, to be offered hospitality by the 'home' reporter who would ensure the away man had a telephone (which was working) in the press box and maybe take him for a beer before the game. So it was at Burnley and I arrived to find the local man waiting when our coach arrived at the ground some two hours before kick-off.

The players went into the dressing room while I walked along the road for a pint and a natter with the guy who had set up a telephone for me. We talked about those who would be playing that day and what the match might provide. We then strolled back to the ground and made our way to the official entrance, at which point I produced my press pass.

The official at the gate waved me through but put a hand firmly in the local man's chest: 'You're banned.'

He looked and sounded amazed and said: 'But it's the first match of the season, how can I be banned?'

'It's not for this season, it's for what you wrote last season and Mr Lord has banned you.'

To my amazement there was no protest, merely a shrugging of shoulders and he made his way to the turnstiles and paid to get into the stand from where he could cover the match - without a telephone. He told me being banned was by no means new.

Bob Lord was the club chairman, a big, red-faced man who was Burnley. A butcher by trade, he was often given, almost on a match by match basis, to barring reporters from the press box or trying to keep them out of the ground altogether.

It was an early and classic case of throwing the toys out of the pram whenever he felt offended. And he was always offended. By something someone had written in some publication and so the gateman had a list of those who were banned - which, instead of making the sinners think twice before reoffending, almost made them compete. Everyone wanted to be banned, if only to produce match reports and make Bob Lord wonder how they had managed to do that. He didn't know them, was therefore unable to recognise them and one or two visiting press men, whose newspapers rather than them as individuals had fallen foul of Lord would try to buy a seat close to the directors' box, whereupon they would smile at the chairman as he took his seat.

He, being egotistical enough to consider it was but a humble fan paying him what he considered to be due homage, would probably smile back.

Other hacks who had been stopped entering the ground paid their entrance fee and then sat with fellow interlopers as close to the press box as they could. Those in the box, anticipating it would surely be their turn next, offered every assistance to outlawed colleagues.

The conclusion of all this nonsensical hilarity was the designing and selling of a tie, in various colours, upon which was woven BBB. This stood for Banned By Burnley or Banned By Bob - and many a reporter from titles all over the north of England wore it with pride and sometimes it was around their necks when they were allowed into the ground. Each had his reply ready should they be asked, once inside, what the initials on their tie stood for.

~ ~ ~ ~ ~ ~ ~ ~ ~ ~

But there were moments which ruffled this smooth and shiny surface over which I was gliding - and a couple were sad. Ken McKenzie was still travelling with United for the *Journal*. He was no longer a young man and such was the state of his memory that I would trot around hotels after him at away games, retrieving his pipe, glasses, tobacco pouch, pencil, notebook - whatever. On receiving these he would always say: 'Aye, thanks lad.' There the conversation would end, but it was not difficult to understand his embarrassment at being unable to remember what had happened such a short time earlier.

But we were good travelling companions for four years, never pinching each other's stories and always respecting each other's space. We travelled to many towns and cities without ever knowing them, seeing only the railway stations and the hotel where we were to stay and then the football ground.

The weekends were totally committed to our work and there came a weekend when Newcastle played at Chelsea and Ken and I spent some time on the Friday afternoon train taking us to London talking about goalkeeper Dave Hollins' chances of joining his brother John, the English international, at Stamford Bridge.

That was not to be, but on the following morning, after I had filed for the first edition, Ken suggested we go early to the Bridge and have a drink before the game with some pals of his at a pub close to the ground. Like him, they had been prisoners of the Japanese during the war. All Londoners, they gave Ken a very big welcome - and we talked football. No mention was made of prison camps until Ken, after a couple of pints, needed the loo.

One of the company said to me: 'If it wasn't for that little fellow none of us would be here today. It was Ken McKenzie who kept so many of us going for many years at a time when most just wanted to die. He's a wonderful man - he saved lives.'

At this point Ken came back, smiled at us all, for the conversation had dried up when we saw him approaching and, perhaps understanding something of what had just been said asked: 'Right, who's for another drink?'

We said our farewells, went to the game and after the game interviewed anyone and everyone, dashing from press box to players' tunnel and on to reception areas. Then it was a cab back to Kings Cross for we were booked on a train heading north and home. It would arrive just before midnight and we would get to our beds in the early hours of Sunday morning.

When we arrived at Kings Cross Ken bustled along the platform towards the train - then abruptly sat on a porter's trolley, his overnight bag slipping to the ground as he placed his head in his hands. I hurried back to him.

'You OK, Ken?'

'Aye, lad, OK.'

We both waited, trying to ignore the shouts of the guards as the train made ready to depart.

'Let's wait for the next one,' I said, but Ken made the huge effort and stood up. His world was spinning and I put a hand under his arm and eased him the few steps to the train where we eventually found our seats.

I sat him down and watched until his surroundings came back into focus.

Some couple of hours later Ken McKenzie was able to sit up straight and drink a cup of tea. He looked at me.

'Thanks,' he said and then added: 'You won't tell anybody at the office about this, will you?'

I promised I wouldn't - and I didn't. So much for war; so much for heroes who, in the aftermath, had to worry about holding on to jobs while suffering problems which can only be imagined.

My friend, Ken McKenzie never, in all the time we travelled together, talked of what he had suffered at the hands of the Japanese, though I had seen him, when I worked with him on the *Journal*, walk out of the office, beetroot red when a party of Orientals came on an office tour.

Like so many more who had survived an appalling time, it wasn't easy to forget. The war was locked into their memory. They just didn't talk about it.

~ ~ ~ ~ ~ ~ ~ ~ ~ ~

There was a quite beautiful pub and hotel in the middle of Newcastle which, in those days, was able to boast a gentlemen's bar without being the subject of litigation by hordes of outraged females.

The Douglas was a place where a man could drink with his foot on the bar rail and, leaning on the highly polished counter, admire the wooden walls which had hung upon them quite outstanding black and white pictures. It was an oasis. And when hungry there was, upstairs, a restaurant.

Ted Hoggard, who was the racing tipster, Silver Spur, on the *Sunday Sun*, and I were one lunch time enjoying a posh pie and pint when a recently retired reporter came into the room. Seeing us he crossed the floor to our table.

After the big hellos there was a silence and then, to the horror of Ted and I, Stan started to cry. We were shuffle footed in our embarrassment as we waited for him to regain control and his composure. When he did it was to explain he was virtually broke and had been to the labour exchange to try to claim benefit of some kind.

I was sitting among the riff raff of Newcastle, said Stan, queuing among people who were living on the dole. Me, who had been one of the best known people in this city. I couldn't stand it. I had to walk out.

There was little point in saying that people who didn't have money were not, necessarily, riff raff and there was no dividend to be gained by explaining that the dole could be a life saver for some folk who had not had Stan's chances in life.

We listened and then pointed Stan in the direction of the Newspaper Press Fund, a charity which had been established to try to get journalists through hard times and Ted went off with him to a place which would be rather more private than the upstairs restaurant of the Douglas.

I was left feeling like the thief of a man's good times for Stan had, most assuredly, kicked up his heels and been something of a roisterer around town while covering stories in this city. But it was time itself which was the thief and not me.

In the days which followed this meeting Ted remained discreet about what had happened to Stan and that was right and proper. The lesson was: Keep a few bob on one side for, as Geordie would have it: You never know to the minute - but sometimes you have a darn good idea.

~ ~ ~ ~ ~ ~ ~ ~ ~ ~ ~

In Newcastle's Second Division days I had been invited by the BBC in the city to broadcast match reports. I loved it for there was an art to writing just the right amount of words to fill a one minute twenty second slot of speech - and then being capable of delivering it in a manner and style which sounded as though you had been preparing the broadcast at your leisure.

I covered for BBC Newcastle and, occasionally I had an opt out for the national programme, *Sports Report* on Saturday nights. All this work was done at away matches for Arthur Appleton, the Beeb's sports editor in the city, usually covered United's home matches.

I always checked, before the game, the point from which I was to broadcast and so it came about that I was knocking at a pub door in Swindon on Saturday morning around 10.30. We had stayed overnight, my copy had gone to the *Chronicle* an hour before, and so I presented myself at the pub's closed and locked portals... and knocked.

There was no reply and so I knocked again. And again. And again until, eventually, a man dressed in vest and shorts, shoeless and sweating opened up and snarled: 'Waddyawant?'

I knew what he had been doing, he knew I knew - and probably was as displeased as the lady waiting, panting upstairs. I tried my brightest, most disarming smile, announcing I was from the BBC.

He was not impressed: 'There,' he said, pointing down the hall to what looked like a closed dart board. I thanked him and he went back upstairs to resume his business while I opened the 'dart board' doors to examine the SOOBE (Self Operating Outside Broadcast Equipment).

It was easy enough to operate with instructions on the inside of the doors saying: Plug lead A into socket A and plug B into socket B. Now lift the telephone receiver, wait for the word - and start your broadcast.

I reckon Rommel had better radio equipment in the desert, but it seemed to work and the BBC, never given to praise, would signal approval by telephoning a few days before the next match and ask for a repeat performance at Little Puddleton or wherever Newcastle were playing.

Indeed, it was at the next away match, after I had interrupted the publican's amorous morning, that there was to be another surprise.

But for me, and not a reluctant third party. We were playing at Portsmouth and the broadcast was to be made from what was a most civilised small room in the corner of a very large civic building.

Such luxury, for there was a live-all-round microphone which enabled speakers to sit anywhere at the table and two lights were attached to a wall, one of which illuminated to show that Southampton, who were feeding my golden words into the network, were receiving me and they would give me a minute before the red light came on when they wanted my polished prose to fracture with sheer joy listeners country wide.

Again, I arrived early to check all was well, climbing a flight of steps at the front then picking my way through builders' debris for there appeared to be very considerable reconstruction work being done on the hall. I lifted the telephone in the studio, Southampton replied, said all was well, old boy - and so I was set fair for the evening's broadcast.

I knew that, when the game was over, it would be futile to try to get to the centre of Portsmouth by any other means than running and so, as soon as I had given the *Chronicle* the final score, nominated my Man of the Match and done the front page Verdict on the Game, it was get out of Fratton Park as quickly as possible and leg it through the going-home fans and Christmas shoppers, still busy with the big bags of goodies under Portsmouth's illuminations.

The game finished at 4.40; my broadcast was to start at 5.08 and the train to London was at 5.50. If I caught this then I could get across London to Kings Cross make a connection with a train back to Newcastle and all this would see me in my own bed sometime after midnight. The *Sunday Sun* had their own man at the game, which was a blessed relief and I was free to broadcast.

Not only was the whole of Portsmouth shopping that Saturday but every schoolgirl and boy seemed to be on the streets - and they were all going my way. I pushed through this jostling, giggling crowd of thousands - and kept running.

I was in the studio a minute or two after 5 and, breathless, lifted the telephone, waited for Southampton to answer and, sure enough, a voice said: 'Hi Roy, a couple of minutes and we'll give you the lights. You OK?'

'Sure,' I lied, trying not to sound as though I was about to expire.

There was just enough time to read aloud my copy in the empty studio and tailor it as well as I could to the allotted time - then I waited those few precious seconds to catch my breath before the 'let's go' light came on.

It did - and the combined schools' choirs of Portsmouth came in at precisely the same time as I uttered my first syllable with the first notes of their carol concert. The studio's sound proofing had not been completed and so I broadcast to the nation in direct competition with several hundred school kids' voices belting out *Silent Night*.

I kept talking, they kept singing. I reckon it was a draw.

~ ~ ~ ~ ~ ~ ~ ~ ~ ~

By this time I had seen the Metropolitan Police Band accompany their splendid tenor at Highbury and marvelled at the memorabilia at the top grounds.

I had stayed at the Adelphi and, while trying to visit the Cavern (which turned out to be full) fallen about with the joy of hearing a brass necked scouse cabby telling Joe Harvey, who similarly wanted to see the Beatles, his team would 'get stuffed at Anfield termorrer' and thereby kiss a good tip farewell.

I had visited most of the grounds that mattered, Anfield and Highbury, Stamford Bridge and Villa Park and nothing insurmountable had presented itself. I was very well used to working to the tightest of deadlines and, in moments calculated to raise the readership of my column, had indulged in sheer mischief.

Before a derby game with Sunderland I wrote that football fans on Wearside had little idea of loyalty and didn't know too much about the game. The roof, duly, fell on me.

The letters poured in and one was written on the inside of a soap powder packet. The crayoned message thereon read: 'You are a prejudiced black and white bastard.'

It was signed: 'Yours In Sport, A Well Wisher.'

But the sentiments were not merely calculated to start a row, I truly believed that Sunderland supporters were intolerant and massively biased towards their own side, unable to appreciate anything not dressed in red and white. Maybe they were ahead of their time, for that seems to be the way of things today.

I was now 29 and 36 years of covering Newcastle United loomed before the presentation of the big clock and goodbye speech No 3 was read out by whoever happened to be editor at the time. It was time to move on.

~ ~ ~ ~ ~ ~ ~ ~ ~ ~

When I resigned Eric Dobson, the editor, found it hard to believe that a comparatively young man was leaving one of the plum jobs on his newspaper. He asked whether I was sure the decision was right and would the job I was going to be right for me.

I told him I was moving to a national newspaper in Manchester, starting at the bottom as a down table sports sub editor and hoping my track record would help me to become a top writer, covering all the national soccer sides in Europe.

I also told him that I didn't think Newcastle United would win anything at all worth having (the League, the FA Cup, the European Cup) for 25 years. The last time the Magpies had won the title (1927) Stanley Baldwin was Prime Minister.

They just don't have the structure, I said. Too many people at the club feel they have a right to be there and Newcastle's supporters will forgive them anything. It was an arrogant comment, but even I did not dream United would not win anything worthwhile for the remainder of the century - and beyond. For a city of such passion and loyalty it is a tragedy.

But I was on my way to new times and big challenges. Eric looked at me as though I was crackers. His opinion would have been shared by all of Tyneside - and for a few miles beyond.

Being paid to travel and watch Newcastle United was a dream which many Geordies would have sold the proverbial granny for - but for me, for now, there was a career to be pursued for already I was being labelled the *Chronicle* sports writer. And I reckoned I could do better than that.

Cottonopolis here I come.

~ ~ ~ ~ ~ ~ ~ ~ ~ ~

When I started at the *Sun* on a warm Sunday evening, just before England were to start their World Cup games in 1966, I began to think Eric had been right.

Jack Saltman, now working with the BBC in Manchester, had fixed me up with digs with a colleague at Chorlton cum Hardy. The first floor flat, in a modern block, had two bedrooms, overlooked a graveyard and was just fine until I sorted out a regular billet.

On that first night I drove up through Didsbury, heading for Oxford Road, in the city, and anywhere I could find to park the vehicle. It was 4pm and days on the *Journal* came flooding back for, while I have never had a problem with working nights, Sunday was always different for it seemed the rest of the world was still enjoying the weekend, lounging around in their collapsing kit while I was wearing collar and tie and making ready to present myself to new colleagues at the office.

The sports editor was nowhere to be seen which, I was to learn, was the way it always was on Sunday nights - and there was a huge metal tea pot on the subs' table.

I looked around, saw far too many staff with not enough to do and so the night, as all it successors did, would drag interminably on in a flood of luke warm beverage and a supper break at the pub across the road.

It was the way I was always to perceive national newspapers with a layer at the top who were deeply involved in whatever they were deeply involved in - probably filling a supervisory role over lunches at pub or restaurant where, with the first course, they ensured their peers did not get close enough to usurp them.

We had a sports editor, a deputy sports editor, a chief sub, a deputy chief sub - and then came the troops among whom was a racing desk of three. How they filled their time in heaven knew. The *Chronicle* had one man, Frank Taylor (occasionally helped by Ronnie Hulse, who also covered golf and subbed) who wrote a column under a by line of Juvenex and looked after the same number of race cards and tips.

Among this happy band of tipsters and tickers up of routine Press Association runners and riders' copy was Paul, a Longsight worthy who was not averse to a drop of alcoholic beverage and was possessed of unusual habits, particularly around breakfast time when he was recovering from a glass or ten the previous night. He would tell us he brought to his solitary table at home a glass of water, a knife - and a bottle of Guinness.

The knife was to scrape off his tongue whatever gunge and garbage still resided there from the previous night's revelries. As the coating came away so he dipped the blade into the glass of water to wash it; he would the repeat the exercise. Eventually satisfied things were as good as they were going to get and life would not taste much better as the day went on, he would then drink the Guinness to give him a kick start to whatever the next 24 hours would bring. Paul lived alone.

His breath carried on it enough alcohol fumes to torch the entire editorial floor had a carelessly discarded match been dropped anywhere near him. Whether he ever tipped any winners is unknown; racing 'experts' will trumpet to the skies their wins and say absolutely nothing about their losing bets, though these could be checked in the *Sporting Life* tables.

The truth is if any of them were consistently good they would not be working on newspapers but reclining on a sun drenched beach on the terrace of a considerable pad in the Windward Islands. I knew. I had been Underhand.

On the writing side there were Frank Clough and Len Noad, each believing he was the lead sports writer and not being best pals as they disputed it. Sometimes sarcasm almost gave way to promising something rather more physical and the gentle columnist Arthur Walmsley who worked alongside them and who had joined the paper when the *Manchester Evening Chronicle* had folded, would step in.

He brought lots of good writing - and lots of common sense and calm to these ego-fired situations which, thankfully, never quite got out of hand.

Arthur was also quite a pianist and could be found many a late night in one of Manchester's better clubs, cigarette hanging from the corner of his mouth, playing gentle sweet music.

Allan Cave wrote about Rugby League and Clement Freud presented a weekly column which was sometimes funny... and the *Sun's* Long Acre office in London, close enough to Fleet Street to believe it was part of it, ruled us all as they weighed in with their writers and production staff.

Manchester reported to London and though we had good writers north of Watford who were close enough to our readers Oop North to matter in terms of what was appropriate, if London said kill that and substitute one of our stories - we killed and substituted.

On the desk, alongside me, were Karl Kershaw and Rob Hughes. Kershaw was to go on to be a top national sports writer while Hughes was to have a highly successful career with the *Sunday Times*. And there we were, ambitious, capable, but stuck - all together, incarcerated on the desk of what we all quickly perceived to be a critically ailing newspaper.

I did manage the very occasional midweek trip to Old Trafford to see Charlton, Law, Best and co., always worth watching and my seat, tucked up high in the stand, offered greater comfort than photographers' viewing positions, for they had to lie on the grass behind the goals.

They took with them to the game two ground sheets, one to lie on, the other to pull over their backs, covering themselves from toe to head, this to collect phlegm. Numskulls in the crowd, as part of their afternoon's entertainment, would spit on the photographers.

When it was all over the lads slimily sought the sanctuary of the refreshment room looking en route before they discarded the ground sheets, like something from the Black Lagoon.

Occasionally, on Friday nights, I managed to attend Stockport County's home matches where, at full time, in the boardroom, stars of Coronation Street would gather for drinks and loud chat.

But that was gloss and show biz and, back in Oxford Street, Manchester, the *Sun* and its management did a great deal of brow knuckling to try to reverse a declining circulation.

Newspapers are particularly good at putting down their peers; they love to see one of the other titles in trouble and the disaster of the *Sun's* launch had been well seized upon by those who wished us anything but well - and they made our plight very public. Our problems had started early.

The title had sprung from the same stable as the *Daily Herald*, a socialist newspaper with its roots in strong support from the TUC. When owners the International Publishing Corporation decided to kill the Herald and launch 'a brand new paper for today' they set about recruiting good writers like the brilliant Nancy Banks Smith, one of the finest and most humorous scribes I have ever read, and the authoritative pair Henry Fielding and Geoffrey Goodman. They bought in other top writers and the pre-launch publicity was brilliant.

The mast head, with a big orange spot on it, could 'float' around the top of the front page. It was uniquely a moveable title piece beneath which was firmly proclaimed: 'The Independent Daily Newspaper'. As the weeks after the launch went by this statement had to be forcibly made, again and again as lost ground was fought over and efforts to distinguish the *Sun* from the previous left wing leanings of the *Daily Herald* were made.

What IPC, quite disastrously, had not done was change the personnel who had laid out and designed the *Herald's* pages. Neither did it change the inherited text and headline types and heaped upon itself the added handicap of still using people who had their own very individualistic ideas about newspaper design and how to lay out the newspaper.

The feature pages looked good and very different, but too much of the *Sun* looked too much like the *Herald* - and so the two titles could not be marketed as totally different. Failure had been built in and fairly hammered home.

Thanks to all the publicity which had preceded the launch more than 2,000,000 copies were sold on the first day, probably as a result of curiosity as the public paid up to see the first edition of a newspaper which they had been hearing about for so many weeks.

They looked at it, they considered it - and then made their judgement. 'It is,' they said, 'the *Daily Herald* under a new title.'

It even had the hero of a thousand working men's clubs throughout the country, Templegate the racing tipster. That was the clincher.

The *Herald's* Templegate had, for many years, given rise to much betting and great speculation on horse racing. The *Sun* should have changed the name, should have called him anything except Templegate. But that was not the only thing that was wrong.

Top writers in Manchester became weary of constantly having to give way to London, to having their copy become old and, eventually, spiked as it became out of date. There began a drift of staff to other titles.

~ ~ ~ ~ ~ ~ ~ ~ ~ ~ ~

For my part drinking gallons of tea, being under-employed and twiddling my thumbs on our desk was no way to earn a living and I longed for the weekends when I could get out to a football match which I would cover for my own paper, our sister Sunday newspaper, the *People* and for Don Mosey, at the BBC in Manchester's Piccadilly, for I had retained my BBC connections and continued to enjoy broadcasting.

What the BBC paid (around £5), alongside my other lineage, put me in financial clover and so I became a property owner, moving north of the city and buying a terraced house in Birtle, a dot on the map between Bury and Rochdale.

Chorlton cum Hardy had been fine - apart from one incident when a passenger aircraft had hit major trouble while making its final approach to Manchester. The pilot, realising he was not going to make it, sent out a mayday and then did a magnificent job despite having to put the aircraft down in the middle of Stockport. He avoided high rise buildings. He pancaked on what he hoped was waste ground - a quite magnificent effort.

But it was a charter flight and the impact concertinad the seats which trapped the tightly packed-in passengers by the legs. A fire started and so many burned to a quite dreadful death. Their fate was not helped by the hundreds of rubber-neckers who, hearing on the radio of the crash, jumped into their cars and drove past my flat as they set off to have as look at the carnage.

As a consequence the emergency services found their routes blocked and police got very heavy with crackpots who took the family to see a crashed aeroplane and, presumably, try to see bodies being taken away. They had succeeded only in grid-locking the roads.

~ ~ ~ ~ ~ ~ ~ ~ ~ ~

My new house was no palace. It was a two up and two down towards the end of a short cinder track which was a cul de sac with six houses all on the same side. Opposite was a garden which belonged to me and which I managed to attack with a cutter once or twice in summer. And I had a garage.

My neighbour had a baby linen shop in town. She was living with a local solicitor who was becoming quite dreadfully unwell with some kind of wasting disease which was a great shame for they had been quite a pair around town, well heeled and much sought after by those who were throwing the posh parties and seeking street cred.

For me Red Bank was a place to get the head down - and entertain. To reach me the visitor had to turn off the Bury to Rochdale road at the sign-post to Birtle, drive through a mill yard and head up a steep hill, climbing through the trees and past properties rather more grand than my very modest pad.

But the night time view from the bedroom in my small spot on the hill-side was spectacular for all the lights of Greater Manchester were spread out below and stretched for many miles in every direction and, if the night was clear, then I fancied I could sometimes see, many miles away, way down in Cheshire, an aircraft making its approach to Ringway.

It was a splendid vantage point, as I frequently pointed out to visiting young women who found the night time view... captivating. Especially when we both saw stars.

The house was off a road which terminated at the very top of the hill where those with real money ate. The pleasures of eating at the Normandie were to escape me as I used the pub at the bottom of the hill, the Pack Horse where the food was wholesome, the booze acceptable - and it was all very much cheaper.

Many a lock-in was enjoyed at the Pack, well off the beaten track and when, in the early hours of the morning, I was driving back from work and turned off the Bury-Rochdale road and up the hill, I would stop and, several first edition papers in hand as an open sesame to those already inside, would knock and find a welcome which could stretch until two or three in the morning.

Outside the Jaguars, Mercedes and Beamers, whispered their way on up to the Normandie where, it was said, though the food was exquisite there were those who had booked a table who never managed to taste it.

They had asked for salt and pepper, which made the chef apoplectic or they had been late. No matter how they had sinned they were given marching orders and probably wound up sitting further along the bar from me at the Pack Horse.

Such tough treatment served, of course, to endear the place to creme de la creme diners who flocked to a restaurant which didn't cater for the languid and casual and where those who considered that to be late for every appointment was chic were shown back to the car park. Down the hill why... we just got on with our casual, easy drinking.

~ ~ ~ ~ ~ ~ ~ ~ ~ ~

Kieron was a gentleman. Irish and smiling he was a top class sub editor and was everyone's common-sense friend, never slow with the help and advice and in this sense was highly regarded. Until he had a drink - and then it was not unknown for Kieron to clear an entire bar and pitch onto the pavement all who had been inside with the style of a Hollywood hero.

Fists would fly everywhere and those who had witnessed Kieron in action (which was most of us) would keep a wary eye on him at the start of any supper break knowing the gentle, softly spoken Irish friend of all the world could, in minutes, indulge in a little jaw breaking.

There was a club across the road from the office, above a tailor's shop, run by an Italian who said he had lost his leg during the war, but had now forgiven us all and was in business to make us happy.

When the evenings drew on he would come swinging past the bar on crutches then sit himself on a high stool to dispense wise words and buy a very occasional drink.

During a pre-Christmas celebration at the Italian Club, while sports writer Cloughie, the boulevardier from Sheffield, was smoothing it around on the dance floor with Miss World 1952 and the remainder of the editorial staff concentrated on the holiday spirit, Kieron got close to putting the world to rights.

Sure enough, he strode to where the Italian was perched and, thrusting his face to within inches of the man, made unpleasant reference to the war and called him a wop so and so. It was unnecessary and very badly out of order even to we who were, and are not, known for the delicacy of our feelings.

Appalled and not wishing to be associated with another of Keiron's rages, half a dozen of us adjourned to the Manchester Press Club where we joined another colleague, a Jewish guy from Cheetham. Within 15 minutes Kieron arrived, weaving, and asked why we had left him.

None of us had the courage to tell him and studied the bottom of our glasses. He turned on our other colleague. Again he was mightily abusive this time about religion but on this occasion the Jewish lad broke the mould and stood up to him.

The barman, by threatening to call the busies, persuaded them to go outside while the rest of us, filled with curiosity at this turn of events, filed out with them. They found space in the grounds of the Quaker Meeting House and there, in the Garden of Peace, the Irish Catholic battled with the Manchester Jew.

The fight was not of any significant duration. Kieron went down, stayed down and we left him to find his way home - not because we didn't care about his welfare on a dark night in December, but because we knew that, when he did come to his senses, he would still be in fighting mood and Samaritans might swiftly find their noses bent and their ears thickened.

The following night Kieron arrived for work with his right hand in plaster from fingers to elbow. He had fractured several bones while swinging at his opponent and connecting with something more solid then flesh and blood. He suspected he'd hit a statue.

Charming, affable and eloquent as his sober self always was, he apologised to the previous night's opponent and shook hands - with his unplastered hand. But, the reality was, he had the style of Captain Hook trying to thread a needle.

~ ~ ~ ~ ~ ~ ~ ~ ~ ~

It was 1968 and by now the *Sun* was losing even more circulation and was well on the way out. Big time. No newspaper, when sales are declining, will tell of its misfortunes; but the Audit Bureau of Circulations exists to officially relate such tales of joy - or unremitting gloom.

Despite this some titles have been known to try to fiddle their circulation, claiming higher figures to tempt advertisers. The reason is simple: The higher the circulation the more can be charged for advertising. But the Bureau will get very tough with those discovered cooking the circulation books.

Even harder times were also looming, for free sheets were about to make a mark - productions where advertising had its way and editorial, to quote a hundred gleeful advertising managers who had always been second-rated by journalists, filled the space in between.

These pushed-through-the-door efforts were to make some of their owners a fortune and as the word spread there were queues to chase this paper trail. Many of them were to claim good 'circulations' which is a total nonsense. They can say they 'distribute' so many thousands of copies, but they do not circulate a single issue.

Circulation comes through readers buying the product, thereby making a financial commitment to see what the newspaper contains. Free newspapers are an uninvited, often intrusive and sometimes politically offensive product, which frequently end up in the householder's rubbish bin without a page being turned.

But they presented a threat to journalists despite the editorial content of these productions being too often of a miserably poor standard with some containing little more than badly written PR hand outs. They are then filled with the reason for their existence - classified and display advertisements.

Free sheets are good news for company accountants and number crunchers; they generate easy money. There is no need to employ many journalists, boundaries between reporters, writers and sub editors are blurred or obliterated as the functions become integrated and so costs stay low. People are the most expensive commodity in any company's budget; the fewer you have aboard the better that year-end figure will look.

The face of newspapers was changing and here I was, on a gasping, expiring national title - and this just three years after joining the Big National Newspaper League. It was time to look around.

~ ~ ~ ~ ~ ~ ~ ~ ~ ~

I came over quite unnecessary when I read of a plan the BBC had for the 1970 World Cup. They wanted a commentator to go to South America to cover the finals. What an opportunity.

My application was sent by first class post and with it went my ambition for an escape route from the setting *Sun* and maybe a permanent job with the Beeb. After all, I had been a freelance broadcaster for them for years and I was young enough to be able to make a full time move from the written word to talking steam radio.

I was later told they had 11,000 applicants which, through looking at CV's and assessing suitability they narrowed to a field small enough to journey to a film studio in Holborn, in London, which we would occupy for two days and where we would-be Ken Wolstenholmes, with a lip mike in our hands would watch a cinema screen for half an hour and commentate on the silent football film which flickered before our eyes.

I loved it and it came easily to me - so much so that I was selected for the final 12 from which the Football Commentator of the Year would be chosen. So far so good.

The final stages of the event took place at Wembley in the summer where England were playing Wales in the home internationals.

I travelled south from Manchester on a Friday, took a cab through the teeming streets and reported to the BBC at Broadcasting House with other hopefuls the following morning (among them Ian St John, the former Liverpool player). We were taken off to Wembley by coach, all of us quiet and apprehensive.

Decanted, we trotted up a considerable flight of stairs at the back of the main stand and then walked out, above the heads of the crowd, on a gantry which ended at studios slung above the pitch and suspended under the front of the roof. It was a superb vantage point - ideal for the job.

Six positions had been set up for us with the working studio a little further towards the centre line and it was here that David Coleman's attendants waited for him as we, even more nervous and shuffling, watched. The main man, who was broadcasting for real, arrived, went into one of the rooms and was made up by glamourous and attentive ladies.

We left The Presence to await our briefing after the man who mattered had met with his crew. And so there came into our small area of the box the director for the day and he spoke to us in a manner well known to journalists. It was, shall we say, direct.

'I have,' he said, 'been known to swear. In fact, I swear a lot and if any of you are likely to be offended by that then you can leave right now.' We straightened our shoulders, smiled cynically awhile - and looked suitably tough.

'I have,' he went on, 'cameramen around the ground' (and he pointed out where the cameras were positioned) 'and if they don't do what I tell them and do it at once, then I tell them their fortunes.'

'You will hear this as you will hear everything that I say, through the cans you'll be given. You will therefore be aware of what is coming. If the centre-forward scores or does something notable I will tell (I might even shout at him) one of the cameraman to zoom in on that player and it must be done at once.

'You will be able to follow everything as we do it for real - and we can't afford a slip up.' Only he didn't say 'slip'.

We were allotted out positions each to cover one half of the game, six to take the first half and the remaining half dozen to commentate on the second.

I was first on and began badly. Being somewhat long in the leg I was not comfortable with what was a restricted seat offering limited leg room. And between my knees was a TV monitor which showed what the viewer was seeing at home.

So there were two 'pictures', one on the screen, the other I could see by marginally lifting my eyes and looking down between my legs at what was happening below on the pitch. Balancing these twin views was not easy for, in addition, the director was talking incessantly. And so one had to listen to him through the headphones with, occasionally, a woman's voice breaking in to say: 'Fifteen minutes gone, clock coming up in five seconds.'

The clock would then appear in the top right hand corner of the screen and, if you were sharp enough, you could announce before it happened: 'England move forward again after 15 minutes play...' and the clock showing exactly that would appear almost as you finished speaking.

Too quickly it all went by and Idwal Roberts, the eventual winner, took over for the second half in the seat I had occupied. I had hoped for better luck, but hadn't all of us who had gone to Wembley looking for a new life?

Back to Manchester, the eternal tea pot - and make the best of it while waiting for the inevitable axe.

~ ~ ~ ~ ~ ~ ~ ~ ~ ~

Being comparatively young and unmarried was good in late-sixties Manchester. If London's world was swinging well, we weren't doing too badly in deepest Lancashire.

Ours was a world of clubs and when graveyard shifts for national newspaper hacks were ended there was a choice of early morning venues, some of which probably amounted to no more than an upstairs room and a bar, behind which was an aspiring film star aiming to catch the eye of a reporter and we, ever ready to oblige, would talk loudly of the many times we met top show biz people. For her part she was ready to serve booze until the money or the equilibrium failed.

At the other end of the scale there were high class night out establishments which were bigger and better than Newcastle's Dolce Vita. They made most of their money through initially happy punters gambling and then departing, very unhappy, and nigh on penniless.

There was one such city centre establishment which had baby crocodiles swimming around a shallow moat which encircled an illuminated stage. Inevitably chumps unlimited, after an ale or six, tried to impress their girls by dabbling their fingers into the warm, blue-tinged water. There is no record of any fingers being bitten off, but several of these guys suffered in other ways - most frequently by being bounced off the pavement outside.

The Manchester club scene was, indeed, taking off and was quickly to become worth a great deal of money - so much so that, so the tale went, the Kray twins journeyed from the east end of London seeking a meeting with a couple of the big club owners.

A rendezvous was arranged at the Midland Hotel in the centre of the city - where the London gangsters were met by several big lads with flat vowelled accents and were presented with return tickets to Euston, an escort to Piccadilly station and an emphatic word which declared that to travel north again would not be the best idea they had ever had.

~~~~~~~~~~

The personalities abounded among the national newspaper writers. Our own man, the aforementioned Frank Clough, Yorkshire and Leeds United to his pit boot straps, was a one man variety show. He had, he said, done his National Service in the Royal Marines, serving as a commando - and he surely was tough enough for his story to be wholly believable.

He covered a Newcastle United midweek game and, travelling from Manchester, sought overnight accommodation on Tyneside. After the match he had filed his copy and before he returned to his hotel for Horlicks and a bourbon biscuit he sought a little light entertainment - and went to a high flying club in down town Grey Street where the action took place below pavement level.

Frank tripped down the stairs seeking a small refreshment and what-ever would present itself, soon becoming engaged in deep conversation with a young lady. But the call of nature took over before Frank could build up a head of acceptable chat - and he headed for the loo.

As he pushed open the door a massive fist was coming the other way; the two collided and Frank was left feeling somewhat disorientated and possessed of considerable damage to his teeth. It seemed the lady had a boy friend who was not given to rational conversation... nor perceived competition.

The next morning Frank sought a dentist, had artificially replaced that which was absent, travelled back to Manchester and presented himself for work. His mouth was badly swollen, his nose reddened - but he completed his shift and we joined him for a pint at the pub across the road. You surely believed he was a tough guy.

Frank spent much of his working week on the telephone or on the road, travelling around the north of England interviewing or covering games.

It was the professional life style I had sought when first I came to Manchester, but which was not to be for by now recruitment was at a standstill, expenses were kept to the minimum and while the average journalist's knowledge of matters financial is around abacus level, all of us were aware, on an ever worsening week-by-week basis the *Sun*, in its present form, was in deepening trouble. My failure to get full-time work at the BBC was taking on an added significance.

There were many chapel (union) meetings when the Father of the Chapel (shop steward) reported... nothing we didn't already know. We were in shtuck and there was nothing the National Union of Journalists, or any other union, could do about it.

In the autumn of 1969 the *Sun*, which had been launched with such vaunting optimism and massively high hopes, was sold to Rupert Murdoch who told an expectant newspaper world that his new paper, also called the *Sun*, would be a tabloid and run from offices in Whitefriars Street, in London. He then announced the closure of the Manchester office.

~ ~ ~ ~ ~ ~ ~ ~ ~ ~

Many of the staff were married and they, particularly those with children, were offered jobs in Manchester with IPC's sister papers, the *Mirror*, the *Sunday Mirror* and *People*. Those with neither wife nor kids were left to find work elsewhere - and so I started looking.

One of Murdoch's chiefs came up from London to interview those without prospects and I was offered a sub editor's job in London. But at about the same time a former colleague on the *Sun*, who had moved to London before the expected bad news became reality, telephoned to say the *Daily Sketch* had a vacancy and would I be interested?.

Nothing was moving on Manchester's other nationals and, being unsure about the future of yet another new product, I turned down the *Sun* and, heaven help me, opted for the *Daily Sketch*.

I put my house on the hillside on the market, turned the key in the lock and my back on a view to die for - and headed for Fleet Street.

I was interviewed by the *Sketch* sports editor who, after expressing himself satisfied, said he would take me along to see the editor, David English.

'Not many new people,' said Bob Findlay as we headed along the corridor, 'get to meet the editor.' I wondered whether I should kneel or bow.

English, young, trendy, long-haired, said welcome, looked down at his desk at something much more interesting than a new sub editor, and so after the briefest of welcomes, we left the presence almost walking backwards and genuflecting.

I was to be on the paper for nearly two years and never spoke to the editor again, though I occasionally saw him getting in or out of his chauffeured Jaguar or drifting through the editorial floor. His reputation was to become huge; his time on the *Sketch* produced abject failure.

We at the bottom of the Christmas tree got on with what we were told to do and, sometimes at night when their partying was done, Bubbles Rothermere, the big boss's wife, would bring a party of natty suited gents and exquisitely groomed women through the offices and they looked at us working away as though we were zoological exhibits.

'These,' she would tell her guests, 'are journalists.'

I thought they might throw buns.

If they had I would have been quite grateful for I was living in a bedsit in Westminster Park Road, in Archway, North London in a house owned by two homosexuals who had raging rows outside my window, which overlooked a small, paved area on the street where the dust bins were kept. And they did so almost on a daily basis.

They always argued about whose turn it was to put rubbish in the bins - and they always, when I was at work, went through what possessions I had in my room. I would have thought they would soon know as well as I did what was there, but perhaps they wondered if anything new might arrive.

The stove, which I infrequently used, seemed to consume ten bob's worth of gas upon ignition and so I ate out - sometimes in the *Daily Sketch* canteen. A hit song at the time was *I Beg Your Pardon - I Never Promised You a Rose Garden* and the canteen ladies just loved it. Whenever I went down to hell's kitchen the dreadful tune was blasting out of a record player while the sing-along girls filled the world's biggest frying pan with... whatever the customer wanted.

Eggs, bacon, sausage, bread, tomatoes, potatoes and all manner of assorted pieces of meat went into the sizzling grease and when it came out many a young hack's digestion took a turn for the worse and stomach pills were much in demand. And so the pubs were favourite.

Or a cafe outside the Archway tube station which stayed open all night and served blokes who had, in the early hours, been thrown out by the ever loving, drunks trying to remember where they lived, down and outs wanting to stay as warm as they could for as long as a cup of tea could last - and hungry hacks.

~ ~ ~ ~ ~ ~ ~ ~ ~ ~

There were, initially, jobs to be enjoyed before I realised I had swapped a dead duck for another newspaper about to cough its last: the *Sketch* was heading the same way as IPC's *Sun* as Murdoch's 'new look, soar away *Sun*' ravenously tore into our circulation - and that of many other titles. But the *Sketch* was easy meat, incapable of fighting for its future.

Circulation was declining and while we watched we were not aware that our editor was being lined up for the editorship of the *Daily Mail* with, perhaps, a chosen few to join him when the newspaper he was currently editing went down the river.

We got on with what we were asked to do and Findlay sent me to interview one of his fellow Scots, Billy Bremner, who was playing for his country as well as being one of leading players for his club, Leeds. I tried to ring the player at the ground and got back a message which said 'someone' would be in touch with me.

That 'someone' turned out to be the first agent I was to deal with. He told me Bremner wanted £200 to do the interview. I was incredulous. It was 1969 and such a sum was massively more than many folk earned in a month.

I smiled knowingly, comforted in the knowledge that Findlay would tell Bremner and his agent where to go and what they could do with their demand. I duly, and smugly, reported back.

'We'll pay him,' said Findlay.

I had great difficulty getting my head around that - and still do. Paying footballers to stand still and grunt for a few minutes, then try to put into English their pearls of wisdom (we take one match at a time...the boss knows best...there's a long way to go yet...) is arrant nonsense, so stupid it's crass and certainly designed to create the most cutting of rods for sports journalism's back.

It springs from a national newspaper paranoia about stories the opposition might be carrying the next day and the early evening scatter when the 'foreigners' arrive in the office well demonstrates this phenomenon.

The chiefs gathered to compare the first editions of papers and if the *Sun* had a story the *Mirror* did not, or the other way around, or the *Mail* produced a feature which the other two thought they should have had then there would be inquests.

Sometimes opposition headlines and pictures were lifted (pinched) and used in subsequent editions, but what truly grates is sportsmen writing about sportsmen and being paid very large bucks in some kind of kamikaze race to win circulation.

The next 'informed comment piece' I read by Clarence Clogger will be the first for I have never considered sportsmen can hold a candle to sports journalists like Ian Wooldridge or Sue Mott or Michael Parkinson who are, truly, talented.

But Bremner got his cash, a percentage of which was probably paid to his agent. We thus had a foot on a slippery slope. After Bremner it was decided I should interview stage personalities who had a material interests in football.

Eric Morecambe with Luton Town and Tommy Steele, who looked as though he might be getting close to Millwall, were duly selected. I met Eric Morecambe in a tiled classroom in a Shepherd's Bush school which the BBC used as a rehearsal studio when the kids were on holiday.

Morecambe and Wise were top variety pulling in massive TV audiences and selling out every theatre in which they appeared. Again I had to negotiate the meeting through an agent - but he did not ask for money.

I confess to some excitement as I climbed the school staircase and made my way down an echoing corridor to the room where rehearsals were going on. These two were big time.

Eric Morecambe was sitting slightly away from a dozen or more TV folk, among whom was Ernie Wise, deep in conversation. Morecambe was anxious and constantly distracted by what was happening to others around and about him.

He would frequently leave me to talk with people on the set then come back to where I was sitting at the side of the hall, ask me where we had got to and try to carry on a conversation - the last sentences of which he couldn't remember.

It was an uneasy, unsatisfactory interview and showed in the copy I presented. It was published because of the name Eric Morecambe and certainly not because of how it was written.

And so, the next week, hoping for much better things, I headed for the West End and went off to see Tommy Steele, who was playing the lead in the London Palladium pantomime.

My interview was scheduled between matinee and first evening performance. I am always on time for work, for interviews, for parties - whatever. If an arrangement is made I stick to it and people who appear after the allotted time have no business being in newspapers. Courts, councils, most meetings, they all start on time and having a reporter wander in when the business is under way is appalling.

It reflects badly on the individual but, much more important, it reflects badly on the newspaper. Those colossal bores who seek dramatic entrances by drifting into parties or to dinners late are beyond the pale.

So it was I walked up Regent Street with time enough to dally and look into the huge shop windows - and still have a few minutes to spare before I pitched up at the stage door of the Palladium and, along with a good natured doorman, waited and watched.

The orchestra was playing, Tommy Steele was on stage singing and the beautiful chorus girls, in spangles and skimpy costumes and spangled tights with head dresses waving, ran past us to change in no time at all before they scattered back to the wings ready for their next call.

It was enough to keep the average chap happy for hours, just leaning back, loafing and observing the prettiest of girls in profusion. Until the pantomime dame came along. Billy Dainty was wearing huge, curly toed scarlet boots, hooped blue and white football stockings, a purple voluminous skirt and bursting pink blouse stuffed with whatever to give him a colossal bosom. Atop all this was a huge ginger wig and a tall, felt, crazily multi-coloured hat.

He was walking one way, the girls were dashing the other way and as one of the most gorgeous in this wonderfully attractive bunch legged it past him Dainty bent down and grabbed a handful of extremely desirable backside.

She stopped in mid flight, turned on him and with a vocabulary which would have been admired by a press room overseer with the print running late, opened her delectable, rosebud mouth and swore at full volume screech - and at considerable length.

When she'd finished Dainty smiled, his huge, painted mouth and rouged cheeks cracking with the joy of it and said: 'Come on, tricky knickers, give us a kiss.'

Her reply, again delivered at maximum decibels, indicated this was unlikely in the extreme.

~ ~ ~ ~ ~ ~ ~ ~ ~ ~

Tommy Steele qualifies, up there with Bill Shankly, as being so easy to interview. He was warm and receptive as he invited me in. When I saw him he was in the star's dressing room which, in fact, was two rooms, one a shower and make-up room and the other a relaxing and sitting room.

He had just danced and sung centre stage for a couple of hours, the sweat was rolling off him and yet, within minutes, he was prepared to be interviewed.

He told of playing football and breaking a leg just before he was due in Hollywood to make *Half a Sixpence* - and how the film people reacted when he hobbled off the aeroplane. He spoke about the way football was and how it would be. He gave me many personal anecdotes and stories.

After I had left he rang the *Sketch* to say he had enjoyed the interview For my part it ranked alongside the easiest jobs I had been asked to complete and the copy, when I got back to the office, just flowed.

~ ~ ~ ~ ~ ~ ~ ~ ~ ~

Nothing else was coming very easily at the *Sketch* and I couldn't believe my wretched luck as months passed and it became absolutely clear that I was, once again, staring at redundancy. There was a thrashing about and there were ideas which were different as attempts were made to halt the decline.

We had a girl reporter who stuck a hen's egg between her breasts and said she'd hatch it. This caused considerable speculation about what happened when she bathed, and when she was sleeping and whether she was well enough endowed to hatch even a sparrow's egg.

She wasn't, it was a crackpot idea - and it didn't work. 'Bound to fail,' said Alec, one of the sports subs. 'She has a chest like a bleedin' choir boy.'

And that seemed to sum that up quite nicely.

Then there was the woman journo who ingested some kind of goo to turn her skin brown which seemed to be a highly dangerous way of getting a story. When she'd taken enough of the stuff and was dark enough to pass as Asian she went off to live on a down trodden estate in the Midlands from where she filed a series of features on how difficult life was becoming for Asians trying to find work and suffering appalling racism. That did work. She wrote a top series. But it was all rather late and, mixed with silly ideas, was devalued.

Yet another female, complete with judiciously situated cameraman, trekked up from our offices overlooking the Thames on the Embankment, to Fleet Street, and made to 'storm' El Vino's, the all-male drinking house where many of the solid wooden chairs in its gloomy interior bore on their backs names of journalists who had become famous. All of them male, of course - and most of them dead.

A mock battle with staff ensued at the doorway, the invasion was repelled - and the snapper duly took his pictures which made a decent centre spread which probably appealed to city types, but didn't mean too much to those working in Leeds, Sheffield, Liverpool, Manchester, Sheffield...

What were we doing? Where were we trying to sell the newspaper? Who cares outside the people working in the middle of London about a raid on El Vino's? We most assuredly were not strong about marketing the product and the word clueless sprang to mind.

~ ~ ~ ~ ~ ~ ~ ~ ~ ~

Away from the story front, but of considerable interest to the staff, the *Sketch* boasted yet another girl reporter who had a unique way of getting her flat painted - any willing lad was paid in kind and it was alleged by Alec that 'she only did it for friends and strangers' and declared 'her pad out west was pristine'. No one asked him how he knew - we all craved the light relief.

It is worth mentioning that, floating above all this was Jean Rook, one of the first angry women in newspapers. She was to be followed by Anne Robinson and Linda Lee Potter and many more, all of them declaring the opposite to a popular line or taking an extreme angle then professing an insider's knowledge.

It might even have been true; it has surely been tried and well tested over many years.

We Brits love to hear the worst about anyone who has made a decent fist of life and by convoluted reasoning conclude that bad news for them will somehow lift our stock and raise our status; our fortunes will, we believe, be enhanced if someone else is suffering. Or it makes us feel smug

This is nonsense, but it's the way we are and so gossip columns flourish - which was certainly more than could be said for the *Daily Sketch* in 1971. Before it reached its unlamented demise I was able to observe, from the touch line, where the business of which paper was doing what and who was moving where was done - in the Fleet Street pubs.

The Mucky Duck, the City Golf Club or the Harrow were close enough to the *Sketch* and hosted the whisperers, cliques of whom abounded. It was around and about these places, all of them within a few hundred yards of each other, that the movers and shakers gathered to drink and gossip - and sometimes, some of what they predicted came about.

They were now talking, more and more, about the death of the *Sketch,* this intelligence being based on our stories of staff being cut further and further back. Furthermore, travelling to stories was being curtailed - along with expenses. For some time those who left had not been replaced and I could almost sing from the hymn sheet which had been thrust in our hands when the *Sun* closed in Manchester.

David English was poised for his move to the *Mail* and those on the *Sketch* who knew anyone of influence on any other titles in town were calling in favours and setting out stalls for what was to happened after the redundancy package was agreed.

It was the start of the Street of Shame becoming just another road in the City of London.

Each newspaper, in its own Fleet Street pub, had all the gossip worth knowing and this was traded across bars and corner tables over pints of indifferent ale and sandwiches, the gripes and grumbles, the latest word from wherever, all had an almost conspiratorial angle.

Express journalists used the Red Lion, in Poppins Court and this inevitably became known as Poppins while the *Mirror* hacks had the White Hart, in Fetter Lane, better known as the 'Stab in the Back' and it was where careers were, indeed, sometimes terminated. We stuck to the river side of the Street.

I left before the infamous night of the long brown envelopes; the night when redundancy notices were handed out. The staff half expected bad news - but not delivered like this. English took with him the *Sketch* favoured to the *Mail* - where they were disliked. The remainder who suffered the 9pm sackings by handed out letter... just left. Bitterly.

By now I had long gone. The great national newspaper experiment had failed, gone to bag wash because I had chosen to work for titles which hadn't survived and all the National Union of Journalists' chapel meetings in all the halls around Ludgate Circus hadn't made a scrap of difference as the *Sketch* sank with hardly a splutter. Our protests had collapsed and our jobs along with them.

I accepted a job at the *Evening Gazette*, in Middlesbrough, as a sub editor, just to get away from yet another newspaper disaster.

Trying to mitigate what had been hard times I reasoned that, twelve years earlier, I would have given anything to have had just that kind of position and so, it was time for respite and to start again. And I brought north with me the girl I was to marry. London, despite Fleet Street, had produced a huge bonus.

~ ~ ~ ~ ~ ~ ~ ~ ~ ~

The journey north to Middlesbrough for interview took me from Kings Cross to Darlington and the change of trains to Middlesbrough was the usual run into hell.

Scrap yards and smoke-belching heavy industry littered the route and while I knew Middlesbrough well enough from schoolboy days, after London when I was on top money and beating up Shepherd's Market restaurants and drinking at Trader Vics, the prospect was not alluring.

I did not know that another Fleet Street hack was on the same rattler heading east along the Tees for an interview the same day by Ian Nimmo, the *Gazette* editor.

John McLeod had been hit by a lift - and spread sideways. No more than 5ft 2in he was four feet wide and all of it was glorious, teasing ego. He strutted, smoked constantly and, like Jack Lemmon in the film The Front Page (he even told a junior, on one prized, never forgotten occasion when working on a story, to 'cigarette me') would describe a huge circle in the air when he took the fag out of his mouth. Theatrical, surely. And he was a massively great guy with huge style and humour who was to become a friend.

He reckoned all married women, between the ages of 25 and 40, who had left work to raise a family, were probably highly intelligent and therefore frustrated as a convent full of cloistered nuns because of living within the four walls of alleged domestic bliss. He considered it was up to him to bring a little zip and vigour into their sheltered and boring existence.

He set about this worthy task with considerable energy and Celtic charm which, he was later to declare, worked more often than not. Shirley Valentine, he said, lived at Acacia Avenue, anywhere on Teesside, and talked to the wall in gibbering frustration.

Enter McLeod arriving like John Wayne to the rescue (well, a much-shortened version). If, indeed, Wee Mac had looked like a John Ford hero the entire female population of Teesside would have been obliged to make frequent tracks for the Cleveland Hills to escape him.

After some years of great and wide ranging pursuit he was eventually, to find a permanent girlfriend and Casanova, figuratively speaking, was emasculated.

His was a path well trodden by many a romantically energetic hack and McLeod told stories of women living on estates to the south of town who left Harpic bottles on the kitchen window sill to indicate whether the coast was clear for a visit by him. When, in his early days at the *Gazette*, McLeod was not seeking to give the female population of Teesside a break he was a cracking reporter.

A prospective woman interviewee on a top story would receive a large bunch of flowers before McLeod arrived on the doorstep, notebook in hand. This preliminary work by the little chap usually worked and he obtained interviews with those who didn't really want to appear in the pages of the *Gazette*. McLeod could crack them and it was a source of great irritation to him that he did not progress beyond being a reporter in the news room.

There was a murder down Loftus way, in North Yorkshire, and The Wee McLeod attached himself to a Scotland Yard superintendent and his sergeant who had journeyed from London to lend aid and expertise to the local constabulary. They spent much time in pubs around Guisborough together.

Where they went McLeod was sure to follow. And the big break came when the murderer, in one of the pubs which the men from the Yard were watching, began drinking hard.

It might have been his conscience, it might have been his usual drunken boasting, but as detectives sat back, stayed quiet and watched, laddo told the rapidly panicking barmaid how he had hidden the hairdresser's body under slabs of stone.

He explained by building a replica of her resting place with beer mats on the bar top, piling one upon another. Two heavy hands were placed on his shoulders and so the case was solved.

McLcod wrote the story (and did it very well) and sought acknowledgement throughout the four northern counties. He didn't get it - but he sure thought he should have done.

~ ~ ~ ~ ~ ~ ~ ~ ~ ~

The *Gazette* was Brigadoon in Borough Road. The editor was a Scot, as was his deputy. The managing director, his assistant and the Production Manager - all were from north of the border and presumably they all had a great time when Burn's night came around.

This gathering of the clans surely fared well enough together on the social side of life in North Yorkshire.

Middlesborough, meanwhile, when one put to rest first appearances, proved to be a wonderful news town. Even away from ICI.

Taking an early evening drink down Albert Road could see us rubbing shoulders with dockers who had 'the card' which meant they, and their fellow card holders, were the only ones allowed to load and unload the ships in the Tees. Ask what they were doing in the pub when they should have been at work and the reply was crisp and forthright.

Rumour had it that one of the reporters from long ago, who had covered the docks and knew these men well had, some years earlier, died almost penniless and was without a family to properly see him off.

A whip round had produced enough to get the lad cremated and it was decided that it would be absolutely appropriate to scatter his ashes in the river which had been his professional home as he covered stories about the big ships coming in and going out and standing, picturesquely off shore, in the huge Tees bay.

A boatman and his sturdy craft was duly hired and after a libation at the dockside pubs, the lads took Ernie in his urn out into the river as the wind whipped in from the North Sea and the clouds threatened a downpour.

A few words, which were perhaps appropriate, were mumbled and Ernie was emptied over the side - only to be blown back aboard by a strong gust of wind and all over the mourners. They said Ernie was in their hair for weeks afterwards.

~ ~ ~ ~ ~ ~ ~ ~ ~ ~

The Chocolate Drop Kids were offering sex Over the Border. Over the Border was a scruffy, down at heel district of Middlesbrough, embracing the docks. Some of these kids were so young (hence their title for they were almost doing tricks for sweets) they were hardly old enough to leave school but, shimmying and shaking along the pavements around the riverside streets, they learned early in life how to earn a living.

The sailors lined up and the local low life also parted with coin of the realm for a night of powder, paint, heavy breathing - and maybe a little something they hadn't legislated for a few weeks later.

When they were old enough to go into the clubs the Chocolate Drop Kids upped their prices along with their skirts and perched on bar stools at the clubs.

They had the tariff for their favours printed on pieces of sticky paper which they stuck to the soles of their shoes. When they eyeballed a prospective punter, who smiled back at them, they would raise a crossed leg, tilt their toes towards the ceiling - and there was that evening's going rate displayed. It all made for good news stories.

I had only been at the *Gazette* for a very few months when the features editor had a coronary on top of Roseberry Topping during a Sunday afternoon walk, pegged it - and I was offered his job. The title and the number of features offering themselves was enough to hold me at the *Gazette* for much, much longer than I had planned.

But what I had not expected was the strength of the NUJ. There were occasions when I went to lunch and returned to find the entire chapel in a working men's club across the road from the office with the editor and his immediate assistants producing the paper.

There had been a walkout. Many attempts were made over several years to temper and restrain the local union, but all failed until a new MD was visited upon us. Bill Heaps, yet another Scot, came to the covered-in-tartan *Gazette*.

After another round of negotiations over grievances real or imagined and facing a threat from the chapel to work on only one story at a time, or not to use a telephone unless it was cleaned daily and this and that and the other, all stunts and strokes designed to halt production... he fired the lot of us.

In no time at all we were outside the building trying to gain support from a disinterested public, producing a feeble news sheet and distributing it to anyone who would take it off our hands. And we waited to see who would be reinstated and what position they might occupy, for our contracts had been spiked and we were unemployed.

We received national backing from NUJ headquarters who made noises to management about breaking agreements, which was about as much use as a rubber crutch and were accordingly ignored - for the production unions continued to work and the newspaper's editorial was produced by executives (including Heaps).

This happy little band worked all hours, notching up a million Thomson Regional Newspapers brownie points. They never missed an edition and the delivery vans rolled on past our picket lines with the more militant guys pleading with them to stop. The rest of us stood around feeling hopeless and lost, suffering the smiling indifference of passers-by.

The weeks went by and just when it seemed some of the men with large mortgages and small children might crack, we were reinstated - on

Heap's terms. His timing was spot on. The dismissals had worked and we didn't give the management enough hassle to cause them to dismiss us again.

~ ~ ~ ~ ~ ~ ~ ~ ~ ~

Something resembling peace being restored, I started a column called the Maddison Line. It was a good title and one which has subsequently been pinched by other journalists around the country who have swapped their surname for mine. It was great fun for I chose my subjects carefully and there was never a shortage of copy.

ICI was Teesside. The principal employer, it put bread on tables and sold shares to its shift working employees from management to process workers. The work was regular and the pay was good and the organisation was massive.

To drive from the town centre down the coast road to Redcar was to travel a fairy land with flare stacks shooting their flames into the deep blue night with millions of lights, white, orange and yellow giving the journey an even greater air of magic.

The flip side of this was the stink of Teesside where the smell seemed to change daily and was so pungent it seemed possible to chew on the retch-making odour.

After one rainy night I left my home in Acklam, went to my car and was horrified to see huge yellow spots with orange centres which had been washed down onto the vehicle as the rain poured through the air borne pollution. Pampered hacks could only wonder what it was like to work inside chemical or fertiliser or petroleum plants down the river which produced such rubbish.

My first paragraph in my new column read: 'If you were born in Middlesbrough, mediocrity was imbibed with your mother's milk'.

It won huge applause from off-comers at the *Gazette* office, created steaming resentment from locals and caused a local cleric to tell his Sunday morning congregation: 'Here we have a journalist sent to us from hell.'

I might be heading there... but I had no recollection of having been there.

The union settled, some of its more active members clearing off in the full knowledge their professional future might be somewhat clouded if they hung around and so the office got up to speed without further interruption. This allowed those remaining to work.

I, unable to understand how anyone can believe horoscopes which appear in newspapers, discovered on one bright Monday morning that the composing room had lost a week's supply of these nonsenses. And so I 'lifted' from those which had appeared in the newspaper a couple of months earlier, a whole week of fortune telling nonsense.

No one noticed or, if they did, no comment was made and presumably the Teesside population went about their business believing what was to befall them - according to the feature pages of the *Gazette*. Except that they were four weeks out of date.

~ ~ ~ ~ ~ ~ ~ ~ ~ ~

One of the most acclaimed features we produced was about cheating mediums, usually women operating from centre-of-town terraced houses with Chief Red Cloud hovering in the pantry.

They were not allowed to ask for consultancy money from the poor souls who sought help, but the Wee McLeod who, by now was in my features department, knew there was a truly heartless fiddle taking place and so he posed as a recently bereaved person.

We decided a series could be made about it as he visited several houses, looking suitably sad and fed up as he sat, head down, sharing front rooms with those who had recently lost loved ones. And always there was, on the sideboard, a dish 'for contributions'. It was always full.

While McLeod waited among the red-eyed silent ones in the parlour, in the back room, the medium, taking clients through one by one from the sorry collection at the front, spent 20 minutes telling the customers... whatever they most wished to hear.

McLeod, in his element, wrote a series of quite excellent features which caused anger among those who had sought comfort and paid-up for this verbal nonsense - and those mediums he had visited telephoned to use the most unchristian language, informing McLeod he would never go to heaven.

So he went instead home to his Saltburn flat, there to ruminate on such unkindness - with a bottle to sustain him through the trauma. And he reckoned he knew someone in New Marske, which was close by, who might have a Harpic bottle handy... and a sympathetic ear.

~~~~~~~~~~

On a bright summer day when we went into our town centre office we heard, early in the morning of a haunted house very close by. It was, we were told, possessed by the devil - even if it was in the unlikely situation of Borough Road, just down the street. I duly sent a promising trainee down Borough Road to this spook filled property and did so with considerable cynicism.

At that time Thomson Regional Newspapers was trawling universities for trainee journalists and Middlesborough had its share of those they recruited.

Some made it, others found more learning, after being at some kind of educational institution for nigh on 20 years, too much to bear and left without too many tears being shed on either side.

But it was a graduate I sent trotting off to be haunted - and he most surely was. He sat in the front room of a large Victorian terraced house with the young couple who had arrived, very afraid, at our office before the front doors were open. They had not slept all night long and this, they said, was not unusual.

The writer was to come back every bit as frightened as the subjects of his interview and with a story which can still, in more private moments, create a shudder.

~~~~~~~~~~

The morning sun was still shining brightly when he arrived, but the curtains had been drawn in the room he was shown into. The three adults sat in armchairs in an artificial twilight with a smouldering fire in the grate. A baby, covered by a blanket, was lying on the settee. The mother said the poltergeist, if such it was, only operated when it was dark. And so our man sat on the edge of his seat in the gloom. Nervously.

The minutes ticked by with nothing happening until the room despite the warm outside temperature and the fire inside, began to get colder. Soon the temperature dropped so far it stopped conversation which he had been almost desperately trying to keep going to comfort himself as much as his hosts. It became cold enough to make him shiver and wrap his hands around his knees.

He stopped all pretence of speaking normally for the young couple were by now hanging onto each other in white faced fear for this was what they had felt so many times. The difference then was they had got out of the room when the temperature changed.

We had, when questioning them before undertaking the feature, secured their word that, with the writer alongside them, this time they would stay. They kept the baby with them for they were convinced the whole house was haunted and did not want her to be in another room. And even the child, who had been chattering to herself went silent as they all sat in a still, ever colder quiet.

The writer tried to start talking again, though he later confessed to not being too sure about what he was saying when, with a great roaring of wind down the chimney the fire's embers were flung from the grate several feet forward and onto the carpet. At the same time the baby, now howling with fear because of the sudden loud noise was tipped off the settee and onto the floor, among the ashes.

Screaming with terror, the woman ran from room, closely followed by her husband, who had scooped up the child - and in hot pursuit was our man who legged it down the hall and burst through the front door and onto the street. He did not stop running until he hit our front office. Tea was administered when he got back to the features department from not too sympathetic colleagues.

As the splendid Wee McLeod said: 'Gutless so-and-so, he could have had the scoop of the decade if he had hung about.'

He was right, but did not volunteer to reinvestigate the job and we later heard a priest had carried out an exorcism of the house which was then put into the hands of an estate agent. McLeod reckoned it would be a great buy and very profitable if properly marketed as a truly haunted house.

The trainee reporter did not share our amusement and maybe in our quieter moments we wondered why a rational and intelligent guy such as he had been scared witless. There was no story for the owners of the house did not want to be identified and would not co-operate further

~ ~ ~ ~ ~ ~ ~ ~ ~ ~

By now it was the late seventies, a time when Peter Sutcliffe was still murdering women around Bradford - and beyond. The police were floundering as they tried to catch him and a Middlesbrough woman became one of his victims.

A tape was sent to the police bearing a message from a guy with a Geordie accent who began by saying: 'I'm Jack...' He then went on to taunt the policeman leading the investigation.

The tape was a played at Roker Park before a Sunderland home match for the voice had been identified as belonging to someone who might have been born in the Grangetown area of the town. The plea was for anyone who recognised the voice to come forward.

No one did and the hoaxer is still at large - and a massive time waster he surely was for Sutcliffe proved to be a Yorkshireman. Before he was eventually caught, almost by accident, the Ripper murders seemed to be unstoppable.

~ ~ ~ ~ ~ ~ ~ ~ ~ ~

During this time there one day came to my desk a call from a man in South Bank, a place of blessed memory for it boasted a club which was guarded by big lads of sometimes unpleasant disposition. Their method of dealing with rowdies was... different.

Two of them would pick up the miscreant, run him across the dance floor and hurl him at twin doors marked: 'push bar to open'. They opened quite easily as the unfortunate's momentum crashed him through these doors and deposited him on the cinder track which surrounded the club. Many a silky suit glittered its last at the South Bank Club.

Beyond this I knew little of what was happening at this small conurbation whose terraced houses ran alongside the river as it headed for the sea.

I spoke to the caller from South Bank who said: 'I know who the Yorkshire Ripper is and where to find him.'

I took a deep breath. Was this it, the really big one, the story which would paralyse the nationals and make the *Gazette* the newspaper which was instrumental in grabbing the Yorkshire Ripper?

Mindful of a request made to all newspapers, by the police, which asked us tell the incident room if we had anything, anything at all, to report on the Ripper, I spoke quietly to the man.

I asked if he was sure and he said he was. I asked whether he had told anyone else and he said no, he hadn't. Could I drive out to see him?

'Yes,' he said, 'I could.'

I duly rang the number supplied by the police and a woman said: 'These tips are coming in barrow loads. But,' she added kindly, 'do let us know how you get on.'

I headed swiftly for South Bank.

~ ~ ~ ~ ~ ~ ~ ~ ~ ~

The semi-detached house had an untidy overgrown front garden, not helped by deposits of discarded cigarette packets and sweet papers. I walked up the path and knocked at the panelled door which was answered by a middle aged woman. She invited me in to meet her husband, the guy, she said, with the knowledge that was to shake the civilised world. Through him, she added, young women would once again walk Yorkshire's streets in safety.

She waved me into the living room and I sat down on a filthy settee and waited for the man with the murderous secrets to appear.

He was small, fat, balding and wearing a dirty sweater and stained trousers. He came into the room accompanied by his daughter, who was infinitely better dressed. She stood behind him making faces which suggested father, who had his back to her, was crazy. His wife, however, looked suitably serious and supportive.

The younger woman stopped rolling her eyes heavenwards and looked at me in a most unpleasant manner, wishing I was miles away. I tried to smile sweetly, which is not, perhaps, my forté, and then the man started to speak.

'I get these voices,' he said. 'They come all the time and everything they tell me is true.'

'Really?'

'Yes, and I know where the Ripper is.'

My attention became more focused.

'I was told in bed last night when the voices started. They always come just after midnight and I tell her' (he nodded towards his wife) 'what they tell me.'

I looked at the wife and wondered what she had been whispering in return. She looked, stolidly, blankly, back.

'He's in Yorkshire,' said the knowledgeable one, 'and he's close to us here in Teesside. In fact, he's in this town.'

'Really? Middlesbrough? Can you be a little more specific?'

'I get my information straight from God,' said he, ducking the question... and looking at the ceiling. He turned the palms of his hands up as he sought verification and heavy support from a higher authority. 'The voices never tell me lies.'

'Really?'

'Oh, yes,' said he and rising, began to walk around the room with fists now clenched to his chest and eyes tight closed, but managing to avoid bumping into the furniture which led me to believe this was not a per-ambulation unknown to him. The silent prowling went on for minute after silent minute while we watched and waited.

It now became too much for the offspring who tossed her head and, grumbling, headed haughtily back to the kitchen.

Eventually the holy man spoke and pointing to an oily stain on the brown wallpaper said: 'There is the face of the crucified Christ. See its shape? It's from there that I get my voices.'

I rose from the settee, thanked them for their time and headed for the door. He scuttled after me, down the cracked garden path, came through the broken gate to the kerb side and resting a hand on the bonnet of my beloved MGB GT, closed his eyes and whispered: 'Yes, it's coming through now, you have a sick motor car here. And it will cost you a great deal of money to have it put right.'

The last sentence was delivered with some vehemence. I was clearly a non believer - and an impatient one at that. He was determined I, a dis-believer, would not escape unscathed.

I put aside this cheering news, wished him and his by now furious, grizzling wife, a very good afternoon and expressed the wish that his voices would guide him along a path to a safe and prosperous future.

The car fired first time and they stood to watch me drive off, shaking their heads, unable to understand that anyone could pass up a chance to discover the name and whereabouts of the Ripper. Back at the office I rang the police incident room, told of my encounter and concluded by saying the guy was crazy.

And the polite police lady said: 'Oh... really?'

~ ~ ~ ~ ~ ~ ~ ~ ~ ~

I was frequently writing the newspaper's daily leaders, attending early morning conference with the editor, his deputy and his two assistant editors. We would look at the morning's national papers, discuss what had been on the early radio programmes and then decide a line for the *Gazette* to follow.

Back in my own department I was getting down to the problems of rats in the town centre and detailing the appalling cost of dying - all of which made good features, particularly the cost of a decent burial.

Everyone is at a low ebb when a relative dies and their last concern is about money. And so when the undertaker arrives he could charge what he wanted - and some of them did. It all made good copy and the weeks rolled quickly by.

~ ~ ~ ~ ~ ~ ~ ~ ~ ~

Mike Hope had been a trainee reporter in the West Hartlepool branch office of the *Northern Echo* when I was an apprentice at the *Mail*. He had married a local girl and, when last I had heard of the family, they were in the Thirsk-York area which is a fine place to be and he was on the news desk of the York evening newspaper.

It was some surprise, therefore, when I arrived at the *Gazette* to find Mike on the news desk in Middlesbrough. He had moved, he said, because the salary was better and so we picked up on a good relationship which had bloomed all those years before. And we did some work together.

We were particularly intrigued by stories of a North Yorkshire solic- itor who was alleged to be defrauding clients. The information had come to us from some of his colleagues who were seeking to clean up their profession and were very fed up with him and so Mike and I set about trying to interview the man himself.

He heard of our interest, said he would not see us - and then let it be known through a third party, who telephoned us, our legs would suffer severe damage if we persisted.

And so one night we drove some 20 miles south of town, close to where our target lived and parked up to consider our future health, recap on how far we had got and whether we should press ahead.

Mike had been morose and said little as we drove. When I turned off the engine I realised it was me who had done all the talking while he had been staring through the windscreen straight ahead. I asked whether he was okay.

He was silent for a short while and then his face creased and tears started. I waited until he had control again and asked again what was wrong. He took a deep breath and paused.

'I have,' he said, 'been diagnosed, this morning, with multiple sclerosis.'

A routine medical check for an insurance policy had revealed the illness. I struggled for an answer or even a marginally intelligent comment, but I was lost and mumbling and unable to make a meaningful contribution. We abandoned the evening and I took Mike home. We were both in our thirties; I was fit and fine and he was facing a slow death.

He continued to come to work but very soon was walking with a stick. The wheelchair quickly followed and though he would walk around the office pushing the chair in front of him it seemed to be no time at all before he couldn't get out of it.

I have no idea about the terms of his leaving work, I only know whenever I visited his home he was in such low spirits he would not allow me to push him down to the pub for a pint - or even out of the house for a change of scenery.

He had bought a Yorkshire terrier and found some comfort in the little dog, but all too soon, much, much too soon, he was dead. I was, as I still am, unable to come to terms with the slow and dreadful demise of a comparatively young man

By now we were living in Great Ayton, one of the delightful North Yorkshire villages which, though close to Teesside and its smelly industry, was light years removed from the clatter, the odour and the choking ICI traffic.

Ayton nestles in the bowl of the Cleveland Hills, the River Leven meanders through its centre and our bungalow looked out on to the Wainstones, a line of high and distant hills created by Wain the Yorkshire giant who, many centuries before, scattered pebbles into the horizon and created a wonderful environment for mere mortal man.

In the heart of the village the Royal Oak pub fronted the Green at the other side of which was the Friends School, a Quaker boarding school.

The Oak was the best early doors pub I had come across with Major Dick Kirkup and son John hosting a 6pm collection of lawyers, estate agents, building society managers, newsagents, accountants - and the local hack.

Many is the night the straight-from-work drinkers would see the hours slip by, eventually ring home and invite the ever loving to join us and, around 10, we would all head for Middlesbrough and Linthorpe Road and the best curry in town.

They were days good for remembering, days for talking about wondrous sporting achievement of some ten years earlier - and as the stories were told so the accomplishments recalled became more inspiring.

After one considerable trek down Memory Lane where the lads had thrashed cricket balls all over the park, bowled county batsmen with one that came back off a length and took out the middle pole, when catches had been held with the ball travelling faster than a pigeon could fly I, in a flush of what we could do then we surely can do now, bravado, formed a cricket team.

Dick Kirkup weighed wholeheartedly in with the idea and so the Royal Oak Taverners was born. We played on the Friends' school pitch with the hills all around the ground and no matter who the opposition and what the result, cricket was never more enjoyed.

Wives and girlfriends made wondrous teas and afterwards it was back to the Oak and summer Sundays just slipped by in a haze of sun and alcohol and enormous fun.

It was a character forming time at the *Gazette*, too for as union activity mellowed at the office, so Geoff Walker, the personnel officer, began to introduce management courses which he offered to the heads of department. The object of these weekends and day-long out of office activities at Otterburn in darkest Northumberland was not merely to form teams and find a leader and then cross invisible rivers with nothing but one's ingenuity for support, but to attempt to clear a path for advancement.

My editor sent me on several and then we really got to grips with our own affairs when Geoff organised an in-house presentation to the managing director and those closest to him. He asked me to lead the team, I said I would - and in doing so probably set back my career by a decade or three.

The presentation had its roots in the fun and frolics which went on at the Marton Hotel and Country Club, which was on the edge of town and many a night of high kicks and good times were had as the *Gazette* organised dances, discos and cabarets at the club.

Charlie Amer, a local millionaire, owned the place and, just now and again, after a late night knees up, some of us would be invited back to his place for more drinks and a battle or two with some inebriated person who wanted to throw you and yours into the indoor swimming pool. But this was occasional stuff for us while the *Gazette* first team knew Amer well.

At office parties at the Country Club there was, at one end of the main hall, a raised platform with half-a-dozen tables thereon. Around these sat the *Gazette's* great and good with the rest of us some six inches below in the body of the kirk and very much knowing our place. It was dreadful management.

It gave the occupiers of the platform a sense of importance which was probably not their due, created toadies from the rank and file who nearly did themselves permanent damage as they tried to ascend the magic six inches to spend the night socialising with the chosen few while the rest of us boogied and bopped our way through the evening with our peers... at a lower level.

Quite what the top order types thought they might catch by mixing with the hoi polli heaven alone knows, but there it was. It was a management issue which had to be addressed - by a foolhardy person. Geoff asked me to lead the boardroom presentation which would detail how this 'us and them' management style might be approached. And, heaven help me, I agreed.

Some of the top managers got their excuses in early and said they could only stay for half an hour and had an urgent job, which just couldn't be missed, at 6pm... probably the pub or golf club. Others expressed marginal interest at such 'a novel idea' from the lower echelons who were, quite clearly, setting themselves up in 'a grand manner.'

And so, to a bored audience, we pitched in - with flip charts, cartoons of the country club and those who emphasised their superiority by sitting on the platform away from the other ranks.

The time for those who 'had to leave early because of urgent business' came and went - and transfixed they sat in the boardroom as we told them theirs was really not the best way to behave and, with managing director Heaps looking on, each of his first team watched and stayed quiet as they waited for his reaction. There was not a blink from him as, after an hour or more, we closed.

He eventually thanked us for our 'most interesting' efforts and so we picked up our charts, our marker pens and chairs and made our way out of the boardroom - probably leaving behind careers on the boardroom floor.

The next day Geoff was ecstatic and said we had been brilliant; it had been a successful experiment and we had graphically told those who decided strategy for the company where they might improve their relationships with the troops, for we had, additionally, widened the project way beyond the Country Club to attitudes in the workplace and on the shop floor.

Geoff's was a lone voice. It became apparent very quickly we had not scored too many points with the chiefs, one of them telling me the presentation had been fine 'as far as it went'.

Quite what he meant by that Lord alone knows, but it was the same guy who would say 'leave it with me' which meant that whatever was left with him would disappear into infinity. It was like dropping a cricket ball into a jar of syrup: It didn't make a noise, quickly sank without a sound - and never left a ripple. And wasn't that the style of management which we had just highlighted?

Geoff, his wife Gerry, Jane and I became good friends, always enjoying the glories of the North Yorkshire moors, driving to restaurants and pubs and walking the cliff tops through magnificent scenery.

We journeyed to Newcastle to enjoy my old stamping ground and such wonderful memories and, on one big night out at a music hall on Tyneside, I stopped smoking after hours of inhaling cigarette smoke and almost expiring the following day when walking on Saltburn beach. It was midwinter, the sun was brilliant and the air so sharp and frosty it almost seared the lungs. I decided I hadn't much breathing tackle left as I coughed and gasped my way along the beaches and so finished with the weed for ever on that glorious morning.

It was a similarly cold and bright day when the four of us journeyed into County Durham to Sedgefield, me doing a little bit of strutting as we entered the racecourse for, let's face it, hadn't I been Underhand of the *Journal*? Had I not gone through the card on one miraculous day? Did I not know what I was doing when it came to horse flesh? I waxed long and loud.

I told them what to look for in a nag and this being a jumping meeting I extolled the virtues of a horse with a big rump, one strong enough to charge the fences and, if necessary, go right through them, and in the hurdle races be able to skip over the birch twigs. The horse, I said, must have a rear end like the back of a Sheffield tram.

By now we were drawing level with an absolutely superb horse box. Highly polished and immaculate, it was long enough to transport three or four horses and, as we approached, a groom was leading down the ramp the most magnificent chestnut.

I paused, stood awhile attempting knowledgeable contemplation and said: 'That's surely one to look out for, the build is right, the eye looks good and it will surely be there or thereabouts today. We must follow it through to the paddock and get a good bet on it.'

Heads were nodded; it was agreed that we must, indeed, make sure we followed the sure thing. At this point a member of the Durham Constabulary came through the crowd, threw a leg over the beast - and rode off to control the crowds.

I could have lived in Great Ayton for ever. Indeed, there are those who were happy to do so and, rural North Yorkshire presented, as it still does, an aspect particularly agreeable.

But the *Gazette* had served a purpose - and I had served them. For seven years, which was longer than I had stayed at any job. My inclination was, by now, to move on and this feeling hardened after an interview, in London, with Nick Herbert, the editorial director of Westminster Press.

He said he wanted me to edit for him. WP's empire was vast, ranging from the big morning, the *Northern Echo*, to evening titles in York, South Shields, Swindon and, at that time, Darlington.

The company had weekly newspapers by the score and, in 1978, Nick appointed me to be editor of the *Shields* and *Wallsend Weekly News*, two of his titles on North Tyneside. I was to be a newspaper editor for the next 18 years.

I headed up the A19, drove through the Tyne Tunnel and emerged into a town which had seen better times. Indeed, the Meadow Well estate was particularly deprived and the 'club men' flourished, these people being leeches on the face of mankind who loaned money to those in desperate need and charged interest at a rate so high it was villainously obscene.

If payment was not forthcoming then the unfortunates were visited by the heavy mob who took cash in kind or in skin. But stories like these were to come.

My predecessor, Robin Thompson, had picked up an ailing production and set about putting it on the road to recovery. He had injected a life and vitality which had turned around the circulation.

His predecessor had been cautious enough to shove into a drawer any story which he considered to be vaguely contentious and his out-of-sight-out-of-mind philosophy had seen the paper drift downwards.

Robin had now moved to Darlington to try to pull back a declining evening paper. It proved to be too far gone for him to do to do so, but he went on to a successful career in training.

I parked near the town centre and walked to Nile Street where the offices were situated. The front office presented a pleasing enough prospect as I gazed through the window with the most elegant front counter of gleaming mahogany.

The street was busy, there was the prospect of a new shopping centre to be opened by then miners' leader Joe Gormley, and we were, eventually, to have offices there.

It was only when I got inside the Nile Street building that I realised just how dreadful the present accommodation was. The prospect of that new office was all that prevented me turning around and heading straight back to North Yorkshire.

The editor's office was filthy and had long been abandoned for the heating system was well and truly broken. I shared a room with the deputy editor and we, like the reporters and photographers in their rooms, had a mobile gas heater which the first in every morning had to light. We would then stand around it, taking turns to warm our backsides against the heater and then thawing fingers.

One of the antiquated loos was permanently locked. It was rumoured an old sub editor had gone up there just after the war with a copy of the *Daily Mirror*. He had expired with the paper open at the racing pages and his skeleton remained with the form guide still spread on his bony knees.

The electricity supply would have sent a Fire Brigade inspector apoplectic for, I was to discover, an employee of a company which shared the offices would mend fuses, which had blown with great regularity, by opening a packet of cigarettes, taking out the inside wrapping removing tissue paper from the silver paper - which he then rolled up and put in the fuse. The fuse did not blow again and, mercifully, the building did not burn down with us inside it.

The local butcher would burn whatever butchers burn in the back yard and the smell and the flies which the stench attracted, would almost overwhelm us.

The chief reporter needed a sneck lifter at Charlie's pub, some fifteen yards away, at 10.30 every morning. But he was a very good reporter and was to live another 20 years.

All this I could stand. What I did find difficult was, within a few short weeks of starting at the *Weekly News*, the NUJ called a national strike and there I was, with my only help being my secretary Olive, producing two newspapers on my own.

I really couldn't believe my luck. After Murdoch and the *Sun*, after the *Sketch*, after the union shenanigans at Middlesbrough which had seen us all on the streets here I was, once more, being beset by the union.

Before the staff went through the door and onto the streets to wave placards to beseech folk not to buy the *Weekly News* I didn't endear myself to them by berating them for their actions - and that, of course, probably made them more determined to strike. I could not have cared less. I would either live with it and manage it - or the paper would expire and me, professionally, with it.

It went on a long time; it seemed to be for ever. Christmas came and went. Trying to put out two tabloid newspapers without journalists was exhausting. The production unions, as usual, ignored the pleas of the NUJ for support. They kept on working and drawing their salaries... and producing all the Northern Press titles - including my two - if I could get the copy to them at the South Shields offices.

My titles were dreadful. Full of PR rubbish and stuffed with anything I could get my hands on - plus what I could glean from any court or committee meeting I managed to find time to cover. But I made it onto the streets every Thursday.

My managing director, Tony Boore, who was based at South Shields, telephoned every day to ask how I was holding up and, when Thursday came the telephone call could run to half-an-hour as he said how delighted he was with the paper.

It was top management for, as the festive season came and went and the hours I was working began to make me look like Marley's Ghost, I needed something to keep me going - I was still living at Ayton and travelling up and down the A19, a return trip which was more than 100 miles a day.

If I had to go through that again I would try harder to better understand the staff's problems, but my plea in mitigation would certainly be that the union's actions had overwhelmed me too often and for too long - and I was thoroughly fed up with them.

The strike eventually ended, as all strikes, do. The banners were put away, the folks came back into the office (and I was more pleased to see them than I could ever say, so I didn't say anything at all) and we started to put back together again that which had been staggering.

I recruited a feature writer who had written for me in Middlesbrough. Jim Crawford was one of the funniest men I have read. A process worker at ICI, he invented a pub in Middlesbrough and brought to hilarious life the characters who boozed there. They became like Damon

Runyon's people - but with a north east flavour. It was massively entertaining copy. Jim changed the location of his pub from Teesside to Tyneside and quickly endeared himself to our Geordie readers.

I raised money for a school for the handicapped in North Shields, Ashleigh. Its head teacher, Cynthia Chicken and her staff, looked after children who were dreadfully disabled either physically or mentally or, sometimes, both. I wouldn't do it again. A newspaper's function is to report news in a balanced and well written, readable manner. Charity work is not our brief.

But I was new, very keen and so I started a scheme which I called Star Cheque. I wrote to screen and stage stars, sportsmen, politicians - anyone whose names were well known. I sent them a letter explaining what the appeal was about, who the proceeds were for and enclosed a one pound note asking them, in the stamped addressed envelope I included, to send back to me a cheque for £1 with the payee space left open.

So, if a reader wanted to boast of his relationship with, say, Les Dawson, he got a cheque signed by his hero. He put his own name on the payee line and produced this to his friends. The cheque would then read: 'Pay Joe Bloggs one pound' and the signature would be Les Dawson's.

Once the celebrity had returned the cheque it would be auctioned around Tyneside and the comedian, Spike Rawlings would do some of this for me at celebrity boxing nights at the Gosforth Park Hotel.

Bobby Thompson, once a nationally known comedian and still so much a Tyneside character, gave a concert for the appeal at Wallsend. It was a sell out despite the fact he hadn't changed his act by one syllable for decades.

From a Durham pit village he had been a radio star, but failed to make it south of Middlesbrough because no one could understand his accent - made worse as he became an alcoholic and almost unintelligible.

He, eventually, would turn up at the club which offered him most money - thereby breaking booking arrangements with another club, whose offer was lower, for the same night. His stock sank to the point of him not being booked at all

When I asked him to appear he was back on top form - and off the booze. He turned up as I had requested, was right on time - and demanded £200 in cash up front despite being told it was a charity night. The club was jammed with punters, Bobby was brilliant and everyone was satisfied... except, maybe, the tax man. But it was a big earner for the appeal.

~ ~ ~ ~ ~ ~ ~ ~ ~

James Mason sent a cheque for £50 with the kindest of notes for the school and singer Blondie, from New York, sent $100. The names of everyone who contributed appeared every week in the newspaper and not one of them failed to send back to me the £1 note... which was promptly sent off with another letter to another celebrity.

The whole deal cost - £1 plus postage and many, many hours of my time for I toured pubs and clubs auctioning the cheques - and that was a very good way to get to know the readers. The staff weren't too supportive, perhaps they were not happy because the paper had published all the time they had been on strike. So, once again, I did it on my own, and it worked.

After several months the children got a large vehicle with an automatic lift at the back which allowed them to gain access, in their wheelchairs, into the bus and be driven... wherever.

~ ~ ~ ~ ~ ~ ~ ~ ~

The circulation of the *Weekly News* was on its way up once more and soon we hit the best figures ever recorded by the title which was a great source of personal satisfaction. The staff had settled back to work and I was able to move house - to Monkseaton Drive, in Whitley Bay - and commute to work in minutes rather than hours. And I could set about getting to properly know my patch.

The lighter side was always with me and the Grab a Grannie Night (Thursday) at the Rex Hotel, in Whitley brought loads of reps with business in town to the bar, then the ballroom and then into the arms of some of the mature local ladies.

In the main street, upstairs in another pub, two grand old dears played classical music as though they were at the Palm Court rather than a front street boozer. Well, Whitley did consider itself to be quite swish.

North Shields, where I was based, had seen glory days when the boats had come in with cigars and fine wines and spirits and the community had boasted rich merchants and traders.

The ferries still headed across the North Sea to Scandinavia which could be a rough old voyage. Indeed, one of the vessels was known by locals as the Vomiting Venus and many a passenger en route for Norway had, half way there, wished for an early death.

The quayside's workers manned a large fishing fleet, these a special breed of men, tough enough to endure winter at sea off the north east coast. The town's other residents worked on the quay's markets or headed for work in the city of Newcastle.

The fish quay was a revelation. Just to stand and watch as the girls gutting the fish chatted and laughed and, with lightning flash of knives so sharp they could remove a finger in a single flick of the wrist, cleaned the catch after it had been sold on to merchants who came from all over the north east.

The Tyne was wide, busy and lively at this point just before it entered the North Sea - but it presented a problem for us. Copy created in our office had to be transported to the other side of the river and South Shields for setting in hot metal and then locking into pages.

Amazingly, this task was done manually by, on our side, a retired and elderly woman who visited the office several times a day, picked up the editorial and advertising copy, then walked through the town's streets and down the bank to the ferry terminal.

She would then hand the package to a crew member of the boat and he, on arrival at the other side, would hand it over to another pensioner who had walked from the South Shields office. He made the return trip, walking up the bank, through the town and eventually got it back to the overseer in the composing room. It was long and tortuous and the difficulties of lost copy and arguments about who had sent or seen what and where were interminable.

It seemed Northern Press didn't know about the wheel being invented, this being followed by newspapers using dedicated telephone lines and copy takers. We were locked in a time warp with the process of producing all our newspapers, the *Shields Gazette* six nights a week, the *Whitley Bay Guardian* and the *Blyth News Post Leader*, along with my two titles, sometimes verging on miraculous.

Tony Boore, after producing the first set of good, profitable figures at

Northern Press almost within living memory, had departed. To my regret. He had fought hard battles with the production unions at South Shields, undoubtedly deserved promotion to bigger titles within Westminster Press, was not given them and so went to Teesside and a free newspaper which, with his advertising background, just took off.

His achievements were quickly recognised by his new company - which made him managing director of the much bigger *Bolton Evening News*.

His first action was to take on a circulation battle against the giant *Manchester Evening News* - to such good effect they head hunted him and made him managing director of their company. He was to spend the rest of his working days as MD of the MEN.

I sometimes wondered how Westminster Press felt about all this. Boore had risen through the ranks, from being an ad rep to successfully tackle the grinding, stuttering, geriatric Northern Press. And they had let him go to much greater things.

~ ~ ~ ~ ~ ~ ~ ~ ~

The amazing transportation of copy was to continue but, on one bitter winter's morning when ice had formed on the pavement thanks to leaking guttering above our offices which had cascaded water on to the footpath, the woman who took our paperwork to the ferry slipped, fell and broke her wrist.

It was clearly our fault for we knew there was a leak. It had been reported, was not repaired and when the temperature plunged after rain the pavement outside our front door could have hosted Torvill and Dean.

I made approaches to head office for some form of compensation to the messenger and in double quick time was rebuffed and told to ensure the copy got cross the river without her - somehow. I considered this and until a replacement could be found said I would send a trainee off to the riverside twice a day to meet the ferry.

This caused some union rumblings about journalists not being employed as labourers to which I invited their practical solutions about alternative means of completing the job. Fortunately, within 24 hours the problem disappeared for our lady was back, wrist plastered and ready for work.

I implored her to take more time off, said I would ensure she would be paid for she was, indeed, entitled to her wages. But she said she was just fine and please could she carry on.

Again I said she should take a few days off and this time, clearly disturbed, she said she wanted to talk to me confidentially. We went to what had been the editor's room and I waited for her to speak.

She eventually said she just didn't want to spend more time at home than she had to. Her husband had become disabled and they had moved his bed into the front room where he drank - heavily. And when he was drunk he hit her.

She didn't want to be hit more than was necessary and looked hard at me when I suggested social services to look after him, a separation order for her and a place in care for him.

For an old lady such solutions were not practical, that kind of talk was beyond her ken and so she smiled tolerantly at me, said she wanted to keep on working - and stay out of the house. She then finished the conversation, took herself and the pot on her wrist down to the front office - and made for the Shields ferry.

~ ~ ~ ~ ~ ~ ~ ~ ~ ~ ~

The streets of North Shields were home to a man who had been one of the best known figures on Tyneside, though T. Dan Smith, who had spent his most active years designing and dreaming of a new City of Newcastle, was now cutting a poor aspect as he walked, in a far from new gabardine mac, around town. A great man, now unprepossessing and sad.

Some of his ideas for the city came to fruition for they had been good and he had been driven by a vision strong enough to keep lighting dark corners after his demise.

Indeed, so admired had he been when life was all sharp suits and first class travel that, it was rumoured, he was Harold Wilson's right hand man when it came to many Parliamentary decisions. He was that close to the heart of government.

Some said he had been invited to serve in the Cabinet as an adviser. But he loved his north east and its people and rebutted advances from those who worked by the Thames.

There then came, disastrously, into his life, and into the lives of so many others in England, an architect called John Poulson. It was the early seventies and Poulson, of vaunting, corrupt ambition, in concluding deals in smoke filled rooms in London, the Midlands and the north east, offered bribes which were greedily taken by those elected to serve the public.

It surely wasn't the first time public figures had allowed themselves to be corrupted, to cheat the tax payer and those who elected them - and it surely would not be the last. This time, however, it led to the conviction of the Wakefield-based Poulson along with senior civil servant George Pottinger and many local politicians and officials.

Among those who went to prison were top Labour men Andrew Cunningham, the Chairman of Durham County Council and T. Dan Smith, the former Leader of Newcastle City Council. Tory Home Secretary Reginald Maudling resigned and the pot bubbled for many others who scrambled then leapt to comparative safety... just in time.

And as police got closer to the shady deals and fraudsters it was said Teesside and Newcastle airports were filled with many worthies seeking extended sick leave from book lined council chambers and offices, all desperate to be aboard early flights to Spain and the Mediterranean's golden beaches - before more collars were felt in the UK.

It could be said Smith and his co-plotters received just what he and they deserved for their dirty dealings. But that was then when they were nationally great and glorious and this was now, in North Shields, and T. Dan Smith was working on behalf of the Howard League for Penal Reform, which tried to look after prisoners' welfare after they had been released from jail. His world had, with a massive jolt, moved on.

In the brief conversations I had with him there was a deep sadness about the man which did not solely spring from his transgressions, or why he had thrown a career away - nor did he mention his time in prison.

But those who had lauded him and wished to be seen in his presence just a few short years earlier had gone to ground when he went inside - and had not re-emerged when he came out. And this was enough to sadden any man, a compounding of the miseries in a life which had been famously notable, but gone so very wrong.

The *Shields* and *Wallsend Weekly News* continued to make progress though the chief reporter nearly came to a sticky end when, before covering magistrates' court, he sought the sanctuary, just down the street, of Charlie's Bar for an early door's beer, this very necessary tincture to brace him for the rigours of the remainder of the day.

The polished wooden bar was a horse shoe and David made his way to one end, there to occupy a stool, taking up his usual position. His pint was placed before him and, as he tilted his glass so his gaze lifted to the other end of the bar where a baby gorilla in dirty, open necked shirt and sweater was scowling at him.

Not being made of heroic stuff, and very definitely a non fighter, David swiftly decided he should sink his ale and get on his way. As he moved towards the door the odious one sprinted to block his path and, confronting our man from a very few inches asked, menacingly: 'Were you at court last week?'

David thought a while, realised denial was not possible for he had surely been recognised and so admitted it was, indeed, he - and prepared himself for a hefty smack for citizens do not appreciate having their names in a newspaper report of court proceedings, particularly when they are found guilty of... whatever.

The reason is simply that the neighbours are inclined to talk, prefacing their chatter with something along the lines of: 'I knew that Geordie Broon would come to no good...'

Such lineage also brings shame upon the family and this is so often a greater punishment than anything a milk and water magistrate might hand down. Fines can be paid - or not - but those reported in the local paper as being before the court can suffer a domestically hard time.

David waited, in an agony of anticipation. The aggressor drew himself up to his very considerable height and, putting hands on hips and sticking out an unshaven chin said: 'Well, mind, next time I'm up and you put it in the paper make sure you spell me name right. OK?'

David assured him it was, indeed, OK and, scattering for the door, he almost tumbled into the street so great was his relief.

The late seventies and the eighties were times of great industrial unease and our industry was right up there, at the forefront, when the banners were unfurled and the marches undertaken. We were beset by industrial troubles which frequently spilled over from niggles and groans into full blown and very muscular strike action.

The *Nottingham Evening Post* had, in 1976, got rid of the NGA and gone for direct input which allowed the journalists to bypass the compositors and, for the first time in publishing history, not hand their copy to them for retyping. The reaction was swift and emphatic. The picket lines were formed and, it was said, that on one occasion the newsprint had to be flown into the offices by helicopter to beat the protesters on the pavements outside the office. It was a long and bitter dispute - which the newspaper, eventually, won.

The unions, whose Fleet Street rule had been absolute for years, who had, at national newspaper level, claimed all kinds of money, legally or otherwise, who had regularly twisted the arms of insipid management were now to go ballistic with rage. Sensing their easy times were ending, they went hard for continued recognition and employment, by whatever means.

In 1978 the *Times* and *Sunday Times* ceased publication for eleven months and in 1983 Eddie Shah, at Warrington, stood with back braced against the big metal doors of his offices as activists, who were certainly not always printers, hammered on the outside and threatened everyone inside and anyone who had the nerve to try to get through their lines.

At the same time Andrew Neil was made editor of the *Sunday Times*. Three years later he was to take the paper to Wapping, in London's dock land when the owner, Rupert Murdoch, took on the craft unions and, eventually, beat them. Neil writes, in his book *Full Disclosure*, about lying on the floor of a chauffeur driven car with a blanket covering him as he tried to get through the picket lines and into work.

It was a long and bloody battle. Horses were used to hold back demonstrators and police lines were strung across pavements to get the journalists into work, for now the printers, who had so often ignored the NUJ's disputes and carried on working, had the situation turned around on them. Their protest rose to the heavens for this was a period which was to herald a change as basic and fundamentally far reaching as anyone could imagine.

The printers were on strike and this time it was the journalists who carried on working. The craft unions were about to be defeated and were on their way to oblivion. What Murdoch did the remainder were swift to follow and management which for years had jelly where their spines should have been, suddenly got a little backbone and, almost gleefully, joined in. The revolution was under way. Northern Press was not at the forefront.

~ ~ ~ ~ ~ ~ ~ ~ ~ ~

There was, however, a printers' strike in 1982 and it came amid the by now inevitable threats from the management of closure of the entire division if it was to continue.

Having been made redundant twice and sacked once through the actions, direct or otherwise, of the newspaper unions, I took a decision which was to have far reaching consequences. I called upon my time spent as a compositor and went through the picket lines at South Shields to try to get some of the copy set and the newspapers out.

This made for a jolly little interlude as the NGA lads on the picket lines, hearing of this all too soon, stopped my car at the garage gates, rocked it, presumably to try to turn it over, which they nearly succeeded in doing, hammered on it with their fists and spit on it so hard and often their throats must have been quiet dry by the time I got through.

The managing director, at that time, was David Spencer Crow, who had arrived from Slough. He jokingly boasted of carrying a heavy piece of wood in the boot of his car, this to dispel all troublemakers. He also said he would buy a house with a fan light above the front door to enable him to stand on a chair, strategically placed behind it, and look through the glass to see who was calling. He, certainly on London's orders, had put the compositors on strike.

In his office, which he seldom left except to use his private lavatory, one door and two yards from his own front door, he operated from behind a large desk, empty except for a pen holder. He brought with him a nickname given him by the unions. They called him Black Jake. In the years I was to know him I got to know exactly where I stood with him. He usually let me down. I tried over the years to find a soft spot for him; if I had I would surely have found medication to apply and get rid of it. But it was his job to save us from extinction and it could be said that, as we were still publishing when he left, he had succeeded well enough.

His presence made for a lively old time at Northern Press and sandwiched between all the problems - we on the north side of the Tyne still tried to get two newspapers onto the streets.

Always aware of the budget, constantly being told what we could not do, we operated on a shoestring and, with an undefinable perversity for suffering, joked and almost enjoyed it as the messages drifted in from South Shields, inevitably threatening financial disaster and always starting Thou shalt not...

~ ~ ~ ~ ~ ~ ~ ~ ~ ~

Meanwhile the Meadow Well estate was always a source of good stories, 'good' in the journalistic sense, for the problems endemic on the estate were almost to become the stuff of legend.

The health clinic had to have wire mesh fitted to the windows and the doors strengthened for attacks on it were frequent, which was beyond belief. The staff at the clinic existed to help people, to bring to them all the assistance which fell within their ambit, to ease their way in what was a difficult life for so many of them. And so they tried to smash their way in at dead of night to steal drugs. Or burn it down if the break-in failed.

It was decided more help was needed for these deprived folk and so a sports centre and staff was planned - next to the clinic. In no time at all the sports centre was torched and razed - all this just a part of the many millions of pounds spent on this small area of North Shields.

The clergy lived among the people and alongside them were all manner of good works and sympathetic souls were put in place. Help was there in abundance.

But it remained a social disaster despite everyone trying to help, social workers, health visitors, clerics, charities - and we gave favourable publicity to them as I tried to support all the good souls dedicated to the welfare of the Meadow Well residents.

Good intentions pave the road to hell and so, unfortunately, they continued to qualify for the worst kind of headlines, all of their own making, as they battled with each other, got drunk and fiddled the benefit system. When they were caught they were hauled before the beak and so the estate earned a reputation which made other folk in North Shields very keen to keep away from the place.

We wrote features and did in-depth pieces as we, too, tried to fathom the problems of the Meadow Well estate. Yet, perversely, when Star Cheque was in full swing the people who lived there were first to put their hands in their pocket for 'the bairns'. So many did not appear to want to help themselves and continued to get into the most dreadful trouble with the law, the revenue and anyone else who came near with hands outstretched to help; but ask for help and they were there.

The council placed disruptive families in the estate and so it became a ghetto with all the whizz-bang ideas of the socially well intentioned coming to nothing on the case hardened residents. Eventually there were riots and many streets bulldozed.

~~~~~~~~~~~

Remarkably, but gratifyingly, our circulation was still growing, despite the newspaper's ratio being cut. This saves money, is easy to do and the offence it causes readers is conveniently forgotten. The 'ratio' is the centimetres of advertising to editorial. Journalistic paradise is 50-50. We were now being trimmed to around 70% advertising to 30% editorial, which is as cute a way of increasing revenue and alienating the guy who buys his paper as you could wish. It is also a move which drives journalists to distraction as their copy lies in a basket, unused because of a lack of space in which to accommodate their stories.

Protests during management meetings were always met with the same response - hard times and disaster just around the corner. Such blank responses achieve their objective. I am ashamed to say that, after weeks of appealing to raised eyebrows and deep sighs I stopped complaining and forecasting what might happen to the titles if we continued down this path.

My predictions were not particularly brow-knuckling, but obvious. They had not sprung from profound economic contemplation and assessment of readers' opinions but they were, a few short years later, to come about.

The *Shields* and *Wallsend Weekly News* would fold and be amalgamated with the *Whitley Bay Guardian* with both titles, under a single banner, becoming free sheets, stuffed with advertising.

151

But that was to come and now there came an event which, from a particularly unpromising beginning, was to present a unique, but initially deeply resented, opportunity.

~ ~ ~ ~ ~ ~ ~ ~ ~

Because of my production activities, working in the composing room when the lads were on strike, I was bottom of the NGA Christmas card list when they all, eventually, trooped back into the office. It was said they had not suffered too badly financially and, indeed, some thought they had won their battle. So much for the firm action we wished to happen.

And when I had to go into the South Shields office to put my newspapers to bed there was, let me put this gently, 'an attitude' from the chaps who had so recently spat on my car, tried to turn it over and me with it - and now had to work with me and do what I told them to do to get my titles onto the street and looking the way I wanted them to appear.

This I could live with. My principles were intact, all the division's newspapers were still being published after the strike and the days of the strikers were, because the whole of the newspaper industry was moving technically forward, numbered.

It only needed time for them to settle and get on with whatever was left of their professional lives. But looming on the horizon of my personal career prospects was the fact that Frank Morris, the editor of the *Northumberland Gazette* and *Morpeth Gazette* was about to retire.

Many people within the Northern Press would have given much to have succeeded him, not least his deputy, Bob Bingham, a journalist born in Berwick who had worked for many years in Alnwick and was one of the most diligent of men for whom no amount of hard work appeared too much.

I never thought this would be for me. The Chair in Alnwick would better fit the backside of a guy wearing cords and big boots with studs in the soles than a bloke with a suit and black, polished moccasins.

But on a bright, sunshiny Friday, Westminster Press editorial director Nick Herbert headed north from London to the Moat House Hotel on the Coast Road, near Wallsend to see one of his chief officials (me) and as he bought sandwiches and a beer and we settled to talk it soon became clear good news was not to be served with the coffee. He asked me to go up to Alnwick and replace Morris.

I couldn't believe it. It was like being sent to the edge of the world - you could look over the precipice and not see a thing in front of you. Here I was a townie to my woolly black socks, being asked to pull on green wellies and Barbour and remove myself to a place where the sheep outnumbered the people by umpteen to one.

It was a move sideways which bruised, for my first editorship with WP had seen me break circulation records, produce newspapers for six weeks without any journalistic help and work through a printers' strike. What else had he required? Handstands? It was exile.

Deeper and subsequent thought made me conclude the compositors at South Shields had won, for they would not weep too many tears as I headed, every day, 50 miles up the A1 towards Scotland.

The management, too came out of it well. They had got rid of a problem by removing me from the proximity of the case-room (Alnwick had its own production department). Therefore the lads south of the Tyne would no longer be upset by my weekly presence.

~ ~ ~ ~ ~ ~ ~ ~ ~ ~

I drove north from Whitley Bay for the first day in the new job. The sun shone, I passed fields of oilseed rape and sheep scattered over vast acres, by passed Morpeth and kept on going, trying to remember the *Northumberland Gazette* had a long history and sound tradition which was precious over many, many years of looking after the community. Furthermore, it had retained a circulation which, though small, was consistent and steady.

I could handle that. I could even get my head around the memo which awaited me in my office on that first morning. I expected a good luck in your new position message. Instead Spencer Crow said he had fired my secretary, who was already working her notice, 'for economic reasons'.

It was a rather different way of saying welcome - and the billet-doux also threatened me with emasculation if I recruited anyone without reference to South Shields. It was a happy introduction to my new, sober life in the sticks.

I read through the files for the past twelve months and it quickly became clear that good news stories, good stories by my definition, did not readily present themselves, and readers looked to the *Gazette* for information rather than a front page which would pin their ears back. But all my news instincts rushed to the fore on one well remembered week when I received a telephone call from a freelance in London who made a living sitting in magistrates' courts in the West End and selling the cases to regional newspapers throughout the country.

It was money for old rope for many a provincial lad (or lass for that matter) goes to town, in all senses of the phrase, for a whoopee time, there to throw aside home town inhibitions and rural rules and blast a way into what they considered the high life.

And sometimes it was legal, but when a hack calls from a magistrates' court there is always a whiff of unpleasantness about to drift under the nostrils. Something very illegal was afoot.

For those loose in the big city can find life going very wrong. They might even be arrested, appear in court and there, on the press bench, is our man, the freelance journalist, who will ring the miscreant's home town newspaper with details of misdemeanours and misbehaviour, as presented by the prosecutor, and the court's verdict.

The London freelance asked if we had, on our patch, a teacher called Little. I asked Bob Bingham who said Little was not merely a teacher but the headmaster of one of the biggest, most prestigious schools in the county, the Duchess's School, in Alnwick, in which the Duchess of Northumberland took more than a passing interest. Her home was the quite splendid pile, Alnwick Castle where she lived with her husband, the duke, in the centre of town. She was not about to be best pleased.

Little had, said the freelance, been caught behaving extremely badly with another teacher in a cinema in Shaftesbury Avenue - and the other teacher was also a man. Patrons had complained, the manager had telephoned the police - who had nicked the pair of them.

We were about to break a national story of some weight; we tried to get as much information as we could.

A reporter was dispatched to Little's house, in Alnwick, which was empty. The school buttoned up tight and refused to comment and the teachers' union stayed silent. But we were able to find out the man had resigned his post.

I ran the story as the page one splash and waited all through publication day for sleepy old Alnwick to rumble all across the county's acres and explode, bringing hell and damnation down on me - but the telephone stayed silent. No one came through the front office door demanding the editor's head for sensationalist reporting (which it wasn't, I was merely being accurate).

Bob Bingham, who lived in the town, reported back the next day to say the townsfolk were already aware of the story before we printed, but had kept it to themselves. Small town equals no secrets? Better believe it.

~ ~ ~ ~ ~ ~ ~ ~ ~ ~

Shortly after arriving in Northumberland I fought off a bid by Spencer Crow to stop paying my petrol as I continued to travel the daily century of miles between Whitley Bay and Alnwick and back again.

If he had succeeded it would have cost me considerable cash I did not want to afford for already we were into having to produce receipts for everything. But buying the local council leader a half of beer and packet of peanuts would not see a claim going into South Shields, for we were too embarrassed to ask the barman for a receipt after we had spent a couple of quid.

But the directive was - no receipt, no recompense. And so I paid for... whatever. My staff also put their hands into their own pockets and, while drinking the first pint bought for contacts, did not add an under-the-breath toast to Northern Press.

By now I was settling into what I had first perceived to be a hill billy world and finding some sense of starting to belong. It helped that the Whitley Bay house was sold, eventually, and we moved north. The long car journeys ceased and Morpeth presented a very pleasant prospect.

Just as the house sale and purchase were taking place I attended the annual lunch of the Army's Northern Command, in York. It was, as it always had been, quite an occasion.

The regimental silver was laid out on long tables covered with snow white linen and the top brass from many regiments were there for the general's speech and to entertain regional editors, TV and radio people. It was an event organised and completed with great style for when the Army undertake such a venture you can be sure it goes with... regimental precision.

Quite what the squaddies, both male and female, thought of serving such very decent fare to a load of civvies was not known. But when they got back to their barracks and chatted to their mates over spaghetti hoops on toast they might have had a word for it.

I am not much given to appreciating Public Relations people. Too many have little sense of what newspapers are about, know nothing of titles, readers, their social status (A, B, or C), know nothing of deadlines, either for last pages or copy times and churn out all manner of semi-literate copy which hits the hacks' bins with a thud.

In fact I have long considered companies really do need educating about publicity and what is offered on their behalf to the newspaper and, they hope, to the client.

My concern was highlighted when I once received a handout from a well known PR company about a bank. The bank did not even have a branch in my circulation area, which was considerable. And it was written in Welsh.

I presumed they thought Cumbria was Cambria. It was astonishingly inept and it went through my mind that I should inform the bank of how they were spending their money, but decided if they did not monitor results, if they had not seen the copy before submission - then they deserved to pay handsomely to be laughed about, for it became a tale well told.

But Bill Holmes, a former Army Major, stood out from all of this. He was good. It was he who organised the lunches and afterwards, as was now our habit, he and I would retire to the Judge's Lodgings, in York, for a small refreshment and talk of what I could get out of the Army which would appeal to my readers.

At the Northern Command lunch in 1982 I was prepared to really press my luck for it was autumn and, in the summer, the Falklands war had ended. It had started with much flag waving and ships' hooter blowing as wives and girlfriends lined the docks to wave off the lads in the convoy heading for the South Atlantic.

To old sweats, those who had fought in two World Wars, had been in uniform to Korea or Vietnam, it was a sight to make them weep for many of those lining the decks and smiling and waving down through the bunting would not come back. They never do; there are always casualties in war and inevitably men die. Gung-ho attitudes change when the first body bags come back to Blighty.

It was to be a brief and costly confrontation, after which Prime Minister Margaret Thatcher had proclaimed an outstanding victory, though time was to tell a story which highlighted a rather more sombre tale of massive military errors and the deaths at Bluff Cove and other locations in the South Atlantic of many British servicemen.

Top national newspaper journalist Max Hastings had managed to be there during the action and while I was to thoroughly recommend his book on what he saw in the war, I had not seen a word written by any regional journalist. The output of information was strictly controlled by the Ministry of Defence, many press briefings being dictated by a man who spoke so slowly it was as though he was addressing children.

And so, at the Judge's Lodgings, I asked Bill: 'Is it possible for me to go to the Falklands?' (and here I took a deep breath and crossed my fingers under the table). 'I could cover it for Westminster Press and all its newspapers.'

Bill paused, smiled and said: 'Leave it with me.'

By the end of the following week I was given permission to fly to the Falklands. I hardly had time to very briefly bone up on my military history and get up to date with the British War in the South Atlantic before I was on a southbound train from Newcastle Central Station. It was a thrilling prospect. And Northern Press did not object - the trip was at the Army's expense

~ ~ ~ ~ ~ ~ ~ ~ ~ ~ ~

The overnight stay at Brize Norton, Oxfordshire, was in barracks. Dinner was in the mess and we went early to bed for we were to board, before the sun was up the following day, a most acceptable RAF aeroplane for the flight to Ascension Island, just off the west coast of Africa - a base of considerable military importance.

We had aboard various personnel, some of whom were to journey onward with us via the air bridge and thus to the South Atlantic. Stewards served our meals and it was all very civilised as we flew towards the equator.

At the rear of the aircraft were three men in dark suits who made a very deliberate point of not mixing with the rest of us. A steward told me one was a doctor who was flying out to tend British car accident victims.

Why, I wondered, would military physicians travel all that way? Who had been hurt? Must have been Top Brass - like whom? I was never to find the answer.

We touched down at an airport in west Africa and the captain, as he made his approach, said we might wish to stretch our legs, adding we should not stray far from the aircraft and certainly not go into a concrete building which, he said, was reception. He didn't say where we were, why we had broken our journey and the air of mystery became one of acute apprehension when we did touch down and began to taxi towards the buildings.

Steps were lowered down which the Suits disappeared with the rest of us filing slowly after them and onto the tarmac. We were at once surrounded by soldiers dressed in immaculately pressed light fawn, lightweight uniforms and holding what looked to my inexperienced eye to be machine guns.

They looked at us totally without curiosity; rather they were, as they shifted, almost flicking their weapons from hand to hand, belligerent in their body language. Their cocky, slow sauntering around the aircraft was extremely intimidating, as it was designed to be.

In the face of these cold, hard, hostile looks the leg stretching was forgotten and we made our way quickly back up the gangway. Our relief at the quick take off to the safety of the wide blue yonder could have been measured. The shocking rise in outside temperature, which had hit us like a blow when the doors had been opened, aided by great apprehension, had brought the sweat cascading down our faces.

After that Ascension, we thought, was going to be beautiful. Well, it might have been if we'd been allowed to see it.

~ ~ ~ ~ ~ ~ ~ ~ ~ ~

As we made our approach I looked down at the biggest aircraft I have ever seen. Its wing span was so wide it seemed the tips were touching the ground; double decker buses could have been driven inside - and probably were. It was American and just part of a considerable NATO fleet on the tarmac, but as we flew closer I wondered how such a massive structure could ever get airborne. It was huge.

I determined to try to walk around it after we landed only to find, when we had disembarked, wire was everywhere, sometimes barbed or razored, usually for perimeter guidance. The warnings from the permanent staff on the ground made it very clear we were only allowed to stay near our sleeping quarters, walk from there to the mess for meals - and that was it. No trespassing. Any attempted excursions beyond these bounds would be very severely frowned upon for security was absolute.

But Ascension smelled of warm spice and the pollen of flowers and a breeze wafted smoothly in from the Atlantic and so we forgot about military aircraft and sat on verandas with gin and tonics and watched the dramatic, so sudden disappearance of the sun as night fell. Then, tired after the long flight from the UK, I turned in.

The next morning, after breakfast, we were given a boarding time for the air bridge and waited in the embarkation hall. I wondered why the military types began elbowing and pushing their way forward while the rest of us sat - and watched. We still had many thousands of miles to travel and I was unable to understand their anxiety to get aboard the Hercules, a pot bellied, grand old lady of aviation, which was to be our home for the next twelve to thirteen hours. So, why the rush?

When the hall's doors opened and we were allowed onto the apron to walk towards the aircraft the service guys started to sprint towards the short flight of stairs which led into the Hercules' interior. Bemused I followed at a normal walking pace. It was only when I got inside I realised the reason for the rush.

Passengers were up in the rigging inside the hollow shell for the Hercules is a transport aircraft, not designed to carry people and those who had travelled in one knew the only way to get any comfort was to rig up some kind of space in the ropes, arranged much like the inside of a removal pantechnicon, with top coats or anything soft which could make a pillow or blanket and where they could stretch out in something resembling a hammock around the shell of the aircraft.

The rest of us, the strollers aboard, the uninitiated, were issued with ear plugs for the noise of the engines would deafen without them, and we sat on benches, knee to embarrassingly close knee with the person opposite. We were desperately cramped and appallingly uncomfortable.

The most attractive blonde girl with the flashes of her squadron bright on her olive green neck to toe coveralls, was in charge of the interior and she tiptoed around the inside of the rigging, her rubber-soled boots seemingly impossible for the job she was doing. But she smiled while sometimes swinging monkey-like around the inside of the plane, stepping from wooden slat to sagging ropes as she handed out shoe boxes.

Inside these was a carton of orange juice, a couple of rounds of sandwiches, a packet of crisps and a chocolate bar. She put her mouth close to my ear, which was enjoyable, and then did something less welcome. She shouted: 'Don't eat it all at once - they are your rations until we touch down at Port Stanley.'

Wonderful. I looked around for signs, something to indicate where the facilities might be located. Nothing I shouted at the chap next door who nodded to a space between the benches. The loo was a bucket and chuck it affair behind a canvas curtain. It sure wasn't Club Class.

The flight crew looked to be fifteen years old - and they were going to fly us to the Falkland Islands in the South Atlantic. As we flew to the left of us would be Africa, to the right America and our flight path was, more or less, directly between the two which left around 1500 miles of only sea and sky to port and to starboard a similar distance. It was not a prospect to dwell upon.

And a very good morning to you, Bill Holmes, I thought as the crew switched on the four turbo prop engines, warmed her up and slowly turned at the end of the runway. And then we were off, climbing ever so slowly upwards and heading due south into what was probably a clear blue sky.

We couldn't know too much about that for the Hercules is not strong on windows so there is nowhere to look except straight ahead. And if you don't like the face of the guy sat directly opposite and all of a metre away, which is all you're going to have to look at, well, you will be rid of him by the time the clock had gone round one full circuit. I could have sworn I heard Bill chuckle.

~ ~ ~ ~ ~ ~ ~ ~ ~ ~

The mid air fuelling during the air bridge was a miracle of flying. Or it seemed so to me. The Hercules is ponderous, designed for work and, as my squared off backside indicated at the end of the flight, definitely not built for comfort. Indeed, it is so slow the aircraft which was to pour into us more fuel had to throttle back a long way to match our speed - and still would be travelling too quickly as we tried to fly together in level flight.

I was invited onto the flight deck to watch a manoeuvre which was a massive tribute to the RAF pilots. We were several hours out of Ascension and still climbing when the lights went out and a huge shape appeared above, between us and the sun, as the fuel arrived in spectacular style.

Our pilot had to pick up speed and co-ordinate this with the speed of 'the shadow'. Already at maximum revs he had to put us into a shallow dive which, allied to our full revs roaring engines, managed to work up enough knots to match the Vulcan's speed.

Down came an umbilical cord from the big aeroplane which our pilot, one hand on the throttle and the other on the steering column watched and edged towards us as the cup on the end of the cord swung and looped in the air above and ahead of us.

The professionalism was immaculate and we locked on to the cup, maintained our dive and the pilots of each aeroplane talked to each other while a series of lights went on under the Vulcan first indicating a connection had been securely made and then showing refuelling was taking place. And so, to my increasing admiration, we held our positions as the fuel flowed from Vulcan to Hercules and the minutes ticked by.

When the job was done it was with a considerable thwack the bigger plane peeled up and away at a great speed and we were left to gain height and continue heading south, alone again, but fully fuelled once more and heading into the blue South Atlantic. I felt like applauding.

Before I left the flight deck I asked why we had not been able to take on board enough fuel to get us to Port Stanley before we had taken off.

'Oh, we did,' said the pilot. 'The additional fuel is not to get us there, but to get us back. The fog can come down in minutes in the Falklands - and we would not be able to land. We would then turn around and fly back to Ascension.'

The thought of this happening and having to make a return trip when we were so nearly there, well, it was not appealing. I staggered back to my bench, eased into my cramped sitting position, repositioned my shoe box on my knee - and the lady of the aircraft, from up in the rigging, smiled sweetly.

I wondered how she coped with flying to and from the Falklands on a regular basis and whether she had ever made a return trip without touching down when the fog descended. She kept on smiling.

In the event we touched down neatly enough and the military folk unravelled themselves from the rigging, stretched and headed off for the Jeeps awaiting their arrival.

We civvies made for the Goose Green Hotel which, like the rest of Port Stanley, was getting used to a very new role in the world as politicians continued to focus on the islands. And the hotel owners were learning to cope with the aftermath of war.

December is the middle of summer in the South Atlantic. Hostilities had ended in June and Governor Rex Hunt, whom I was soon to visit at his house to sign his visitors' book and even ride in his red London cab, had resumed his work in Port Stanley. And the people tried to live with the influx of troops, the roar of trucks up and down their narrow main street and thousands of military people around town.

There was a very lovely young nurse from the tiny local hospital who was the centre of much attention as the troops sought girl friends among the island's 1,800 inhabitants.

She had taken to wearing a kind of sailor's hat and around the band were a series of stickers and badges with some of the slogans verging on the obscene. While these were good for military belly laughs it seemed to me almost like the despoiling of innocence. And like the girl maybe the Falkland Islanders just didn't know what had hit them, but the people were smiling, nervously, through it all as they tried to find out and come to terms with life being turned upside down.

To help them a considerable amount of work was being done by the forces to win applause and respect from the locals who had spent their lives so quietly it was, as I moved among them, like turning the clock back half a century. Concerts were being staged as entertainers from the UK headed for Port Stanley to entertain the boys. Local dignitaries occupied front row seats at these shows though I sometimes felt the quality of the basic humour on stage was a little too much for them... but the troops were loud with their applause.

Islanders had been overwhelmed by events when, in March, Argentinian scrap metal dealers had come ashore to lay claim, they said, to what belonged to their country. They had been quickly followed by soldiers and diplomacy between the UK and Argentina deteriorated quickly and in no time at all descended into the awful reality of war. They told me how it had been.

Rex Hunt, governor of the Falklands from 1980-85 took a lead role, they said, when Margaret Thatcher declared she was not be taken lightly and, after Argentine invaded on 1 April, taking South Georgia on the third of that month, the first Task Force ships upped anchor and sailed from Portsmouth. He never wavered, they said.

A 200-mile exclusion zone was thrown around the islands and on the 9 April the P&O cruise ship, the Canberra, left from her home port, Southampton, crammed with troops and ready for war.

Islanders said they had heard she had left as the bands played and tearful wives and girlfriends waved and cheered. It was as it always had been at time of war; the men were off to fight leaving behind families who had not been prepared for their lads to be called into action.

Falkland Islanders, like me, wondered how anyone can join the forces and not expect, at some time during their career, to be called into action. It's what the forces are about. In the early stages of the Falklands War neither side was to fare well.

We, amid great controversy for it was said the ship was outside the exclusion zone and not posing a threat, torpedoed and sank the Belgrano.

HMS Sheffield was hit by an exocet missile and Ardent, Argonaut and Coventry were bombed. Atlantic Conveyor, which had been pressed into military service, was hit by an exocet. So it went on and though the war was to last a mere three months the damage and casualties laid bare any claims to our invulnerability and any arrogance we might have felt when we went into active service quickly evaporated as men were killed and hurt and strategic errors abounded.

The retaking of the Falkland was completed at great cost, sometimes with passages of hand-to-hand combat and bayonet fighting, which had taken place on Mount Harriet and there was almost unbelievable acts of heroism with posthumous VCs awarded to Col H. Jones and Sergeant McKay of Third Para.

I was to visit what was said to be the site of the dreadful skirmish which resulted in Col. Jones charging up an embankment above and around him from where the Argentinians were firing down. He was, without doubt, incredibly brave though it seemed to me, a hack abroad and not knowing much of these matters, that it had not been prudent to try to take such a well defended ridge. But VC winners do not take the cautious, diffident line.

And now it was my job to report on the welfare of the troops at the end of the war - and to look with a sadness I had thought was beyond my sensitivities down San Carlos Water at the blue sea in the far distance at the bottom of the world.

Then, merely by turning around, I could see, within a few feet, the white, semicircular stone memorial to British servicemen who had lost their lives in the Falklands. Beneath it toys children had sent to be placed on the graves of fathers who would forever look down and out over the fields and towards the South Atlantic, so many thousands of miles from home.

I was to visit Tumbledown and Wireless Ridge and Mount William, see spent cartridges all around and about me still as I walked through these macabre memorials to the so-recent fighting. There were sheets, crumpled and thrown into the bottom of dry stone walls on which injured men had been carried to helicopters. The linen was marked with their blood and excrement where battle hardened troops had been shot, bled - then lost control of their bowels and dignity in the agony of war.

I was to fly everywhere by helicopter, for the defeated Argentines, a force said to have been made up of boys and amateur soldiers, had laid many miles of minefields only to forget, some said conveniently for they were the vanquished and could be behaving spitefully, where the mines were.

Local farmers had tried driving sheep over many acres where they suspected the mines were located, but the animals were not heavy enough to detonate the charges and so there will forever be parts of the Falkland Islands which are no go areas.

These vast, empty spaces added to the aura, the silence, the distance over nothing but fields and the sea beyond and the sighing of the wind. It was the loneliest place I have ever known - or wish to know, made worse by the fields of danger where no one could tread.

I met some of the farmers who raised sheep for the wool which would be sent back to the UK, people whose isolated lives were beyond my comprehension for I could not understand why anyone would wish to live in a place where the wind seemed always to blow, be it zephyr or hurricane force, lifting skin off the face and hands and where the loneliness was so acute it made northern hemisphere hearts ache with the want of seeing another soul.

Maybe because they could look out over a sea so pure so unadulterated and so prolific that fishermen sailed for many miles to catch and take home fish so easy to net they merely had to cast, they tolerated it. Many had cleared a strip of shore, allowing the boats to arrive close in to unship supplies and these were hauled, by tractor, to the farm buildings in the middle of nowhere.

The school teacher, a jolly, plump guy carried on his profession by short wave radio and, when he could, he would set off on visits to the children of the Islanders. Maybe he, too had an agenda which meant solitude was important.

I was flown to the sea shore of South Georgia where I stood as close as I dare to many hundreds of King Penguins and, farther down the beach, made tentative steps towards enormous sea elephants, big as a living room with the males waving their long snouts and so ponderous they turned by throwing themselves around. But woe betide anyone close enough for them to lumber after, catch and attack.

The stench of them verges on being indescribable, rotten fish and worse after they came out of the sea to bathe in the sunshine. Then it was back to the helicopter and the mess and supper.

~ ~ ~ ~ ~ ~ ~ ~ ~ ~

Journalists are awarded the honorary rank of Second Lieutenant, the lowest form of commissioned Army life, but it allowed me to eat with the officers and move around fairly freely. My principal reason for being there was to see how the Northumberland Fusiliers were coping - and they were doing just fine.

I got from them the stories I wanted, cheer-up encouraging yarns for the folks back home - and I also got enough off beat material from other regiments which would be appropriate for other Westminster Press publications around England.

The objective was a couple of general features around which would be tucked tales of local guys appropriate to the Westminster Press titles. There was loads of material.

An Army flier called McCorquerdale, tall languid, very laid back and with an Edinburgh Morningside accent, was nicknamed the Green Baron by the troops who regarded him as some kind of superman. I privately scoffed at the title - the guy flew helicopters which was no more than a job. Until one day he took it upon himself to transport me to an assignment.

Dressed in survival kit, designed to keep me alive for a short while if we had to ditch in a freezing sea, I waddled like a Michelin man to the helicopter. A mist was beginning to drift in, but the green helmeted McCorquerdale took us straight up and through it - only to find when we were up there the adverse weather was more widespread than we had imagined.

In fact it was coming in thick and fast... which presented us with something of a dilemma. Going straight up through the weather was, in a helicopter, not a problem. Coming down was somewhat different.

The Green Baron was up to it and while I, in a sheer funk, sweated inside my layers of survival suit he circled a while then dropped the 'copter down through the swirling mist and landed it as easily as putting down a cup on a saucer - and with as little fuss. I agreed with the lads - he was some flier.

There were other such tales to tell and the Army were super, never denying me access, always prepared to talk which we did long after supper and aided by the odd tincture as the late hours became early hours and just rolled on by.

The flight back to the UK was uneventful and I quickly resumed, without too much enthusiasm, my editorship at the *Northumberland Gazette* in Alnwick.

~ ~ ~ ~ ~ ~ ~ ~ ~ ~

I took to walking around the town at lunch time, a trip which lasted around ten minutes, looking for stories which might be readily available. I read notice boards, discovered what was happening where and to whom... and none of it was very exciting. You can't find what doesn't exist.

I would buy a lunch time sandwich and head for the villages which fell within our massive circulation area and sit and watch Northumbrians, our readers, going about their business, before walking down the main street and then... I would wonder what I was doing there.

Amble, Alnmouth, Craster, Walkworth, Beadnell, up the road north towards Berwick and on another day west to Rothbury, I visited them all and everything in between. I even volunteered for talks to WI clubs, Mother's Union, Round Table and Rotary clubs, et al. But there remained nothing much doing to blast the front page off the newsagents' stands.

I had inherited a good, sound staff. Indeed one reporter, the highly prolific Terry Hackett, covered an entire town on his own and filled the pages of my secondary title, the *Morpeth Gazette*, which sold around 2,500 copies in that most pleasant conurbation - where I chose to live. It was close to my favourite city, Newcastle, just fifteen minutes drive, and there was a railway station in town.

When, each morning, I left Morpeth and turned north to head for our office in Alnwick, it was like driving to the edge of the world and being so close to the edge of Northumberland did not make my heart pump with eager anticipation as the hot and high life spots of Felton and Swarland were by passed.

The only answer to this, and to do it before torpor set in, was to work. There was, in Berwick, the Tweeddale Press, a newspaper company which had titles along the Borders. Just before my arrival in town they had started the *Alnwick Advertiser*, which did not seem to be a master stroke for there was hardly enough business to enable one of us to flourish, let alone keep two titles going. But they were in town and constituted an itch which had to be addressed.

Taken as a single entity the *Advertiser* did not present a mind bending problem. The editor had been a photographer and my reporters just blew the *Advertiser* away in terms of professionalism. We were, in addition, skilled enough to look typographically sound.

But they needed to be taken care of and so I decided to launch a free newspaper in the heartland of the Tweeddale Press. My deputy, Bob Bingham and I took off one Friday morning, after press day, and headed north from Alnwick.

He knew his way very well around the towns in southern Scotland and we drove through Coldstream and Kelso, Jedburgh and Hawick and thus to the very heart of Tweeddale Press country, Selkirk.

The towns seemed to have their very own identities and, rather than be united under the heading of the Borders, they viewed neighbours in adjoining towns with less than good favour. Hawick did not seem to be too concerned with what was happening in Langholm and so it went, but there were shops and factories and councils and enough commerce to make the prospect of selling advertising at a rate substantially less than the Tweeddale Press was charging a very real possibility... which was to become reality.

We returned to Alnwick and I set about a business plan part of which was a request for a full time reporter and one part timer for the new Berwick free newspaper.

South Shields told me I couldn't have either, the new title would have to be staffed from my present reporting strength and, furthermore, there would not be an office for us in Berwick or anywhere in the Borders. We would have to operate from Alnwick, approximately 50 miles away. And so, overwhelmed with such support and snowed under by so many good wishes, I went ahead - anyway.

I sent a reporter up north whenever the mini van was not being used for the *Northumberland Gazette*, we used a freelance in Berwick for the bulk of the copy and the photographers' patch now stretched from the very fringes of Newcastle to the edge of England and into Scotland.

Well, it kept us off the streets and so we started to produce our third newspaper. I launched the *Berwick Gazette* in 1983. It has expanded and is still publishing. The *Alnwick Advertiser* has gone to the wall.

~ ~ ~ ~ ~ ~ ~ ~ ~ ~ ~

Craig Stamps is, quite simply, the best circulation man I have ever worked with. He was in charge of all the Northern Press titles, evening and weekly, and waged a one man war with the big boys from Newcastle who stuck their multi-coloured, extremely expensive contents bills all over Tyneside.

Most of these very quickly ended their gaudy days in the boot of Craig's car to be replaced by our less glamourous black and white efforts. While doing this meritorious work he parked anywhere - and every-where, usually illegally and got away with it by switching on his hazard lights and lifting the boot lid as he parked all around Durham and Northumberland. He said the busies (police) thought the car had broken down and so he bought the few minutes of time he needed.

The hours he worked were crazy and testified to an iron constitution, stamina sufficient to keep going as the clock completed a twelve hour circle - and he did so with hardly a break.

It was not unknown for him to complete a day's work with evening and weekly titles to the south of us, go to his home in South Shields, in the early evening, pick up a cup of tea and a sandwich, his wife, his deaf and handsome Old English sheepdog, put the lot in his car and drive to Alnwick.

The Stamps' entourage frequently arrived very late at night and Craig would set about his business, sometimes climbing lampposts there to attach our contents bills on the main drag (the only drag?) in town.

This excited the interest of the local constabulary who were informed by a midnight telephone call that there was a guy climbing lampposts in the middle of the fair city of Alnwick which was against local practice and custom and was frightening the horses.

The bobbies duly arrived suggested to Craig he was drunk, swiftly understood he most certainly was not - but told him to move on anyway. He did so, waited an hour and returned to climb more lampposts. He was worth many newspaper sales to the Northern Press; I hope he was appreciated by those in head office who paid his salary.

~ ~ ~ ~ ~ ~ ~ ~ ~ ~ ~

Our titles were hanging on in and we were proud of them, but complacency was never to be our lot - and yet another cacophony of unpleasant noises drifted up from head office in South Shields.

Northern Press, still desperately struggling for cash, had decided to cut back our pagination - drastically. The news came on a Monday when I was not feeling chipper for the day before I had been playing in what was to prove my last cricket match for my team in Great Ayton.

A very young, very quick bowler, bursting out of his eager self, was digging the ball in short on an uneven wicket (what did I expect, Lords?) and it got up high. I tried to hook, missed and with a click heard around the ground the ball broke my right forearm as neat as you like.

I was already the possessor of a couple of fingers which had been broken playing the great game and now wander hither and thither at funny angles, but a broken arm was different. It was time to stop playing cricket. It was a very sad day.

I had been to the local hospital, in Alnwick, they confirmed the break and so I sat at my desk with an aching wing, trying to remember the golden days when I could play the game well, little knowing I was about to get pain from a totally different source.

The headache came with the first layout for that week which detailed a massive reduction of editorial space. There had been no discussion nor warning from South Shields.

It was to be the start of real problems as we began to operate on reduced paper sizes. Week after week reporters' copy was not to see the light of day. I once again tried to take the management line for, after all, I was a chief official of Westminster Press and therefore duty bound to uphold decisions taken by the managing director. But in my private moments I fumed.

Good operators, tip top weekly journalists who spent many hours working beyond their statutory hours as they travelled miles in the office mini van to jobs in a cave near nowhereland and came back with stories were to see their work pinned as the stories were squeezed out, then became dated.

More important, the readers, loyal all their lives to the *Northumberland Gazette*, began to write to complain, gently at first then with greater vigour as their newspaper became less to be relied upon to serve them. And still the story count diminished.

I complained many times to the managing director who, eventually, refused to accept my telephone calls. I then parcelled up, every week, all the carbon copies of my reporters' copy which had not been used, crowded out and sunk into oblivion for there was no space in the ridiculously small newspaper. Together with the bundle I sent to him readers' letters of complaint.

There was no response. Not a word not a call, not a written line. Spencer Crow had long since refused to have me attend management meetings in South Shields, saying the cost of travelling was too much and communication could be by telephone - but, too often, he didn't return calls. There then came a master stroke.

We had an aged set of office premises in Alnwick's main street, a location which was ideal, for we had the name above the door, the readers and advertisers knew just where we were and could come in to see us whenever they came to town. It was the perfect site.

Northern Press said they were going to sell this office to Greenwoods the tailors. We were to move to share accommodation with compositors and stereotypers in a side street, St Michael's Lane.

Privately I thought we were now really beginning to commit suicide. The arguments were still of lack of cash; not being able to afford two lots of rates; trying to secure our future.

And so, again, as a chief official of Westminster Press, I defended the move to the staff and tried to sound convincing as a couple of lads from South Shields arrived with plywood and battens and hammered up partitions. I attempted to talk of togetherness rather than photographers and reporters being remote (no more than a flight of stairs apart in the old office). I was by no means convincing and not one of my journalists believed life was going to be so wonderful. To their lasting credit they remained loyal to me and their understanding made me even more sad for it was clear there was not a thing I could do to change the situation and I felt they were being cheated.

I tried by saying we would carry very big 'puffs' in the newspaper telling of our move and detailing our new address, I said folk would quickly get used to us not being around in the town. I said the only way forward was upward. And, of course, it wasn't. And no one, least of all any of my very bright hacks, was fooled.

~ ~ ~ ~ ~ ~ ~ ~ ~ ~

There had to be diversions, something to relieve the unrelenting battle of a professional life on a shoestring. I was watching my staff, good operators all of them, becoming increasingly despondent as they worked diligently all the while knowing much of their copy was not to appear in print. It was no way for a journalist to live and I found myself almost wanting the threats from South Shields to become reality and for us to go bust, fold up - and have done with it.

In need of something to do away from newspapers, and I had never thought I would even contemplate such blasphemy, I took myself, on a dark winter night, off towards the town centre and, turning off a side street, strode up a cinder path towards the Morpeth Rugby Club pavilion. Behind me a hastening stride brought level with me Bernard Dick, local solicitor and a club stalwart.

'Hi,' said he.

'Hello,' I replied.

There was a silence as we crunched along together before I said: 'I want to join your club.'

'Oh, good,' said Bernard and went on: 'Who have you been playing for?'

I chuckled, blessed the darkness and said days of playing active sport were long gone. I wanted to be a social member.

It was to be the start of several years of good times and excellent fellowship - which led to me taking a very different view of the Northumbrian and what they are as they set about their business. Many of the club members were farmers, but others sought a living in the city, travelling into Newcastle every day.

It was a good mix, the team were okay - and match days were a joy for, after the game the clubhouse would fill with steam as cold and damp spectators crowded the bar, behind which was a picture of Erica Rowe, a large, attractive young lady who had decided to take off her top and dance around the pitch at Twickenham, the home of international rugby.

Such bravery, for it was a chilly day when she might have been wearing a woolly vest rather than nothing at all, was generously applauded by the tens of thousands watching and one of the England players who, like the remainder on the park stopped to watch a performance which could have cost serious money in Soho, told a bemused skipper, Bill Beaumont, that Erica's chest bore a passing resemblance to the size of his backside. This caused something of a debate after the game, but was deemed to be a reasonable comparison.

And so Erica had a place of honour behind the bar at Morpeth RFC where custom and etiquette demanded the visiting team had first bite at the after-match pie and peas. When they had been fed they were followed to the trestle table by the home team. But while the rest of us touch line supporters waited one of our number would go through all manner of convolutions to disturb the order of things and get to the eats first. It was a cabaret which, after a couple of pints, was very amusing for he was not blessed with height, but as he tried to hide among the towering players his considerable girth identified him.

And when the winter was over and the lads took off their boots and folded away their cherry red and white hooped shirts until the autumn there were, aplenty, the joys of the summer shows. Agriculture and farm produce and carvings of shepherds' sticks and fancy goods and stalls selling tweed jackets and leather hats and sweets and ice cream and tea and scones fought with the frequently damp summer weather to sell their goods. And when the sun shone there was no better place to be.

Willie Poole, who went on to write for the weekend *Daily Telegraph*, had moved close to Alnwick and despite me buying him lunch, for which I paid myself rather than go through the 'was this expenditure really necessary' routine with Shields, told me he didn't want to write for the *Northumberland Gazette.*

He could have only have done so for glory, a largish picture of his largish self in the paper and a few bob - just about enough to buy him a bottle a week. Can't imagine why he chose the *Telegraph* - but I consoled myself that this considerable talent, this splendid writer who so understood the countryside, had received an offer from me first.

Rural life was starting to have an appeal, fostered to a considerable degree by the Shepherds' Meets in wildest Northumberland. Usually held up near the border, they were not like any function I had ever attended. Men who had donned best gaiters and/or wellies, then put on their posh cap and breeches and taking a few quid from the brown teapot on the mantelpiece have set off for these gatherings - and gone missing for days. For these are wonderful, colourful and intensely alcoholic occasions.

Aside from the hard drinking the laughs and me deciding at a very early stage not to shake hands with farmers who could, without thinking and, assuredly without malice, snap a finger or two on a journalists' skinny bunch of fives, there are tales which are legend.

At one show, which is close enough to Scotland to smell the porridge and heather, there is a summer marquee erected for the event. This magnificent canvas is so big the central pole which holds up the tent, designed to hold hundreds, stands many tens of feet tall.

When the young bucks have shouldered and jostled each other and shouted the length of the long bar to their mates they then take on board a pint or six of the brown ale... aka lunatics' broth. Each beer is quickly followed with a wee dram and it is around that time they decide they are Mister Universe. To prove this they shin high up the pole, touch the canvas ceiling and slither down to the begrudging applause of their mates.

As the afternoon wears on and more lads go up the pole the feat becomes less remarkable and the clapping less spontaneous as the visitors set about more serious supping and telling tales of how life has treated them since last they saw Geordie.

But in looking away from the climbing lads every one of them kept an eye on a small lady, not in the first flush of youth and with a limpet attachment to the bar. The reason for this close scrutiny? Everyone knew that, at sometime during the afternoon, when the ale has scattered prudence and decorum to the wind, she would take her turn to shin up the pole.

This event, greatly anticipated by the lads, was preceded by her faltering movement among them, progressing slowly along the bar, drinking with them, as she went, pint for pint. Despite what might have been considered a handicap to pole climbing she always wore a skirt.

This left her unfettered and most assuredly unabashed for, as the encouragement grew more vociferous and the clapping became synchronised, she would judiciously pick her moment and, moving to the foot of the pole in a crescendo of applause, would grasp it then, with theatrical twirl, spin all around its circumference.

The encouragement by now would be deafening and, suddenly, up she would go, with the gathering crowd moving directly beneath her as she went higher and higher. She would touch the canvas at the top, pause, look down and smile in victory.

She would then take one hand off the pole to wave to her enthralled audience - before she swooshed down to the grassy floor, her skirt flying around her ears.

This brought huge cheers and roars of appreciation for she never let them down... so to speak. For she did not wear them. Underwear and the lady at the show were not associated.

The story goes that she, being a country woman, and living where she did, found work around the county. But the police, after issuing many warnings about her penchant for alcohol followed by erratic driving, eventually charged her and the magistrates imposed a deserved driving ban.

And so she relied on lifts, these being offered by fellow workers, two of whom called one mid morning to take her to business. There was much pounding at her door and shouts of: 'Are you awake?'

After beating on the wooden panels for many minutes the upstairs sash window was flung up and out she leaned, again without under clothing but, on this occasion, without any outer clothing. Togless she displayed herself to the amazed Samaritans below.

'Come in,' she shouted, pulling her naked top half back into the bedroom and slamming shut the window.

The boys entered cautiously into a chaotic front room on the floor of which was a bemused budgie whose cage had, some time ago judging by the evidence, been lifted from its stand and placed on the carpet. The bird had not come to any harm, but the same could not be said for the carpet which was covered in guano.

~ ~ ~ ~ ~ ~ ~ ~ ~ ~

It was while I was editor of the *Northumberland Gazette* Britain's miners went on strike. It was 1984 and no doubt encouraged by their successes against the Heath government in the early seventies they followed their leader, Arthur Scargill, once more and walked off the job.

But this time it was different. Coal stocks were massive, the police were well paid - and ready for action. And we, in the north east, were to suffer badly. Not as journalists, not as traders and workers going about our business in other industries, but because we observed the passing weeks and months when men stood outside the pit gates picketing and hoping to win what was patently a hopeless cause. Our scars were cerebral.

Their women brought soup and bread to the strikers and it was the thirties all over again with wives standing by their men who could only become more despondent as the months dragged by.

The country town of Alnwick, castle, duke, duchess and all saw miners who did not go on strike bring driven to work hiding the faces with pulled down caps and hands raised to their foreheads as a shield against recognition. The buses' windows were covered with grilles and the drivers sought anonymity under balaclava hats.

While Arthur Scargill raged about not crossing picket lines, about the centuries of struggles of the workers, about how the fight was there to be won, Margaret Thatcher was digging in her high heels and the police fought with pitmen on the front line.

I sent a young, attractive trainee to interview the men in Northumberland, for I was advocating in my leaders settlement at almost any price. The coal stocks were massive and the government was not showing a sign of surrender. But there were those, almost spoiling for a fight, pushing their heads further and further into the noose of permanent unemployment by continuing to stay on strike.

Sue Shepherd was a good reporter, well able to talk to the men outside the gates who, like the civilised Northumbrians they always were, would not hurt her.

Cowardly on my part? No way - prudent. We needed the story every week, she withstood some harsh comments about me and the *Gazette* - and a man from my newspaper which was urging miners to settle for what they could get might not have received a warm welcome. Sue was super. During the long, long strike I took two weeks' holiday and headed for the Mediterranean.

~ ~ ~ ~ ~ ~ ~ ~ ~ ~

The sun shone, the pool was clear and inviting and industrial problems at home were well behind me until I met, at the hotel, a mining engineer from North Yorkshire, a man with his own business who was on vacation because there was now nowhere for him to work back home.

I suggested he must be furious with Scargill who would probably, by continuing the strike, put him right out of business.

'No,' said he, 'I've heard him speak and he understands miners and their dreams and aspirations. And he has the ability to put their dreams into words and tell them he knows what they want for themselves and their families. He delivers to them a message they want to hear in a language they understand.'

Within two day of returning home I watched, on television, Arthur Scargill being dragged off a picket line and arrested. The strike was about to be broken and when it was all the east Durham coal field, where I had spent time in the early days of my career with their boxers and footballers, the area which had produced Labour leaders by the dozen, went with it.

Billy Elliots were about to populate the streets of Easington, Horden, Blackhall and Wingate and when houses in the streets became boarded up so the winding gear at the pit head became quiet and rusty and was, eventually, pulled down as surely and as certainly as the miners had been taken down.

~ ~ ~ ~ ~ ~ ~ ~ ~ ~

There were other stories which caused concern, though none which hit as hard as the miners' strike. In Morpeth town centre there was an amusement arcade with blue facade and vases in a display window alongside a notice which said, inside, there was free tea and coffee.

On the outskirts of the town there was sheltered accommodation for the mentally handicapped and most of the residents would wander into town there to look in shop windows or maybe watch the ducks on the River Wansbeck. But they also found their way into the arcade which was warm and almost welcoming on a cold, wet day.

Once inside they put whatever money they had into the slot machines and the one armed bandit duly ate their cash - and in return a member of staff gave them a cup of tea.

We tried to contact the owners of the place to talk about the morality of the situation, to ask whether they felt comfortable when taking cash from people who were probably not totally aware of what was going on and where their money went.

There was never anyone available to comment; the manager, Mr Bloggins would 'get back to us' - but, of course, he never did. We went ahead with a piece which described this outrageous behaviour and said that, try as we might, the owners would not speak.

The result? The arcade stayed open, indiscriminately allowing anyone into the place - and still no one from the company would speak to us.

The ultimate frustration for any journalist is to encounter stonewall silence, though one or two national tabloids have been known to invent what they can't glean by legitimate means.

~ ~ ~ ~ ~ ~ ~ ~ ~ ~

In 1986 Westminster Press sold their Northern Press Division to Peterpress. Nine years of being a chief official ended and though the new owner told me he saw 'great things' for my Northumbrian titles, which I would still edit, I was not convinced what these might be and he was not making concrete promises.

I felt he, before relieving WP of their Northern Press burden, must have seen either profit somewhere in the company which others had missed - or he was about to make us a more worthwhile proposition for reselling.

One of his first acts was to say he would retain the South Shields MD, Charles Barton, who had moved in when Spencer Crow had headed back to London. Barton was no longer a young man and had been an account- ant with the company for all of his working days, so it did not seem too much might be changing in that direction.

And it didn't. The reins remained tightly pulled and there was no indi- cation of any positive editorial changes which would enable me to produce the newspapers I wanted to put onto the streets.

After less than a year of Peterpress I'd had enough. It was time to move on, but this time I determined to do so after thoroughly research- ing the company I would join. I'd had my fill of years of newspapers hanging by their fingertips above a financial abyss, some dropping off or operating under such restrictions they might as well have given up the losing struggle and coughed their last.

An advertisement appeared for an editor for the *Whitehaven News*, in Cumbria, land of lakes and industry. The town had around 28,000 peo- ple, but the circulation area included places like Cleator Moor and Egremont... beauty (for Whitehaven is an emerging Georgian town with enormous potential) and the less lovely areas of ribbon development. A good mix.

A ring around of people I knew would be privy to such information also revealed the company was solvent. It had one evening newspaper at Carlisle (later to be two when it bought the *Barrow Evening Mail*) and three weekly titles, the *Whitehaven News*, the *Cumberland News* and the *Times and Star*, at Workington.

It was into contract printing, produced business newspapers and it was said the Burgess family, who owned the whole lot, had large interests in Border Television and Reuters. They looked to be sound - and so did their company. I applied and had my first interview with Robin Burgess, all 6ft 6in and around seventeen stone of him. It went well.

My second was with his father, Sir John Burgess, and again took place in the elegant, panelled boardroom at Newspaper House, at Dalston Road, in Carlisle. It was this talk with the moustachioed, white haired Sir John which swung it for me.

He had been commissioned in the Border Regiment during the war, seeing action in France, Syria and Burma. I was to find out his troops had a loyalty which, when I was out and about with Robin saw conversations run along the lines of: 'Robin Burgess, eh. Aye, well, I knew your father... he was a wonderful man.'

Robin bore these comments with a smile but the inference was clear: You have a devil of a lot to live up to young man. Like me, Sir John had been a journo on the *Journal* and the *Sketch*. Then he had entered the family business.

And now here he was, regrettably very unwell in late 1986. Indeed, he died within two months of our only meeting, but he stood with some difficulty and as I entered the room he walked around the huge boardroom table with his hand outstretched. He could have remained sitting, or stayed at his side of the table. The effort he made to greet me was considerable and told me all I needed to know about the man and his attitude which, I hoped, would spill on down through the company.

There was a third interview, this time for Jane, which saw us being given lunch at the Trout, in Cockermouth, presumably to pass muster with Robin's wife, Alex, and with Terry Kirton, editor of the *Times and Star*, in Workington and his wife Linda in attendance. We were to become good friends.

I knew, as we headed back across the Pennines to Morpeth, the job was mine if I wanted it. Salary was acceptable and there was the bonus of being made a director of the company, taking my place on the management board.

Robin asked me to have a medical, I did so with a consultant at his amazingly beautiful detached mansion in Ponteland, the Hampstead of Tyneside and was passed A1.

Now, could Whitehaven and I hit it off? One week later the contract arrived but, before signing it, I headed west for the Cumbrian coast and the Irish Sea.

~ ~ ~ ~ ~ ~ ~ ~ ~ ~

I arrived in Whitehaven in December, 1986, after driving along roads which were unbelievably bad. The A595 was, as it is to this day, single carriageway through all its 50 miles and more as it heads south for Barrow.

Every day it is crowded by the thousands of cars streaming daily to and from Sellafield and, because it has to take so much traffic, it is constantly being repaired and dug up. Temporary traffic lights abound in their dozens and lads in luminous jackets have a great old time waving large yellow lollipops which say: 'Stop.'

As I drove I thought I must have taken a wrong turning, reasoning there had to be an easier way into town than along this cart track. I was wrong. The A595 was the only way in - even with its, twists, turns, and bumps.

It is also the only way out and it all seems designed not only to stop normal driving progress, but to prevent any quick getaway if, heaven forbid, there was to be an accident at Sellafield. The nuclear reprocessing plant is situated a very few miles down the coast from Whitehaven and the road is so bad citizens' chances of escaping any problems there would be as a snowball in a hell of a very different kind.

It was later suggested to me the only way to handle such a catastrophe would be to grab a bottle of whisky and walk towards the huge BNFL works reflecting on all the things you wished you had done in this fleeting life - but hadn't.

I parked my car on waste ground in town, close to two huge silos which scarred the sea front. These, I was to learn, were part of the Albright and Wilson factory, the main part of which was sited on a hill to the south of town. It made detergents and frequently cast an odour over the town redolent of cat's urine. It also discharged into the sea a foam which spread, slick-like, for many hundreds of yards. I presumed they got away with this pollution because they employed so many local people.

And so the silos stood, hideous and incongruous as they disfigured what could have been, and now very nearly is, a fine Georgian town. I walked along the harbour side and turned up into the town centre to marvel at the Co-op building, rectangular, windowless, single storied, blank and hugely out of place in the middle of attractive streets terraced with fine houses - yet another utter eyesore. Indeed, I was to write a leader berating the existence of such buildings demanding the silos come down and asking for an explanation for the Co-op being allowed to build their store.

The silos did come down when, several years later, a new managing director, John Markham, left ICI on Teesside to run the Marchon works in Whitehaven. Not necessarily because of my constant complaints in the *News*, rather for economic reasons with the chemicals being landed at Workington quay rather than off shore at Whitehaven then being transported by huge chutes from ships to the silos. To be rid of them was to be a huge environmental bonus for the town.

The reaction of the Co-op to my incredulous comment was somewhat different. They threatened to stop their advertising - which is always a massive joke.

The only reason any business advertises in a newspaper is because the advertising works and that business is, therefore, enhanced. Advertising is not placed for the benefit of the newspaper's staff but to grow the advertisers' sales. Businesses are not philanthropic, they are there to make money. To threaten to discontinue advertising should always evoke the response: 'Fine - just do it!'

When they did not get the reply they wanted, when sackcloth and contrition were not around, they went, as so many do in similar circumstances, to Phase II - and complained to MD Robin. He stood by me then as he did through all the years to come.

But on that first day in town, as the wind whipped rain off the Irish Sea and the stall holders packed up their canvas covered tables in the market place, for there were few folk around in such treacherous weather, I grew more despondent as I headed up Roper Street, asking directions for the office.

I found the old theatre, for that is what part of the *News* office had been, late in the morning and, looking through the steamed up windows, managed to see computer screens and a tidiness and order, all of which were encouraging.

I moved back through town, again battling the winds and, starting up the car, tried to find a different way back to the M6 to avoid the wretched and totally inadequate A595. I drove west through Hensingham, up the incline and through the long road which is Cleator Moor, took the turn sign posted to Ennerdale, where I knew there was a lake and, skirting through that village, headed for the hills. Literally... for the fells could just be distinguished through the rain and mist.

I found the Kirkstile Inn nestling near Lorton and headed inside for lunch. It was warm, friendly, the food and the ale were good, a river running nearby could be seen from the dining room windows and as I left after a good lunch to continue the journey the sun broke through the storm clouds (which is not unusual in Lakeland).

The world was transformed as the light shaded then tinted and broke over the mountains and shone down in widening rays over the fields and onto the trees around a shimmering lake. It was a scene which sold me on Whitehaven... and its environs.

I drove back along the A69 and, the following Monday, signed the contract from Cumbrian Newspapers. Within two weeks I was writing a note of sympathy to Robin for his father, Sir John, had died.

I asked Peterpress to free me from my contract, which required a year's notice to be given by either party. The owner, Peter Fowler did not reply, Barton, aware of how well I had enjoyed Northern Press, said OK and I started at the *Whitehaven News* in April, 1987.

~ ~ ~ ~ ~ ~ ~ ~ ~ ~

It was a comparative paradise as I set about redesigning the newspaper and reorganising so many aspects of the editorial content - receiving as I did so total backing and absolute votes of confidence from head office in Carlisle.

They showed sound judgement. Once again I was to break a title's circulation record and the *Whitehaven News*, selling around 17,500-18,000 copies when I started, burst through 20,000 within two years. And the advertising boomed along with the circulation.

I was, once again, working with a successful outfit and it could have made a lesser man weep with the joy of it all and the relief of leaving Northern Press. They enjoyed me too. My next company car was a BMW. Cumbrian Newspapers and I were going to have a good time.

~ ~ ~ ~ ~ ~ ~ ~ ~ ~

An indication of the difference was, quite simply, style, the way the business of producing newspapers was approached and effected. Robin, like his father, was a Cumbrian without compromise and in those early days of his reign wanted his staff to be aware of his aims and desires.

To help him with this we were sent on management training courses at some of the Lake District's top hotels, learning in luxury with deluxe days at Leeming House and the Hilton in Borrowdale.

To celebrate the 175th birthday of the oldest title, the *Cumberland News*, he brought the Bolshoi Ballet to the Sands Centre, at Carlisle, where they danced Swan Lake for us. Afterwards, at a reception we, the directors and our wives, prepared to meet wonderfully slim and elegant women who walked with feet at ten-to-two, leading with their toes then gently placing down their heels as they glided into the room, every move and gesture accentuated and graceful.

The male dancers were not what we had expected, sometimes being shorter than the woman but all of them possessed of arms like billiard table legs, strong enough to pick up pianos let alone a ballerina. And they wanted whisky - the vodka which we had ensured would be in good supply stayed in the bottles.

Advertisers and good editorial contacts were taken to the Keswick Hotel for summer nights of champagne and canapés then to the Theatre by the Lake for a show.

Every late summer, at their huge and wonderfully appointed house at Scaleby, just outside Carlisle, Robin and his family entertained the first team to a lunch party, taking us into their home where we drank and ate - and then played football on their lawn with Skiddaw, majestic in the distance and the wide acres of Cumbria as a backdrop.

It was a time of times, a series of good happenings which had so recently seemed to be light years beyond my aspirations and, of course, Robin received, in return, a total loyalty.

Iinherited a good team at the *Whitehaven News* - Margaret Crosby, Dave Siddall, Trevor Clements and the sub editors - which got better as I introduced journalists from the south of England, Karen Brodie, George Nicholson and Nigel Jarrett. They brought new ideas which were always needed and which I allowed them to get on with, virtually unfettered.

One of a journalist's joys is being trusted and left alone to get the job done as quickly as possible - and always accurately. This can be achieved without direct supervision, though there might be an inquest back at the office over some stories.

A variety of number crunchers have tried time and motion studies and, because of their stoic natures, are unable to comprehend that when they try to draw graphs with staff employed down the vertical leg and stories produced on the horizontal leg, the point at which the lines meet is not of much consequence.

Newspaper life just ain't like that. Journalists should not work as rewrite people or always be on the diary covering whatever that 'bible' says is there to be covered. This is only a part of the great scheme of things for the day. Hacks need a good contacts book, must produce off the wall stories which come to them through an unexpected 'phone call which they recognise as worthy of a follow-up - or because they are alert and know what they're doing. It doesn't matter how much or how little time passes while they are on a good story.

The guys with the stop watches and stats sheets received short shrift from me but there happened, one evening, a couple of years into my editorship, an event where a telephone caller received anything but a curt response.

Bryan Bone, much acclaimed as one of the best freelances Cumbria had produced, telephoned me at home and asked for a job; it took all of a couple of minutes to promise him work with what was becoming a very good title - being well received and improving - and was to be further enhanced by his highly professional and totally helpful presence. Good operator, great guy.

The paper had been competent without style, full of heavy rules of varying shapes and widths with headline types scattered around the pages like a rash - and we were massively overset as stories were sent to the production unit at Carlisle to where, every Wednesday, the sub editors and I would go to put the paper to bed and where they used to fit stories where they could. Now we planned pages fully and properly.

The composing room guys were good, but handling many titles all of which were lined up on the frames with rolls of copy waiting to be stuck into the pages.

It was called lick and stick and its expectations of life and style of producing newspapers was limited. Journalists were to become able to send their copy from the away-from-centre offices over dedicated telephone lines - and these pages arrived at Carlisle set, laid out and ready for press.

It's hard when good men lose their jobs, but there was an inevitability about it for the days of the newspaper compositor had been numbered all those years before when Murdoch went into Wapping with his national newspapers and stopped the NGA working on them by locking them out of the building. If he could do it then the rest of the nation's titles were quick to follow suit. And did so.

The journalists were going to be in control. But for now I set about changing designs, types and attitudes to news - and there was masses of it about... though there was a hiccup or two at the beginning.

Copeland is a socialist constituency with MP Dr. Jack Cunningham our representative in the House. I began by asking why, when he worked in London to represent us in the north west, did he live in Chester-le-Street in County Durham, in the north east.

Mistakenly, I also queried his role with Sellafield, for he attended dinners at their hospitality house, Sella Park, adjacent to the plant - and then he would stay overnight. I called him an advisor to BNFL - and after doing so the solicitor's letter arrived within two days declaring this was not the case and that he had no professional connection with the nuclear reprocessing plant. It also made the lawyers' bog standard threats of what they would do if the story was not corrected.

It is difficult to say who was dafter - me for making such an elementary error or him for coming over all unnecessary and wheeling out a London lawyer to handle something which we could have cleared up between us with a telephone call. And for him to threaten a new editor, with whom he would have to work with for the foreseeable future, was not the best move to make. He got his correction in the following week's edition in pearl - which was the smallest type available to me.

In all my days in newspapers no one ever successfully sued me - though many tried including a GP who had a lawyer warn me not to mention him (the doctor) in a case which saw us carry a story about an irate West Cumbrian father whose doctor had, he said, assaulted his teenage daughter who had been undergoing a medical examination.

It seemed the doc was well known for his unprofessional habits and young women who went to him with a sprained ankle were told to take off their blouses while he made further, essential, examinations.

There was great hilarity on publication day when some of our readers said they knew about the man and had done so for years. They had always warned their female off spring to beware his clutching hand when visiting Dr Grope.

~ ~ ~ ~ ~ ~ ~ ~ ~ ~

Trevor Clements was chief reporter and, taking his stint at magistrates court one day in 1990 wrote-up, quite brilliantly, a case which was to have humorous repercussions for years.

All a solicitor says in court is privileged and newspapers can report all proceedings therein. And when you get a lawyer as eloquent as Marcus Nickson then reporters bent their backs over the notebook for Marcus in full oratorical flood is quite splendid.

It was he, defending a man appearing before the Bench on two charges of indecent assault. Marcus won, the man walked free, but not before Marcus had regaled the court in wonderful, quite splendid style, all of which was reported by Clements whose story ran thus:

'To the locals it was the quiet village pub, decent ale, good grub and a quiet game of dominoes.

'But once the towels went over the pumps and the owner's back was turned the whole scene changed.

'The staff were said to have indulged in after hours drinks parties and sordid sex games.

'Solicitor Marcus Nickson said: 'The goings on at this hotel were nothing short of startling.'

'He was defending a man who admitted touching a waitress's breasts, but contended that this horseplay was tame compared with what went on in other areas at the country pub.

'The staff would get drunk at after hours parties and a housekeeper would lead the fun.

'He said on one occasion she sat on the chef's knee and made sexual advances to him.'

'On another occasion (which Marcus referred to as 'the Phyllis Diller affair) a woman teased onlookers by intermittently covering up her breasts with balloons while lying on a pool table.

'Once a young man, on his bachelor night party, was led into the cellar for sex but was so drunk all he could do was to be sick.

'It was not unusual for waitresses to be picked up and put in the kitchen freezer and they would retaliate by putting ice cubes down the trousers of the men who put them there.'

I put up a headline which read: 'The Phyllis Diller affair - hotel sex parties' and thought to myself... my oh my... welcome to sleepy West Cumbria, fringing the glorious Lake District, where blue rinse widows reign with little fingers crooked over bone china teacups in hotels with flouncey floral curtains being served by courtly waiters. But I reckon the client numbers at the hotel must have doubled in the months which followed our story.

~ ~ ~ ~ ~ ~ ~ ~ ~ ~

There came a Thursday afternoon which brought a little offbeat happening into our always expectant lives, for this was publication day and when the pubs rolled out between three and four o'clock in the afternoon those who considered they had been wronged, their indignation fuelled by a gallon or so of ale, would arrive at our front counter.

These callers were quite often women, paid up members of our child-obsessed society and hell bent on protecting their young Tristram who had been before the beak for all manner of misdemeanours.

Highly defensive, mother would scream (and, my word, it surely can be noisy) that their noble lad was not guilty and how dare we publish such rubbish about someone destined to be a brain surgeon?

These comments usually were accompanied by threats of bringing father (wherever and whoever he might be) down to the office where he would give us a good smack. They would then detail what a good boy Tristram had been to his granny who had cancer/heart trouble and would surely peg it when she read in the paper these disgusting lies.

They would not be mollified by being told it was the verdict of the court who had listened to police evidence and we had merely reported it - they wanted their say (shout) and were going to have it. Usually our front office could handle the Thursday protesters, employing kind words, common-sense and gentle smiles they would turn aside wrath and rage with aplomb.

But on this Thursday, when the boozers had turned the lads onto the pavement, we had a caller who was known to be particularly violent, having at one time thrown his partner into the dock, which made her extremely damp for the remainder of the day and was an incident which had been of interest to the local bobbies. On another occasion he had bitten off the ear of a man with whom he was in dispute, a happening which again stirred the imaginings of the constabulary.

Both events had put him in front of magistrates who probably looked at his five by five figure, cauliflower ears, shortage of teeth and broken nose - and wished they lived in another town. Not the most articulate of men, what he lacked in education and erudition he compensated for with salty language and quite dreadful chin-thrusting aggression. And he wanted to see me. And there was nothing our receptionists, Ann and Audrey, could do about it.

~ ~ ~ ~ ~ ~ ~ ~ ~ ~

I had designed the interview room to try to take an interviewee 'off his feet' by sitting him at a low level. Men standing up and nursing grievances felt bigger than they probably were and so they became inclined to take a swing - all of which becomes much more difficult when the guy is seated so low as to be almost on his haunches.

I took into the room, let's call him Larry Potts, and sat him down. He couldn't wait for formalities or niceties but launched at once into what had I meant by publishing a picture of his lad and saying what we had said about him. He pointed to a picture on an inside page of a youngster, aged about ten, cheeky and smiling all over his face - but with a tiny nick on his forehead.

The boy had been using a pedestrian crossing and been clipped by a car which had bowled him over and his head had been slightly cut. The piece was not apportioning blame, though it seemed likely the lad had been trying to beat the bleeps and the traffic lights when he'd made his run to cross the road. The point of the story was the lack of time there was for folk to cross at the lights before they changed in favour of the motorist. We made the point that the aged or disabled would have difficulty. Olympic sprinters, we said, would probably get to the other side unscathed. Just.

'Okay,' Mr Potts, I said, 'show me what's wrong and if I agree I promise to correct it in next week's edition.'

He blustered, reddened and shouted: 'It's all in there.' And he jabbed a forefinger at the story.

We carried on like this for several minutes, me asking, him pointing and shouting and then I realised why he couldn't be specific - he couldn't read. I suggested he must have forgotten his specs and he very quickly agreed that this was, indeed, the case. I then read through the story, aloud and slowly.

He assumed his more usual complexion (port stained rather than pillar box red) and, after brief consideration, said the story was OK. He made his excuses and left, apologising to the receptionists on the front counter en route. His boozing pals were probably falling about laughing further down the street, but I found a charm about him in subsequent meetings when we passed in the town.

He would shout a greeting across the street, always called me Sir, enquire after my health and say he hoped I would have a good day. I responded equally courteously, calling him Mr Potts and similarly wishing the world would smile upon him, that day and forever, for I didn't want to end up in the dock - or have my ear bitten off.

It would not have been likely, for the West Cumbrian is, more often than not, the most gentle of people, sometimes used by Smart Alicks who mistake good nature for stupidity and impose upon him that which other parts of the country would not tolerate.

His term of endearment, Marra, is indeed an honour for it means you are recognised as a good guy. If, however, he calls you 'Pal' - leave, for he is extremely angry and when Mr Cool and Easy loses it well, it's advisable to head for the beautiful fells.

~ ~ ~ ~ ~ ~ ~ ~ ~ ~

It seemed, in these early days, that the stories just presented themselves. An editorial change of direction meant the staff were becoming more focused on what I wanted the paper to become.

The eloquent, aforementioned lawyer Marcus Nickson was writing a motoring column which was not what my kind of weekly newspaper was about. Readers look for local news - and loads of it. If they want a new car then they buy specialist magazines. I have never known anyone to buy a newspaper to see what is being written about the latest broom broom with go faster stripes. I stopped the column.

There was a video column which presumably got the writer a living room full of free tapes for review - but they had no value to the *News*. They, too, went out.

A photographer who sent in wedding pictures found his work published from time to time - and complained about the subs cropping his pictures. We were, he said, destroying his works of art. And we were allowing him free space.

I gave him an option; he either stopped trying to interfere with the production of the title and understood the pressure of space or he would be banned. He chose the latter option which was crazy. He'd had his pictures circulating around town in my newspaper with the happy couple having a reasonable chance of figuring in the *News* - and he'd thrown it away.

There was a barrister's column, a Citizen's Advice Bureau column, Youthspeak, a sort of editorial dustbin which looked to contain anything which couldn't squeeze in elsewhere. All were dropped.

One guy who stayed was cartoonist Trevor Green who is so good he could have held a job down on a Fleet Street title. He had been used on an occasional basis; now he was to be published every week and used as big as we possibly could.

I introduced a double column, full length-of-the-page leader, for I so enjoyed writing and never believed in publishing the garbage contained in so many 'voice of the newspaper' columns. Who cares if the

Cleckheaton Accuser demands: 'Stop this shocking outrage?'

My leaders were... different. Highly opinionated, very local, though sometimes I wrote about the latest failure by the England cricket team, or the price of fish or, on one never to be forgotten occasion, after a holiday in Vienna, where the women were so smart and svelte and so absolutely fashion conscious, about the size of a Whitehaven woman's backside which she had crammed into a pair of ski pants.

She then chose to wobble down the main thoroughfare with various bits of her heading in differing directions - and all at the same time. It was a terrible sight.

And the letters poured in, not only from politically correct persons about Miss World 1923, but on all manner of subjects eventually filling a page and then sometimes spilling to another... and maybe one after that for pagination was excellent, the people were interested and they wanted to have their say. We were on the way up.

~ ~ ~ ~ ~ ~ ~ ~ ~ ~ ~

I had my first taste of Sellafield - over breakfast. In those days Sellafield gave every appearance of buying acceptance into the community. The rest of the world, aided and abetted by two-bit radio and TV comics, talked of we residents turning green, setting off security alarms at airports... masses of feeble, oft repeated jokes.

I maintained then, as I still do, that BNFL's plant was so well monitored by their own people, by the government's inspectors and by Cumbrians Opposed to A Radioactive Environment that it is safer to live here, in the western Lake District, than close to industrial plants in other parts of the world.

The top brass at the plant raise their families within a very few miles of the factory gates and, as with many other matters, the 'experts' on nuclear reprocessing had never worked at the plant or been close it.

But in my early days over the Pennines, there was a culture which saw anyone who wanted ten bob and a trophy for the pub darts competition asking Sellafield - and they would come across with the goods.

The unions had a high old time, with one of their leaders declaring I had worked on the *Sun* (which had, at that time, been taken massively to the right by Rupert Murdoch) and therefore I was an enemy of the lads.

He wasn't sharp enough to realise that I had worked on the *Sun* before Murdoch got his hot little hands on it and the title I had known was fiercely independent.

But, in the old newspaper parlance, never let the facts get in the way of a good story. And so here I was, early in my career at the *News*, and contemplating a claim by the union who had turned down an £1,800 per man mid morning breakfast break. Like Oliver Twist at the dining table, they wanted more.

It was gobbledegook language and to emphasise the point I sent the chief reporter across the road to buy enough goodies for a hearty breakfast.

Orange juice, cereal, bacon, sausage, egg, beans, tomatoes, bread and coffee were purchased, the till role, registering a very few pounds, was brought back to the office, a consensus was reached on how much might be consumed per person per week - and I published the results on the front page which showed just how crazily extravagant the title of the wage claim was. But the union won and peace crept back over the plant's chimneys.

~ ~ ~ ~ ~ ~ ~ ~ ~ ~

There came, one late afternoon a call from the receptionists, that Bill Deedes was in the office. I was sceptical. Let me explain that, when a writ is being served, guys will present themselves at the front counter and tell anything but the truth to get the editor downstairs and face to face so they can slap a lawyer's love letter into his unwilling hand. The deed is then done, the writ is served.

These people usually call themselves 'councillors', or someone from a 'ministry' - anything at all when they roll up to deliver the missive which invariably starts with a declaration about how their client has been grievously wronged, his character irreparably damaged and his business suffering to the point of bankruptcy.

The next paragraph says it's going to cost the newspaper hundreds of thousands of pounds to right their 'wrong'. I thought hard... and couldn't recall anything in recent times contentious enough to warrant such action.

Cautiously, and after a few moments, I said: 'Say again, Ann.'

'It's Mr Bill Deedes,' she repeated.

I proceeded cautiously down the stairs and there he was, accompanied by a young female reporter.

I nigh on salaamed as I took him into my office for wasn't this the former editor of the *Daily Telegraph*, the Dear Bill, of *Private Eye* fame, the former highly successful politician? And he was here, in Whitehaven. He was he said, sitting at the other side of my desk, crossing his legs and showing bright red socks above battered brown suede shoes, here to do a piece on West Cumbria.

I had already decided not to allow the national newspapers, who similarly wanted to work on these stories, access to our files, for in those days these were in bound paper form.

It was not unknown for a reporter, heading up the M6 and probably with the Sellafield story already written before they got to the west coast, to come to our library and then tear pieces out of pages out rather than write notes from them. This gave us a mighty problem, for we could not replace the damaged bound files. But this man was very different.

While his companion hung on his every word, Bill Deedes talked about the area, how it had changed since last he had been here when the pits were blasting coal out of the ground and he was, as I had hoped he would be, quite charming and never, not for a moment, condescending about a newspaper in the sticks when he had been so enormously successful for so very long at the top of Fleet Street's sparklingly bedecked tree.

He had arrived late in the day when the troops had fallen out, dusted their medals, wiped their swords - and gone home. And so when, the next morning, I told the staff who had been in to see me the previous day they reacted as I had done when Ann had telephoned from the front office. They assumed more natural demeanours when, within a month, the town starred in one of Sir Bill's features, in the *Daily Telegraph*. The 'oh, aye boss' line was forgotten.

Sellafield and its managers were figuring strongly in our operation for they had fingers in every pie - savoury or sweet or just because there was a vacancy on a board of something or other. There was a cartel of some half a dozen to ten men who appeared everywhere in West Cumbria, in polished mahogany boardrooms even in the directors' box of a rugby league club on match days. Sellafield chiefs were part of this happy band.

The problem, if one existed, is that the same thinking went into half a dozen organisations for the people running the show, the cartel, didn't vary from one meeting to the next.

And BNFL, because they employed so many thousands, also had on their strength councillors who seemed to be given time off to attend their civic duties almost at request. It was a unique mix.

The area was, and is, flooded with organisations dedicated to bringing work/tourism/regeneration/grants west of the Pennines. My in-paper suggestion that there were too many of them costing too much and that it might be a sound idea if they were to get together, talk and even amalgamate brought strong condemnation from those involved. And so they keep going.

It seemed to be an odd way to run an area of limited population, but with one massive employer there was always going to be involvement with Copeland Borough and county councils - and many local politicians spent many of their nights at Sella Park, BNFL's five star hospitality suite in the shadow of the plant's main gates where, if they had enjoyed themselves too much, there was always a chauffeured car to get them back to the bosom of the family when the roistering was ended and the moon had risen over the plant's twin towers.

For Sellafield, always the source of great controversy, with battles between the Greens and the locals who relied on the plant for well paid employment, treated its guests very well.

Claude from Kells, voted in to be a socialist representative for whatever ward, could find himself drinking cocktails and raising little fingers with Humphrey from the House of Lords - and, inevitably sharing in the company of representatives of the sanctum, those who clung to power by representing one of the many committees which sought to get something good going for West Cumbria. And, occasionally, they succeeded.

There was a gag which went along the lines of: 'How many people work at Sellafield? About half of them!'

And indeed, Whitehaven, when first I saw it, had streets jammed with people wearing the pink socks which were standard issue to the plant's workers, or wearing black donkey jackets with Albright and Wilson in large letters on the back

And sometimes the lads were wearing both which was not sartorially sound but kept out winter's chill. Should they have been at work instead of wandering the town's streets? Best not to ask.

John Kane was not only a sound representative of the men but eminently sensible. He was also a first rate darts player. He was always approachable as, indeed was a management which was becoming more relaxed and aware that the press did not always wear big boots with which to kick them as a preliminary to discussions.

And so we didn't have to dig too often for our coverage of the huge plant, which paid its people very well and was, as it is, the lifeblood of the county - and sometimes beyond with people travelling to work in its divisions from as far away as the Scottish borders.

The opposition to the plant was always there, sometimes spectacularly, and in 1992 the pop group U2 and Bono (who described Sellafield as hell's kitchen) arrived off shore to protest about the emissions from Sellafield into the Irish Sea and the Greenpeace boat *Sirius*, which had sailed in at the dead of night in support, stood offshore. Our photographers did a super job with what was a snapper's dream, putting these high profile people on our front page.

Martin Day, a London lawyer, advertised with us for those who thought Sellafield might have damaged their health and offered to look hard at their claims and maybe prosecute.

We were carrying a rich mix and our pagination, like our circulation, was increasing as we became an increasingly desirable vehicle for advertisers.

And when we broke 20,000 copies a week, which had never been achieved by the title in its nearly 150 years, the champagne flowed throughout every department in the office.

It's always easier to go with the successful flow and the staff were at the peak of their form with never a moment's hesitation about accepting less glamourous jobs, even when we started, week by week, spotlighting villages throughout the circulation area and they took it on their toes to get out and about to talk to vicars and postmasters and local worthies in Nowheresville.

Terry Harrison, the assistant editor looked after the hound trailing, a sport as Cumbrian as fell running.

Jos Naylor had been the best runner of them all and still, despite his advancing years, ran up and down mountains while sloths like me stood by the lakes at the bottom of the valleys and marvelled.

Jos would not run up one mountain - but, for charity events, several. And all in one day. He would also enter the Biggest Liar in the World Competition, at the Santon Bridge Inn, at Eskdale which was quite close to Wastwater, the deepest of the lakes where the daunting screes drop almost vertically into the water.

It is here the local diving clubs send their members for sport and training. They built, just beneath the surface, a 'garden' the principal feature of which was a profusion of plastic garden gnomes... surrounded by small picket fences.

Visiting divers would walk into the lake, suitably geared up for a day's sport - and could hardly believe their eyes as they began to submerge among funny little brightly painted models with pointed hats. But there was a sinister story which had unfolded before the gnomes took over.

~ ~ ~ ~ ~ ~ ~ ~ ~ ~

In the south of England, in the home counties, there had been a married couple who had, as the years passed, become increasingly unhappy with each other.

This is not unknown in our society, but on this occasion there was a most definite and evil conclusion. The husband, an airline pilot, decided he'd had enough - and killed his wife.

He bundled her body in plastic and tarpaulin and, at the dead of night, put her in the boot of his car and began the long drive, through the blackness, north to the Lake District. He made good progress before turning off the M6 at junction 40 where he headed west, by passing Keswick and Cockermouth then, turning south, he headed through the early morning for the glories of beautiful Eskdale.

He knew Wastwater was many hundreds of feet deep and one of the loneliest lakes, being difficult to access. It is also majestically dramatic, with the fells dropping sharply into its blackness and it was there, he decided that there was every chance of him being unobserved.

So, weighting the body with tied-on rocks from the shore, he cast off from the lakeside in a small boat which had been moored there and, as dawn began to break, he pulled for the middle of the lake.

Whether he became frightened or whether he was disturbed by man or beast is not known, but he tipped the body over the stern too soon. The ever loving floated down and missed, by a mere foot or two, the ultimate drop to the very bottom. She came to rest on a ledge, still well below the surface - but not far enough down for his purposes.

The weekend divers were quick to spot the bundle but, never suspecting the contents, thought it was some kind of training aid and left it for the club they thought might have placed it there. But as time went by and the package stayed at the same spot one of them brought it to the shore side, unwrapped it - and sent for the police.

The pilot, who had told neighbours his wife had left him, which was not too much of a deviation from the truth, was arrested, charged and convicted of murder.

~ ~ ~ ~ ~ ~ ~ ~ ~ ~

I always insisted that magistrates courts were covered. I believe it is difficult to justify covering one case and not another with the attendant publicity for one miscreant not being given to someone else. Whitehaven mags produced copy much like any other small town with petty crime dominating - burglary, assaults, car thefts and the like.

But one morning on the press bench, one of our chaps set about his duty and read the list of defendants which the clerk of the court produces on the day. And there, in front of his widening eyes, was a familiar name.

It belonged to the wife of one of the very biggest, but now retired, managers at BNFL and she was facing a charge of criminal damage. The story unfolded before a court room barely able to keep a collective straight face.

She and her husband lived in a pleasant spot where the river curls and bends with a cluster of brightly painted houses along its green and grassy banks and life would seem to be fairly idyllic in this snoozy backwater.

But there lurked (it is not known whether he donned a dirty mac before going out) a midnight marauder. A yowling rapist, a doer of foul deeds - and all committed at a time when decent souls were abed and sleeping.

The tom cat stalked the village; it was his patch and many a darling little pussy went home at dawn dishevelled and beaten up. Or expecting a litter. Owners were livid because, when the sun had gone down, their Tiddles had become reluctant to leave the homestead. The Phantom was always at large, though he wasn't much of a mystery - everyone knew where he lived.

Something had to be done and so it was decided, by the wife of the former high flier and her friend that the rapist had to be caught; an end had to be put to his disgusting ways, 'Enough,' they thought, 'was enough.'

And so, one dark night, with the clouds scudding across the moon and the wind rattling through back alleys and whistling around corners, they waited for him to pad along in search of female felines or, if another tom wanted a battle well, he was up for that too.

The hours slid by and it seemed this was one night when the marauding moggie was not to have a strike and then, quite suddenly, luck was with the catnappers and they nabbed him in mid challenging yowl. Into a bag he went, spitting and screaming, claws slashing and scratching, but all to no avail. He was incarcerated. And held that way overnight.

The next morning dawned fair, but not for the beast in the bag for he was put into a car which slipped along the country roads to end its journey at - the vet's surgery. And there, with a flash of a wicked blade, his wedding tackle was removed.

That very same night, the former philanderer, he who forced favours upon every cat in the village, willing or otherwise, was released into the village - in very average fettle, not knowing whether he was in Cumbria or Canton.

He found his way back to his own pad where his owners, delighted to have him restored to the bosom of the family were not, however, best pleased to see him in his new, highly confused and decidedly depleted condition. They prosecuted.

Though the two miscreants received no more than conditional discharges for criminal damage, it made a cracking front page story, cartoonist Green was brilliantly illustrative and the *News of the World* and every national followed it up.

It is not known how the by now docile Tom spent his time, but he probably breathed on his paws and sheathed his claws - and did a lot of sleeping. Well, there wouldn't be much else on his mind.

~ ~ ~ ~ ~ ~ ~ ~ ~ ~ ~

There was much amusement to be found with the characters who abound in West Cumbria and Patrick Gordon Duff Pennington, the charming, clever, self styled Patrick of the Hills, who lives at the fabulous Muncaster Castle where acres of rhododendrons bloom in late spring in profusion such as I had never seen, was a purveyor of wonderful stories.

Born north of the border he always proclaimed to me that he 'wished to die in Scotland' and after such melancholy deliveries would, as a poet of sorts, occasionally telephone me at some very odd hours, once well after midnight, to offer his latest pearls. I struggled to be sociable when dragged from my bed, and tried very hard to be focused on what he was saying, but probably didn't succeed too well.

There was always a line of two in the paper for Patrick and much more than that for other matters for there was no shortage of stories of consequence and junior doctors and nurses at the West Cumberland Hospital not only complained about their dreadful accommodation but sent to us pictures of crumbling plaster and hand basins hanging off walls.

And one council worker, who had been sacked over a mix-up in his payment of the Community Charge (poll tax) had some joy brought into his now jobless life when we revealed that the son of the council leader, the very council which had fired him, who was living at home, had not paid his tax, either. That splendid publication *Private Eye* followed up our story in their Rotten Boroughs columns.

The council workers, some of whom were being disciplined by chief officer Robin Smith for reasons we couldn't fathom, realised they now had an ally and their anonymous letters came through our letter box giving us leads to stories which saw two councillors from the controlling Labour groups visiting me in my office to ask me to ease up.

Smith, meanwhile, threatened to stop the holidays of everyone on the staff and they reacted by sending us ammunition for even more stories. And we always published, though press releases from the council, always of limited value, were issued after we had gone to press - and so we kept them for the following week if there was a worthwhile line in them. And our columns stayed full of hard news - which was very interesting to our readers.

In these heady days, the mayor, came in one publishing day to demand an explanation as to why his deputy's picture had been in that week's paper and not his. He added that, in future, he wanted his name first in any caption and then demanded more pictures of him should appear. He left the office with only a slight limp.

Another mayor commissioned a monument to the children of the area who had died in the Whitehaven pits. Their names were all around the marble structure with which name massively bigger than them all? You've guessed it, the mayor's.

A solicitor with a well developed sense of humour who was probably a bit fed up at the time, weary of the treadmill of trying to say something nice about the local low life he was defending, said of another of the local chumps on an assault charge: 'May it please your worships, this is not in character. He normally commits this type of offence only when blind drunk.'

A blonde moppet, aged around ten, knocked at doors around town and opened wide her china blue eyes before asked for charitable donations to... whatever. What she spent the money on we could not discover.

It was alleged by one or two local shopkeepers some of the lads at Sellafield used the company's brilliant, top-of-the-range photocopying equipment to give them headaches by producing forged ten pound notes and trying to pass them off as legal tender. Sometimes they succeeded.

And a local nurse, living in Kells, which is very close to the Marchon works, arrived in the office to say she would sue if yet another toxic emission from the factory made her four-year-old son ill later in his life.

It had been a bad incident and 250 cars suffered damaged paint work after an accidental discharge of sulphuric acid. It was usual for Albright and Wilson to pay for this damage - and the damage they did to washing on the lines and gardens when the vegetables became uneatable because of the factory's awful blanket chimney discharges.

We published and then tried to follow-up the story up with a visit to her home. She was extremely agitated. There had been a flood of anonymous letters, each threatening her and her boy if she made any more complaints against the company which might result in the writers of this disgusting rubbish losing work. And so she kept quiet. The poison pens triumphed.

~ ~ ~ ~ ~ ~ ~ ~ ~ ~

The unsigned letter was not untypical and many a missive came into the office which was certainly actionable. Not about the newspaper, but about someone alleged to be doing something indecent or unpleasant or illegal - somewhere in town.

I wrote a leader in which I drew a picture of the writer(s). I described a dark attic, lit only by a sputtering candle and the anonymous one, hunch backed, crook nosed with a dew drop hanging from the end, tongue stuck out of a corner of his mouth as he scrawled with green felt pen on lined note paper.

I said he/she then had to go about their business the following day pretending to be normal and not so full of vitriol their entire carcass was contaminated with a poisonous hatred of their fellows.

It worked. Well, it did in one case and a friend who had been receiving these kind letters told me of them later. We had not been alone and now they had stopped. But I always wondered what the writer was now doing, for a mind so twisted could not be relied upon to stay out of trouble. It was not a typical happening.

Like me, the West Cumbrian had been raised close to where men worked hard with their hands and their brawn - and they were not unused to tragedy through disasters in the pits.

There was always going to be trouble when men, working miles out under the sea, be it in Whitehaven or East Durham had sometimes to push a pick ahead of them to chop at a coal face in eighteen inch seams dripping with sea water. These took half an hour to reach after the cage had dropped them 1000 feet and more underground.

These are the guys who are tough as they come and yet stay possessed of a gentleness which seems to be the stock in trade of those who have the bottle to work where softies like me, all briefcase, collar and tie, could never even contemplate earning a living.

Mining communities are close and reliant on each other for support - whether it's when the roof caves in or merely for the friendship between these men and their families. It is they who show the true spirit of survival when the going is really tough... like unto death. I got a whiff of this hands across the Pennines camaraderie from my predecessor, Walter Thomson, who had been at the *Whitehaven News* for 40 years.

We met frequently, he had taken me to his home for supper and, on a day when we toured the town, he stopped the car on the Loop Road, which runs high above the harbour and we looked down on what was essentially a working port and not, as it now is, a thing of beauty with yachts and peaked capped skippers everywhere.

Walter gazed down and asked: 'Isn't that lovely?'

I agreed it was canny, but if he could have seen it now he would have been bursting with pride at the new look of his home town. Regrettably, Walter suffered a cancer which killed him quickly after retirement and many years before his time.

~ ~ ~ ~ ~ ~ ~ ~ ~ ~

One of the chaps Walter had recruited, and I inherited, was Bruce Foster, a sub editor, who was to give me one of my most uncomfortable moments. Bruce was 39, had run marathons in this country and abroad, usually for charity, and was married with two very young children. He, too, got cancer which galloped away with his life.

I stayed as close as I could to him, visiting him at home and, eventually, during his more frequent stays at the West Cumberland Hospital. He was on Melbreak Ward and I last saw him on the eve of his death when a nurse allowed me to walk as quietly as I could on to the ward to visit outside usual hours.

The place was full of patients looking very ill but Bruce, in a bed at the far end of the ward, was clearly close to death and his wasted body and shrunken face upset me so badly I put my hand on his, which was blue vein lined and now so small it was all bones beneath mine.

He was unconscious and so I stayed with him looking out of the window and occasionally down at him, hoping he would come to if I spoke gently about... anything.

And so I told him how things at work were and how all his colleagues, everyone a friend, was thinking of him and willing him to pull through. I told him about that week's front page lead, who had written it and what the follow-up might be. I gave him the Whitehaven Rugby League result and told him who had played well.

Just when it seemed all the gentle rubbing of his hand and seamless, aimless chatter would fail his eyes opened and at the same time his wife, Lesley, came on to the ward. Had he heard, or sensed her coming?

Bruce smiled at me, looked at Lesley, but couldn't speak and the nurse, gentle in her understanding and well used to these awful happenings, came to stand by Lesley and me. He became unconscious again after a very short time and we all looked helplessly at each other.

~ ~ ~ ~ ~ ~ ~ ~ ~ ~

Lesley said Bruce had been making notes during what was to be the last of his several stays in hospital and he wanted me to have them. She produced a few sheets from a reporter's notepad which had been in a drawer in his locker by the side of the bed.

I put them in my pocket, squeezed Bruce's hand one last time and left him to die, with his wife beside him.

In a very few hours news came to me at home, from his family who had travelled to Cumbria from the south coast, that Bruce had, indeed, passed away.

I telephoned each member of staff to tell them the dreadful news. They had expected him to die soon, but when it happened there was still shock and the depth of their sadness could never be overstated.

~ ~ ~ ~ ~ ~ ~ ~ ~ ~

I read the notes in my office, on the first floor of the *Whitehaven News*, asking Jean Hughes, my secretary, to keep would-be visitors at bay for a while and to stop telephone calls.

The notes were, on the first two pages, clear enough but deteriorated, mirroring the progress of the disease and his increasing incapacity to write until they were no more than an illegible scrawl as the pencil had slipped all over the page.

I had spoken to Bruce often enough over the weeks of his illness when his condition was worsening and knew that he was becoming increasingly agitated about the nurses working in what he perceived were very poor conditions. And he was worried about the long hours they seemed to be on duty. And so he had written about his fears.

The sincerity was unquestionable, the intention obvious - Bruce knew he was dying and wanted to make comment on the West Cumberland Hospital's operation.

There were, however, several points to consider: He was desperately ill when he was writing and most certainly on huge doses of drugs to help him cope with the excruciating pain. In such circumstances could he be objective and totally aware of what he was writing?

Had he questioned the nurses (there were no direct quotes from them)? And would they wish to reveal their problems to a man in their care who was so close to death?

Might other cancer patients, still full of hope, be discouraged by his story - and what would be the effect on the morale of the nurses who might have been working split shifts, which could have made Bruce think they had been on duty from dawn until dusk?

It took a long time but I decided to go with a piece which was marginally different, but essentially his and we produced one of the most moving features the newspaper has, in all probability, ever carried. To this day it is still remembered - most often by those who nursed him.

~ ~ ~ ~ ~ ~ ~ ~ ~ ~

Bruce wrote of the early days when the Man in The Grey Suit came and sat on the end of his bed and spoke quietly about the operation Bruce needed and how he would, before that happened, be sent to Carlisle for a scan.

This was done and the next time the Man in The Grey Suit came it was to tell him that the operation which had been proposed would be of no avail. He told Bruce he was dying.

The story went on to say that, at 4am the next morning, Lesley rang the hospital to say she had been awakened by a dreadful nightmare and she thought Bruce had died. A nurse had come to tell Bruce about her call and after this, he wrote in his notes, tears came for the first time. And so the nurse sat with him and, for two hours until he drifted off into sleep, gently held his hand.

The story of the Man in The Grey Suit was read, it seemed, by everyone in our circulation area - and then passed on to relatives and friends all around the country. The letters' page filled and a charity fund to raise funds for cancer research was started by some of Bruce's closest pals in the Sunny Hill pub in town.

Whether Bruce would have thought what I published was adequate compensation for my failure to castigate the hospital authorities we will never know.

He might have been comforted by the response we got to his brilliant, moving last story, written as he lay dying. Lesley, his wife came to help us at the *News* and that was good and practical for two small boys had to be reared - and I was mightily proud to read the liturgy at his funeral service.

Did I do him and his nurses a disservice? Should I have published under some kind of tabloid headline, a 96 point banner with a strap above it along the lines of: 'The thoughts of a dying man... How the NHS is failing?'

I didn't and even after all this time I wouldn't - and Bruce, if he could read this, would understand why I didn't. Much more importantly, he would also know that he was held in the greatest regard by his colleagues, some of whom acted as pall bearers when we saw him off at St James's Church on the top of the hill in his adopted town.

And I reckon he would have settled for that and the affection in which he was held - and the publication of a truly amazing story of absolute bravery, written by a dying man.

~~~~~~~~~~

In the manner of all the good journalistic things which happened down all the splendid *Whitehaven News* days we produced the best schools' newspaper in Britain. The Newspaper Society, at their annual awards bash, gave us a large cup, a framed testimonial and heartiest congratulations.

It had, indeed, been a decent effort and the Prime Minister, Margaret Thatcher had a piece on the front in which she said we had shown great enterprise - and Neil Kinnock, the Leader of the Opposition, doubtless through Jack Cunningham reading the piece, demanded a right of reply, well, the equivalent amount of space, to say he, too, was delighted with our success.

Why he should have been heaven knows. I hadn't met him, none of us had and he was just doing some opposition politicking. But I was happy to give him that space for I'm always delighted to lie back, let the sun shine on me - and receive plaudits.

The same schools' production saw one of the girl feature writers, from Whitehaven School, be highly commended by the *Daily Telegraph* in their national awards for school newspapers - and so we had a party. Robin was always quick to acknowledge achievement.

The special newspaper had happened because I spent hours with head teachers of comprehensive schools in Whitehaven who, eventually, allowed me to appoint reporters, writers and photographers from among their students.

I tried to get them all together on a weekly basis - which was nigh on impossible for when kids don't absolutely have to be somewhere it can be hard to motivate them to attend, though there was much fun and many good times for those who did turn up on a regular basis.

The meetings went on for weeks then it was off to the production unit in Carlisle, with all my young hacks, to see the finished job printed. We carried it in the main edition of the *Whitehaven News* as a supplement - and did so with some pride for it looked good.

The children had by-lines on their work, there were pictures of them; it was a sound effort. But one of the head teachers complained that his pupils did not have as much space as the others. I couldn't believe such comment.

It seemed to have escaped him that none of his staff had shown any inclination to help with the product, he had not attended any meetings apart from the first one and he probably expected copy to come from the Great Jehovah, thereby avoiding any inconvenience or personal effort from him.

It was the first of several national awards we were to win with the *News* - awards which delighted me for there is a plethora of regional events which give awards which don't amount to much. We, a weekly newspaper, on the fringes of Cumbria with limited editorial resources, took on every newspaper, national, regional, evening morning or weekly - and we won.

Some years later we were to repeat the performance with a supplement entitled Cumbria at War which remembered the men of our county fifty years after the end of the Second World War and which again cleaned up at the Newspaper Society awards, this time in Harrogate, taking the national sales promotions award. Once more the top trophy was ours and another glass paper weight and framed commendation was on my desk.

And alongside my sports editor, Andy Gallon, was a certificate commending him in the British Sportswriter of the Year awards. He was just 23, recently out of university and virtually ploughed a lone furrow as so many guys on weekly titles are obliged to do. He covered every sport he was expected to write about - and then some.

And he was right up there with the national writers and all their support teams. The *Whitehaven News*, had taken them all on. And beaten them. It was a very good feeling.

~ ~ ~ ~ ~ ~ ~ ~ ~ ~

The New Year of 1989 dawned after a pensioner Father Christmas had been knocked down, beaten up and had all his presents stolen by youths who were full of some kind of spirit and life took a rather more serious turn after the poor old guy posed for us with a face like a burst mattress.

Nirex, the nuclear waste authority, was looking for somewhere to bury the stuff and, while Sellafield was and remains the favourite location, it was assumed that we as a community, while possessing the expertise to handle the material, would welcome a bore hole which, it was proposed, would be sunk close to the glorious Eskdale valley, at Gosforth.

Christopher Harding, the boss of BNFL, declared the Copeland people were warm to the idea. I was furious and asked how the blazes he knew and said, in print, that he couldn't possibly know - and how dare he assume this was the case?

I brought caravans into town, manned one in the Market Place and took one to Gosforth and conducted a poll about whether we wanted more nuclear waste on our patch. Overwhelmingly, the answer was no we didn't.

Okay, it was no way to conduct a proper poll and Mori would have rolled over in sheer exasperation, but it gave us some indication of what folk felt about the proposal - despite the council leader's welcome for the proposal. He was employed by BNFL. His job there was to be in charge of the suggestions committee.

Don't ask because I surely don't know how many suggestions there were per annum - nor what they were and how many hours per week the job consumed!

But it looked as though the fat lady had sung when in June of '89 Cumbria County Council 'approved without comment proposals for a test bore hole at Sellafield.' It was massively contentious but the decision did bring into our area one of the most amusing and hard working guys. Tom Curtin, the PR man for the organisation.

An Irishman Tom, who graduated in Dublin, had been a restaurateur and in his youth even been a cockroach catcher in a New York eatery. A man of quick wit and enormous good humour he was highly intelligent and worked as a good public relations man should - on the ground and everywhere on the patch.

When John Selwyn Gummer, the Secretary of State for the Environment threw out the whole idea, nearly a decade later, it must have been hard for a man who spent so much time organising local opinion and emphasising his beliefs, to accept the ruling.

Gummer declared protection of badgers and the impact on the Cumbrian landscape as reasons for the refusal as well, of course, as issues of radiation safety. But the stuff has to be got rid of somehow and, as most of it is on site at Sellafield it might as well be in West Cumbria as anywhere.

Any politician suggesting it be buried anywhere else in the country might be advised to walk off the top of the London Eye, a dramatic enough place to commit professional suicide.

~ ~ ~ ~ ~ ~ ~ ~ ~ ~

Down all the years Sellafield and Marchon produced copy. A Dalston man, living some 20 miles from the plant and carrying a radio telephone to let the world's media know what he was doing, breached BNFL security to climb a 100 foot crane inside the factory and unfurl a banner which read: 'BNFL Child Killers.'

A Whitehaven GP said the Albright and Wilson factory was responsible for a high rate of asthma in the area - a claim which was, almost as a matter of routine, denied by the company. You might well ask what we expected the plant to do except say: 'it's nothing to do with us' or words to that effect. Our lack of expectation was realised.

Journalists, in these circumstances, never look for anything other than denials, but we do highlight problems, real or imagined and the *Whitehaven News* was most assuredly the vehicle for printing stories which had been backed by qualified comment.

A few miles down the coast from Whitehaven there is a delightful village, clinging to the shoreline with one of the widest main streets in the north of England. Ravenglass is much beloved of film makers who take over this wide cul de sac, with the waves lapping the beach at the bottom of the road and drive vintage cars and carriages up and down it while cameras roll and actors in period costume do their theatrical thing.

Residents of the village, Christopher and Christine Merlin, who lived at Mountain Ash, tried to sue BNFL because, they said, plutonium dust had been found in their house which had sold for £35,000 rather then the expected £60,000. Their case failed.

Veronica Shilling, she of the amazing ladies' day at Ascot hats wrote to say her family had lived at Linethwaite Hall, St Bees, and her sister had died of leukemia. She asked if there was a connection with the Sellafield plant and the Sellafield PRs duly said no, there wasn't.

Scientists Dr. Roger Berry said BNFL personnel who worked in high risk areas might consider not having children and Professor Martin Gardner linked radiation doses with childhood leukemia.

Their comments created almighty rows and we carried, chapter and verse, claim and counter claim. But Sellafield continued to function, as it still does.

~ ~ ~ ~ ~ ~ ~ ~ ~ ~

Every week I always sought the verdict of the front office receptionists, asking the how the paper looked and whether we might have gone wrong. They were local women, bright and outward looking who knew their patch very well. They were aware of who was thinking what and why and which stories would be of consequence.

I learned a lot - as I did when I presented the Whitehaven News Darts

Trophy at the Calder Club, in Mirehouse. I was then forcefully and invariably told what was wrong with the title. But that was usually bravado for when we had a drink after the awards I could get a more sensible line about what they liked and what they wanted to see.

It is their newspaper. Always has been and the editor is a custodian, keeping a seat warm until he meets the great MD in the sky, retires or is taken into the back yard and metaphorically shot. The only people who matter are the readers and their newspaper is a part of their life.

The *Whitehaven News* is a Bible in Copeland and our circulation had boomed beyond all expectations for there are not enough houses on the patch to make sense of the numbers we were selling.

This, concluded our circulation department, happened because people were buying a copy on their way to work, not wanting to have to wait until they got home at night to read the paper which would be there on the mat behind the front door. Or we were improving our out of town sale.

Good theories and, of course, we cared about the figures which had by now become a matter of personal pride for all of us. They continued to rise and we stayed a successful product. Any story we could angle into the light hearted usually meant front page coverage.

I had two fine snappers in John Story and Chris Morrison (who was to go into the hotel business and be replaced by the splendid Jim Davis). Their pictures, if they warranted such treatment, and they usually did, would boom out of the front page and they always got a by-line.

The picture was theirs: it was their work, they owned it because it said so on the front page and this always gives the originator a heightened sense of being judged on the quality of their work. And it was high.

They pictured Michael Moon, the local antiquarian bookseller, known country wide and probably world wide for his shop and its magical contents is one of the brightest sparks in the firmament and he had devised a watering system for the hanging baskets which adorned the front of his premises.

The system won him an award in the Cumbria in Bloom competition - to which he said he didn't know a plant from a weed. It was Michael not at his absolutely sparkling best, but most assuredly getting there. His style and wit make him the easiest of interviewees for TV and radio; he was and remains highly intelligent, a wonderful raconteur - and absolutely incorrigible.

By now Cumbrian Newspapers, under Robin, was even more heavily into the county, its promotion and welfare. Our export awards saw most of the leading manufacturers in the north west attending a lunch at a particularly posh hotel, usually in our Lake District, with the principal guest being a politician of some weight.

Margaret Thatcher, when she was Prime Minister, Labour's John Smith, who I always thought was such a splendid leader, were each introduced to us at these annual events which were only marginally dented by the local MPs refusing invitations when the top table included a leading member of an opposition party.

It doesn't take too much for the toys to go out of the politician's pram and it was at a local level when, after attending a dinner at which the speaker was Chris Cowdrey, the Kent cricketer (and very good he was, too) I found myself sharing a cab with a leading member of the County Council.

John Major was Prime Minister and my fellow passenger began berating the government over unemployment. The people of his home town, Workington, couldn't, he said, get work and he told tales of people turning up at his house in sad states because of unemployment.

On and on he went until I decided enough was enough. I had been made redundant and moved from Manchester to London and to North Yorkshire to find work. I, along with a complete staff, had been fired and reinstated. I knew a wee bit about employment - and the lack of it. It might help, I said, if a few of them got off their backsides and looked for work elsewhere.

He was instantly close to apoplexy; spluttering and squirming in his seat, while the cabby pretended not to listen.

Eventually he managed to shout: 'You're a damned Tory.'

In his rhetoric it was akin to being described as poxed, diseased, contagious, HIV positive. It was the worst condemnation he could manage. I smiled and silently considered he might like a trip back to the land of my fathers, to Hopps Street.

It is still standing and I might have taken him for a wander along the terraced rows and past the houses where I had played as a child. I would have described to him the families who had lived with the outside loo and only cold water being piped through a single tap to houses without bathrooms - and I would have told of their families and their kids who had got off their backsides and made themselves a life far from such deprivation. Not many of them would be Tories.

~ ~ ~ ~ ~ ~ ~ ~ ~ ~

The new decade dawned with a sadness which touched all of us in Copeland. A partly burned and badly mutilated body of a baby was found on the Redhills tip, at Millom.

The police tried particularly hard to find the child's killer, but were unable to do so and, though the case remains open to this day, eventually, blamed travelling people who drifted through Cumbria from time to time in their lorries and trailers, setting up by roadsides or on the edges of fields.

Whether this was an excuse or a reason none of us knew. All we did know was that a child of unknown parents and without even a name, had been murdered and had to be buried.

The Rev Jim Baker conducted the service at St James's Church, at the top of the hill, in Whitehaven and the undertakers carried in a small white coffin while Jim stood at the church door... and waited for the mystery child.

John Story took a picture which was brilliant and which I used across all nine columns of the front page. It was a piece of work which, better than any words, summed up a truly awful happening.

Jim's anguish was obvious as he stood, head bowed, waiting for the nameless, unknown baby in a coffin bourne by two undertakers, top hats removed and nothing else but a background of trees as the body was carried along the path from the hearse.

It was achingly sad, but there was great dignity in the massive emptiness in a picture which was so touching it was almost beautiful. It conveyed the message.

The child, whoever he might have been, and it was a boy, would surely pass over with the thoughts of many thousands of West Cumbrians with him as he ended his tragic few days on this earth with dignity... and a feeling of great caring.

1 993 started with Santa dying on the job. He was appearing at a local club, distributing presents to members' children - and he collapsed, sack and all, and was dead on arrival at hospital.

Thieves, who like most two-bit operators are not possessed of too much between the ears, robbed a house and took with, among other things, a parrot called Charlie. The bird was in a four foot high metal cage and was valued at £900. Its language varied from foul to profane and among the more acceptable comments Charlie was likely to utter was: 'Sod off.'

Writing the story about the police wanting to interview anyone who had been offered a foul-mouthed parrot for sale cracked smiles all around the news room. But through all this silly stuff there shone a piece of pure journalism which still warmed my heart.

It was still a time when, every Wednesday, two of us had to go to head office in Carlisle where we put the paper to bed in the composing room. This meant we had to have the front page laid out and all the copy in the hands of the composing room ready to be set well before deadline.

Today this is done by the journalists at source and the pages transmitted by wire, from Whitehaven to Carlisle ready for the press. The trip to head office, like the compositors who used to work there, is redundant.

But in January that year we set off from Whitehaven, up the ghastly A595 and hung around waiting our turn as other publications went off stone at headquarters. Almost as we were ready to complete there came the word from the news desk that an aircraft had dived into the West Cumbrian fells, near Ponsonby.

I stripped the front page, colour and all and waited for reporter David Siddall to head up the fells to the crash scene with photographer Jim Davis. Climbing in the Lake District on a dark winter night, with a strong wind whipping the rain off the sea is not be recommended. But up they went while I, in Carlisle, waited... and waited.

Mobile telephones were useless in the fells and so I had a further wait for them to reach the crash scene, gather what information was available - then get back to a call box.

They got close, but the best angle they could get was that the aircraft had dived into the earth just three miles from Sellafield - whose PR department immediately issued a statement to the effect that there was never any danger - though I would not have wished to test the veracity of that comment.

Two men in the 'plane, which was travelling from Southend to Glasgow and was carrying parcels, had been pronounced dead at the scene after being located by police, the Wasdale Mountain Rescue Team and an RAF Search and Rescue squad.

A farmer's wife spoke to Siddall about the appalling weather but considering we had only this quote and the bones of the story, it came together well.

Working with one of the Carlisle overseers, Colin Bee, I put together a black and white page, this in an era when the front pages of newspapers always had colour on them. It was an exclusive and it worked wonderfully well, a classic example of good reporting and clever work by Bee.

A map was included and a picture of Superintendent Phil Park, who had been based at Whitehaven. It showed him up there, on the fellside, in charge of the attempted rescue. It was playing at proper newspapers once more. And I loved it.

~ ~ ~ ~ ~ ~ ~ ~ ~ ~

BNFL are renowned for paying top dollar and this is why they never have any trouble recruiting guys at the very top of their profession or someone to sweep the factory floor. The money and benefits are massively worthwhile.

From the top to the bottom the good times roll every pay day and it was difficult to understand why, again in early '93, Harold Bolter, CBE, a former *Financial Times* journalist, was to admit, following a police investigation, using the company to pay for redecoration and repairs to his big and beautiful house in Cheshire.

He was said to be earning, at that time, more than £85,000 as BNFL's company secretary and director of corporate affairs. He resigned or was fired, take your choice, and then wrote a book about everything that had been wrong with BNFL while he had been there.

This seemed odd. If it had been so wrong while he was there in such a very senior position then why didn't he put it to rights?

I blasted the story which was no more than a tale of unmitigated greed, scratched my head and got on with bringing to Cleator Moor a heavily guarded exhibition of Lowry paintings and drawings which was massively appreciated - as was a visit by Fred Dibnah, knocker down of chimneys and tall buildings and a most charming chap who came to play on La'al Ratty, the narrow gauge railway which chuffs its way from Ravenglass through the glories of Eskdale to the delight of us all.

Diversity in newspapers? Better believe it.

~ ~ ~ ~ ~ ~ ~ ~ ~ ~

It was in 1978 that I was elected to membership of the Guild of British Newspaper Editors, an organisation which lobbies Parliamentarians for continued freedom of the press and which battles on so many fronts, not least against those who would seek to stifle and submerge the truth and our lawful rights to report it.

Editors meet in regions throughout the UK to talk of local battles with various bodies (including, occasionally, our own managements who had been known to try to put commercial interests before the balanced journalism which we all strive to achieve) and how to maintain the status of our titles.

Maurice Brady, who had been the district reporter at Peterlee when first I joined the *Mail* at Hartlepool, but was now editor of that title, brought me into a fold which gave me great satisfaction for now I was accepted by my fellow regional editors, who managed evening, morning and weekly titles throughout Britain. I had arrived in journalism in some style and it was a privilege I was always to take most seriously.

While on Tyneside and in Northumberland I was to become councillor, travelling to London for meetings and reporting back to the region and then, eventually, the chairman of the northern region, which stretches from the Scottish borders, including Berwick, down to south of Teesside.

Some managing directors were not at all keen on the Guild, declaring it was costly and involved editors in spending too much time away from their desks. In truth, it was an organisation which they, often as former accountants or advertising or circulation men, were unable to understand and, therefore, did not like.

Some would not pay annual subscriptions and certainly not dig deep for the annual Guild conference which was held in the circulation area of the current national president. But, as they had been with just about everything else, Cumbrian Newspapers, in the considerable shape of Robin Burgess, could not have been more supportive.

He believed in the Guild, what we worked for and the networking with other organisations through which we, as members, were able to bring back to his company. He supported me by allowing me to attend all conferences everywhere (in addition to those management courses on which he sent me) and so more progress was made and I became councillor and again chairman, this time of the north west region after my move to Cumbrian Newspapers.

Again I had to travel to London, first to Whitefriars Street, just off Fleet Street, for meetings then subsequently to Newspaper House, in Bloomsbury when we moved to premises which were shared with the Newspaper Society, the organisation for provincial newspaper managers.

Battles were always being fought and we tried to circumnavigate threats from various governments, some of whose Members of Parliament felt bruised after being found out morally or politically of some misdemeanour and wanted revenge upon us, the regional press, rather than our more famous brothers, the national newspapers, who had probably broken the story in the first place.

We entertained Cabinet ministers to lunch and lobbied our local MPs. We fought and beat a threat to impose VAT on newspapers and yet it seemed the beasts were never truly conquered, raising their ghastly heads time after time as some gushing new boy to the back benches tried to gain favour with something beyond the sycophancy at PM's Question Time and regurgitated the aged and hoary 'let's have a go at the press' issues.

And so it was we always battled for our freedoms and our integrity and newspaper editors, having been around more blocks than many politicians have seen, managed to win more then they lost.

A sprinkling of common sense; a modicum of understanding, a smattering of good judgement stretched many a mile when it comes to career threatening decisions and young Galahads, MPs for wherever, leaping in with girded loins and making ready to fall on the sword of justice (as one of them might have said) are best left in a darkened room with sliced cucumber on their fevered brow.

It was in 1993 that I became national president of the Guild of British Newspaper Editors. My predecessor, David Williams, from Bury St Edmunds, had employed a team of consultants and we were beginning to undergo changes of name and strive for independence to enable us to be financially independent of the Newspaper Society.

So it came about and, indeed, there was to be yet another change of title as we became the Society of Editors. More top people in the media are now part of this society and national newspaper editors are members rather than it being a preserve of we provincial folk, somewhat farther down the editorial ladder. But the principles remain unchanged and there is still a familiar ring to the battles which are being fought.

My presidency came a year before I was due to take over from Alan Prosser, who was the editor of the *Northern Echo*, at Darlington. But he was promoted as he was about to take over the Guild office.

He understandably decided he couldn't tackle the considerable task of looking after Guild members nationwide while doing justice to his new job and all that would entail.

I had been due to be eased into the job, as all presidents were, but when Prosser stood down as president elect I was asked to move in without serving the customary year as vice president. I spoke with Robin Burgess about it and his reply was succinct - and was to prove accurate: 'Go for it,' he said. And so I did.

~ ~ ~ ~ ~ ~ ~ ~ ~ ~ ~

The only perk of being president of the Guild of British Newspaper Editors was to receive two Centre Court tickets for Wimbledon and an invitation to a Garden Party at Buckingham Palace.

Both were massively enjoyable and though we took a back seat at the Palace while the more experienced party people attending rushed towards the steps leading into the massive back garden when the Queen and the Royal party descended, it was such a hot and sweltering day we escaped to a pub near St James's as soon as we decently could.

We were not first in and women were queuing for the loo where they could remove their tights while downstairs the men took off jackets, loosened their ties and undid the top buttons of their shirts - all the while demanding pints of cool ale.

On the business side I was to travel more then 30,000 miles around the UK, visiting regions, and as I did so drinking more buffet car coffee than any man should have to endure in one lifetime.

The preparation for these trips often saw me driving through the beautiful northern lakes from the coast to Penrith, a journey of just over an hour and frequently undertaken between 4am and 5.15am to connect with the 5.35 early morning London train which would deposit me at Euston around 9.45. Then there was a dash through London's morning traffic to chair the council meetings at Bloomsbury.

To get back I would be booked aboard two evening trains, the 5.30 and 6.30 which removed pressure of a late-finishing meeting. I would catch one or the other to Penrith and be back in my bed around midnight - which made for a lengthy day.

Cabinet ministers, chief constables and many more of the great and good who were greeted by me at the door of Bloomsbury House, would sweep up in their limos, complete with security men and chauffeurs to our door.

They would be given lunch, we would explain why we existed and what we wished to achieve - and one or two of them might have listened. Certainly nothing untoward happened during my presidency and we made progress on sponsorship which took us away from the Newspapers Society's financial apron strings.

The splendid city headquarters of BT were visited and they came good with financial deals which secured our immediate future. Many members did not approve of an organisation which was so fiercely independent being beholden to any commercial outfit. But we needed money and it was either allow a huge outfit like BT to have their logo alongside our letterhead - or raise the subscriptions substantially.

The ever present opposition to the Guild in some quarters from MDs was undiminished so raising cash through higher subs would be a considerable problem. Mercifully, many more groups were enlightened.

But the ground rules were made clear to BT who not only agreed them but were of enormous help at the annual conference which was to be held at the conclusion of my term of office, in 1994.

I organised it at an hotel on the shores of Windermere. The Low Wood has a huge conference room and many of the bedrooms looked over the lake and the Langdale Pikes. The view is so spectacular it resembles the front cover of a glossy magazine with yachts cruising the lake, pleasure boats puttering around with weekend sailors draped all over them and, occasionally, light aircraft dipping in over the mountains to zoom the length of the blue and beautiful lake.

It was quite a venue, but there was much to be done and speakers had to be cajoled into appearing for just their travelling expenses and accommodation. We did not pay appearance money and the small committee which I had pulled together, headed by Veronica Lupton Hird, the Guild secretary, had produced a line up which was awesome.

~ ~ ~ ~ ~ ~ ~ ~ ~ ~

And so it was friends and former colleagues and their partners crowded up the M6 on a wild and wet October day to be part of the Big Weekend and even a motorway smash on the morning of Friday when the conference was to start and which closed the north bound carriageway near Manchester for many hours did not deter one of them.

They arrived from everywhere, filling the Low Wood and spilling over into the Wild Boar and the Waterhead hotels where we had buses to transport them to the conference sessions at Low Wood.

First to appear on the platform was Max Clifford, PR specialist and publicist. Urbane, silver haired, he chatted to and with everyone and there was gentleness about the man which was remarkable for someone who spent much of his life toughing it out in front of national newspaper reporters who were demanding answers about, among other things, the sexual inclinations of the rich and famous.

Clifford's line was: 'If a guy is homosexual and wants to appear 'straight' then I will produce two gorgeous girls, one for each of his arms, and then it's up to you to deny his sexuality. I make the image and I present it.' He was light, amusing and a very good speaker.

He was followed almost immediately by a considerable row as the next speaker, Sir John Hall, then the chairman and benefactor of Newcastle United (ah, memories, memories) took issue, while on the platform, to a story which had recently appeared in the *Newcastle Journal*. As we had the editor of the *Journal* in the conference hall it made for lightening quick reflexes as they verbally set about each other.

Great stuff. Now, where had I heard football clubs declare they didn't get a square deal from the press before?

That evening Conservative MP Edwina Curry was the speaker at dinner - and she, spiky, twitchingly nervous, beautifully dressed, was brilliant... and not a word about John Major who might have been in a B&B down the road on the banks of Windermere.

She took questions at the end of a clever and not too political talk and then visited every table in the dining room to speak to each of the several hundred journalists seated there, full of food and wine and good humour. Well, I hoped they were humorous. She kept right on smiling.

At 9am the next morning, Saturday, we started again. Alan Clark MP and his attractive wife Jane were the only people who said they did not wish to stay in hotels booked by us for the conference. They made their own arrangements and chose Michael's Nook, at Grasmere, one of the smartest places in the Lake District, which could rank alongside Ullswater's Sharrow Bay.

He arrived half an hour before he was due on the platform for a 9am start, looking well refreshed and, despite having recently received a dreadful press for some of his sexual excursions, publicised in his diaries, stood alongside his lovely Jane - and smiled at us all.

Indeed, on the platform he made gentle fun of us for being so interested in his extra marital activities and even said he was delighted to receive so much publicity. It was humour with a message; a smooth and easy message with a conclusion which almost shrugged the shoulders and suggested we just get on with it - if that's what we felt made news.

Not so urbane, but on the same platform, was Sandy Gall who was mightily upset with the press for recent coverage of his professional life and while I would guarantee not too many of the regional journalists gathered before him had carried a syllable about his work this was a good place to make his point.

The third person on the platform was Professor Robert Pinker, the Privacy Commissioner, a title almost elastic if seeking a definition, but he was polite, erudite and warm towards us all.

The chairman for this platform was the television presenter Fiona Armstrong, a most attractive young woman who introduced speakers with me, fulfiling my presidential role, at her right hand making whispered comments like: 'OK, Fiona, if you run into trouble I'm right here.'

'Thank you, Roy.'

'If you need any speakers' background I have all the biographical. notes.'

'Thank you, Roy.'

And so she went into the session, introducing each speaker with great accuracy, presence and style. And she did not, not once, say, during all of this: 'Do me a favour, Roy, just let me get on with it.'

Polite, competent and totally professional, she chaired the session so well and the afternoon was then devoted to in-house speakers, eminent newspaper people who talked our language and were experienced enough to grab the floor's attention.

That evening Cumbrian Newspapers, through the always thoughtful and generous Robin, hosted a champagne reception before the gala din- ner at which the principal speaker was John Prescott, at that time in oppo- sition. He arrived scowling and in foul mood. He had driven, that after- noon, from his constituency in Hull and crossed the Pennines, via the crowded M62, in dreadful weather.

He said hello, hung around for a few minutes glowering, had a drink then went up to his room leaving me wondering why on earth we had invited him.

He sat next to my wife at top table and I sat with his wife - all the while looking apprehensively out of the corner of my eye at him and wonder- ing whether he was going to blast us all after an evening which had promised so much when so many people had been so pleased to meet once again.

My fears were groundless. He excused himself for a few minutes after dinner and on his return stood up, made the standard gag about the last time he had worn a dinner suit he had been waiting on at table on a cruise ship - and launched into funny stories and told tales.

It was as though the man who had walked into reception, wet and weary, had been an illusion. He, like Edwina Curry (and he had asked how she had spoken the previous night) went to visit every table at the end of his speech and the laughter went with him. The transformation had been remarkable - indeed, a remarkable man... a tremendous success.

The next morning was given to Rear Admiral David Pulvertaft, then secretary of the Defence, Press and Broadcasting Advisory Committee and David Rigg, who spoke about the National Lottery, which was about to be launched.

We broke after Sunday lunch and I settled back as the congratulations came in from all manner of delegates and guests. Everyone had turned up, much had been said, much was learned. It had been a great weekend and as I headed for home I took the long way around Derwentwater.

As I drove through the weak autumn sunshine, around the glittering lake and back towards the coast, I considered more than 40 years as a newspaper man from inky tea boy at the *Northern Daily Mail* to national President of the Guild of British Newspaper Editors.

It had, I thought, been a fair old trip. And I wouldn't have missed a day of it. OK... maybe just one or two!

MORE BOOKS FROM HAYLOFT

The Long Day Done by Jeremy Rowan-Robinson
(£9.50, ISBN 1 9045240 4 4)

Odd Corners in Appleby, Gareth Hayes
(£8.50, ISBN 1 9045240 0 1)

The Ghastlies, Trix Jones and Shane Surgey
(£3.99, ISBN 1 9045240 4 4)

A Journey of Soles, Lands End to John O'Groats, Kathy Trimmer
(£9.50, 1 9045240 5 2)

Changing the Face of Carlisle, The Life and Times of Percy Dalton, City Engineer and Surveyor, 1926-1949, Marie K. Dickens
(£8, ISBN 0 9540711 9 0)

From Clogs and Wellies to Shiny Shoes, A Windermere Lad's Memories of South Lakeland, Miles R. M. Bolton
(£12.50, ISBN 1 9045240 2 8)

A History of Kaber, Helen McDonald and Christine Dowson,
(£8, ISBN 0 9540711 6 6)

The Gifkin Gofkins, Irene Brenan
(£2.50, ISBN 1 9045240 1 X)

A Dream Come True, the Life and Times of a Lake District National Park Ranger, David Birkett
(£5.50, ISBN 0 9540711 5 8)

Gone to Blazes, Life as a Cumbrian Fireman, David Stubbings
(£9.95, ISBN 0 9540711 4 X)

Changing Times, The Millennium Story of Bolton, Barbara Cotton
(£12.50, ISBN 0 9540711 3 1)

Better by Far a Cumberland Hussar, A History of the Westmorland and Cumberland Yeomanry, Colin Bardgett
(Hardback, £26.95, ISBN 0 9540711 2 3)
(Paperback, £16.95, ISBN 0 9540711 1 5)

Northern Warrior, the Story of Sir Andreas de Harcla, Adrian Rogan
(£8.95, ISBN 0 9523282 8 3)

A Riot of Thorn & Leaf, Dulcie Matthews
(£7.95, ISBN 0 9540711 0 7)

A Country Doctor, Dr. Isaac Bainbridge, Dawn Robertson
(£2.25, ISBN 0 9523282 32)

Military Mountaineering, A History of Services Expeditions, 1945-2000,
Retd. SAS Major Bronco Lane
(Hardback, £25.95, ISBN 0 9523282 1 6)
(Paperback, £17.95, ISBN 0 9523282 6 7)

2041 - The Voyage South, Robert Swan
(£8.95, 0 9523282 7 5)

Yows & Cows, A Bit of Westmorland Wit, Mike Sanderson
(£7.95, ISBN 0 9523282 0 8)

Riding the Stang, Dawn Robertson
(£9.99, ISBN 0 9523282 2 4)

Secrets and Legends of Old Westmorland,
Peter Koronka and Dawn Robertson
(Hardback, £17.95, ISBN 0 9523282 4 0)
(Paperback, £11.95, ISBN 0 9523282 9 1)

The Irish Influence, Migrant Workers in Northern England,
Harold Slight
(£4.95, 0 9523282 5 9)

Soldiers and Sherpas, A Taste for Adventure, Brummie Stokes.
(£19.95, 0 9541551 0 6)

North Country Tapestry, Sylvia Mary McCosh
(£10, 0 9518690 0 0)

Between Two Gardens, The Diary of two Border Gardens,
Sylvia Mary McCosh
(£5.95, 0 9008111 7 X)

Dacre Castle, A short history of the Castle and the Dacre Family,
E. H. A. Stretton
(£5.50, 0 9518690 1 9)

Antarctica Unveiled, Scott's First Expedition and the Quest for the Unknown Continent, David E. Yelverton
(£25.99, 0 8708158 2 2)

You can order any of our books by writing to:
Hayloft Publishing,
South Stainmore, Kirkby Stephen,
Cumbria, CA17 4EU, UK.
Please enclose a cheque plus £2 for UK postage and packing.
or telephone: +44 (0)17683) 42300

For more information see: www.hayloft.org.uk